INDIAN WARRIORS OF EQUALITY AND SOCIAL JUSTICE

THEIR LIFE, STRUGGLE AND CONTRIBUTION

DR. KULDEEP SINGH

Copyright © Dr. Kuldeep Singh
All Rights Reserved.

Dedicated to All the Champions of

Equality and Social Justice

Contents

Preface

This book attempts to address the issue of equality and social justice in India that has been a central theme of the Constitution of India, which we achieved after a long struggle. This book is mainly based on secondary sources of information and internet based websites mainly the Wikipedia. Attempt has been made to give to the point information through this book on life, struggle and contribution of the great warriors of social justice in India since the times of Mahatma Gautam Buddha to Dr. B.R. Ambedkar. As India is celebrating Azadi ka Amrit Mahotsv on completion seventy five years as an independent and democratic country, it is time to memorise the role of the worthy champions of equality and social justice who sturdily fought against inequality and injustice facing heinous and inhuman brutality of caste system and caste based discrimination. This book discusses the significant issues of equality and social justice and the efforts of the governments towards the equality and social justice. This book also puts light on the constitutional safeguards as far as the equality and social justice are concerned.

But it is surprising to see, even after seventy five years of independence, how little the younger citizens of our country know about the life, struggle and contribution of the harbingers of the social justice. Most of them know about the freedom movement but very few know much about the fight for social justice and what pain and humiliation was experienced by the stalwarts of social justice. Through this book an attempt has been made to fill this gap. It tells you the story of the journey of struggle for equality and social justice since Mahatma Gautam Buddha to the contemporary fighters including Babasaheb Dr. Bhim Rao Ambedkar, the key architect of Indian Constitution and the messiah of downtrodden and women.

This book contains the accumulated information about the life, struggle and contribution of the great champions of social justice such as Mahatma Gautam Buddha, Saint Kabir Das, Saint Ravidas, Mahatma Jyotiba Phule, Savitribai Phule, Fatima Seikh, Shahuji Maharaj, Sree Nraryana Guru, E.V. Ramasami Neiker (Periyar), Babsaheb Dr. Ambedkar, Shaheede Azam Bhagat Singh, Swami Achhootanand etc. However, a serious effort has been made to put light on the stalwart champions of social justice, but some other worthy warriors of social justice could not be depicted in this book. I shall try to write another book in future on the life, struggle and contribution of the left out ones.

The first chapter of the book covers introduction of social justice and second one sheds light on Historical Background of Social Justice. The chapters from third to eighteen offers an overview of various advocates of equality and social justice. Last Chapter covers Indian Constitution and Social Justice. In the last chapter, it has been focused that social justice is the foundation of national unity and a stable democracy. The objective of this book is to equip the readers particularly the youth with information and perspectives so that you can take more informed and well thought out positions regarding the fight for social justice and to aware the students of political science or other citizens of the country about role of the great champions of equality and social justice who sacrificed their lives to create an egalitarian society and inclusive democracy.

The book uses a variety of sources from scholarly books, different newspapers and websites such as Wikipedia to tell the story of the defenders and supporters of equality and social justice. 'Samajik Nyay ki Paathshala', a YouTube channel being run by Dr. Laxman Yadav, Assistant Professor at Delhi University deeply influenced and inspired me to write a book on the life, struggle and contribution of the great warriors of equality and social justice. The cover page of this book contains the photographs of the warriors of social justice. All the photographs have taken from the concerned websites in particular the Wikipedia. I am really thankful towards all the concerned websites including the Wikipedia from where I collected relevant data and information to prepare this book.

This book is a tribute to all the warriors of equality and social justice who played great role to plant the seed of social justice in a caste ridden country and who nurtured the tiny plant to turn it into a huge tree. This book will help the readers to read and understand the thoughts and philosophy of social justice. I sincerely hope that this book will be received in this spirit and will be useful not only for students of political science and social science but also to a wider group of young citizens of our country.

DR. KULDEEP SINGH

CHAPTER ONE

EQUALITY AND SOCIAL JUSTICE:

AN OVERVIEW

INTRODUCTION

Social justice is one of the different dimensions of justice and it is the most significant element of a civilized society as it makes it stable for a long time. Without justice and social justice in particular, a society cannot survive for a long time. Social Justice as a concept arose in the early 19th century during the Industrial Revolution and subsequent civil revolutions throughout Europe too crystallized the voices for social justice. These voices aimed to create more egalitarian societies and protect human labor from capitalistic exploitation. Because of the stark stratifications between the wealthy and the poor during this time, early social justice advocates focused primarily on capital, property, and the distribution of wealth. By the mid-20th century, social justice had expanded from being primarily concerned with economics to include other spheres of social life to include the environment, race, gender, and other causes and manifestations of inequality.

As far as India is concerned, the voices for social justice began to be echoed for a long but these voices became vibrant in modern India. Here, the form of social injustice was different to Europe. In India, the root cause of injustice and exploitation was caste system based on *Chatur-Varna* System that segmented Indian Society into four grades on the basis of birth. In ancient India, Mahatma Gautam Buddha had echoed his energetic voice and initiated a strong campaign against caste based inequality, discrimination and injustice. During mediaeval period, Sant Ravidas and Sant Kabir Das attacked on caste, caste based inequality, discrimination, humiliation and subjugation. but the bigger attack was made on caste based social injustice and much effective voice was echoed in modern India by Mahatma Jyotiba Phule, Shahuji Maharaj, Naryana Guru, Baba Gadge, E.V. Ramasami Naiker (Periyar), Dr. B.R. Ambedkar, Swami Achutanand etc. this voice turned into a decisive fight for social justice later on joined by Manyawar Kanshi Ram, Ram Manohar Lohia, B.P. Mandal, Karpoori Thakur, Ram Swaroop Verma, Lalai Singh Yadav etc.

Concurrently, the measure of equality and social justice expanded from being measured and enacted only by the nation-state (or government) to include a universal human dimension. For example, presently governments measure income inequality by only comparing people within the same nation. But social justice can also be applied on a broader scale at the level of humanity as a whole. As the United Nations states: "Slaves, exploited workers and oppressed women are above all victimized human beings whose location matters less than their circumstances." However, poor and backwards face almost the similar conditions of inequality and social injustice throughout the world. But in India, the situation is different. Here, people face inequality not only on the basis of economic condition but also on the basis of caste and later is much painful than the first.

EQUALITY

The humanity has been a sever victim of inequality world wide. Racism has been a huge ground of discrimination and favourism as far as the Europe, Africa and Americas are concerned. But in India, the situation is different. Here, caste is the most remarkable element which not only supported discrimination but also promoted it. All people had been not considered equal due to caste. A number of people were labled as lower or inferior and they were deprived of all sources of progress and development. They were denied education and schools doors were kept closed for them. There had been inequality in all fields such as social, economic, political and religious. This condition is called inequality.

Here a question rises, what is equality? Acording to Laski, equality is the most difficult concept of political science. As far as the meaning of equality is concerned, it is the absence of discrimination and privileges on the basis of birth, caste, colour, race, gender and religion. Equality means equal treatment with all. But the opponent of equality deliberately oppose the equality and favours discrimination and treatment of the basis of merit or ability. No doubt to say that equal treatment with all in all conditions may not be equality. In true sense, it is absence of discrimination on the basis of social grounds. Discrimination based on birth, caste, gender and religion can not be accepted in a just society. All must be given adequaete opportunities for development. There must be no discrimination while providing opportunities to the citizens of the country.

Laski clarifying the meaning of equality says, "the rights that other people have on the basis of being a citizen, in the same form and to the same extent, those rights should be given to me also. He further says that the meaning of equality on the one hand is that no one should be given privileges in the society. On the other hand, every person should get equal opportunity for his development. It means that equality is not to discriminate with any citizen manly on the basis of social grounds. Society and the state must be just while distributing awards and offering punishments, no one sholud be escaped and given punishment on the basis his actions not on the basis that he belongs to a particular caste or community.

Academically, there are following characteristics of equality:

1. Absence of Discrimination on the basis of Social Grounds
2. Equal Opportunities to all
3. Equality before Law
4. Equal Protection by Law
5. Fulfillment of the Basic Needs of everyone
6. Equality not Equal Income of all but Less Gap between Rich and Poor
7. Adequate Distribution of Resources among the Citizens
8. Fairness while delivering Justice

In short, equality is the essence of a just and egalitarian society that promotes social justice and social justice in turn concretise the unity and integrity of the country.

JUSTICE

Justice is the primary and most relevant component of the state and in the absence of justice we cannot imagine of a civilsed life of people and stable and disciplined state. It is the justice which we can call the backbone of the state indeed. Therefore, a free, fair and competent judiciary is much important in any just state. Lord Bryce was of the view that "a society without legislative organ is conceivable, but a civilized state without judicial organ is hardly conceivable". Justice makes coordination between the all segments of the society and make them agreed to live together. Justice connects individuals and communities with each other safeguarding rights of all without any discrimination. State and the citizens collectively are responsible to ensure justice in any state.

<u>Meaning of Justice</u>

In simpler sense, Justice is the fiber that unites a society and its absence may lead to disintegration of not only the society but also the country. Those who suffer injustice may move to separatism and ultimately to the division of land. For Plato a Greek philosopher, justice was an important virtue of an ideal state. According to him, an ideal state possessed four cardinal virtues of wisdom, courage, discipline and justice. Different scholars and thinkers defined justice variously. Some focused on moral aspect, some on legal and someone natural. Many scholars and thinkers have tried to define justice as under-

Cephalus stressed upon moral aspect of justice and according to him, justice is to tell the truth, being honest in words and deed and paying one's debt.

This point of view of Cephalus was effortlessly dismissed by Socrates and he said that it would be harmful to return the weapon to a mad man. To conceal the weapon of a mad man is much beneficial than return it to him. Therefore, he emphasized upon that the justice should be beneficial not harmful.

Polemarchus pointed out that justice is "giving each man his due or what was fitting".

According to Thracymachus, justice is the interest of stronger or the ruler.

But Socrates showed that justice was not the advantage of the stronger, for the ruler's duty was to serve the interests of the people. A ruler's position was similar to that of a doctor, teacher or shepherd. Any art, which included ruling, should be for the welfare of the object and not the subject.

Plato who was a disciple of Socrates, viewed justice separately in individual and in the state. Justice in the individual meant that every individual should be assigned a place in society as according to one's natural aptitudes and skills. Here most important thing to be noted is that Plato did not recommend role and rights as according to the community or caste unlike Indian Varna system which determined the role to the people as according to their varnas or social category. People belonging to shudra (the fourth varna) were restricted to do work assigned to three upper varnas (Brahmins, Kshatriyas and Vaishyas), however, they were naturally fit for performing those works assigned to three upper varnas. To ensure justice, a just society should educate every individual talent to which he is naturally fit without any social discrimination.

For Aristotle, justice meant virtue in action. He emphasized on virtues as a significant part of a just state.

In words of Salmond, "Justice means to distribute the due share to everybody".

According to D.D. Raphel, justice protects the rights of the individual as well as the order of the society.

J.S. Mill says, "Justice is the name for certain classes of moral values which concerns the essentials of human well-being more clearly and are, therefore, of more absolute obligations than any other rules for the guidance of life".

Justice is of many types like Natural justice, Moral justice, Social justice, Economic justice, Political justice and Legal justice. Out of these all, social justice is most significant upon which all other justices depend. In absence of social justice, other justice like economic, political and legal are not possible. In this book, focus has been put on social justice mainly.

CONCEPT OF SOCIAL JUSTICE

Many thinkers and scholars have defined social justice too in many ways but Social justice simply speaking is the equal access of all to wealth, opportunities, and privileges within a society. The preeminent theoretician of fairness social justice was **John Rawls**, author of the seminal *A Theory of Justice* (1971/2005). Rawls's thought centered on ideas of fair distribution and political freedom that hinge on the existence of basic freedoms and equality of opportunity.

The concept of social justice emerged out of a process of evolution of social norms, order, law and morality. The term 'social justice' consists of two words: one is social and the second is justice. The term 'social' is concerned with all human beings who live in society, while the term 'justice' is related to liberty, equality and rights. Chanakya in his *Arthshastra* admitted social equality as the basis of social justice. Former Chief Justice of India, P.B. Gajendergadkar wrote, "Social Justice is to give equal opportunity to every individual in social domain by ending social inequalities". Thus, social justice is concerned with ensuring opportunity, providing equality and maintaining individual rights for every human being in society. In other words, securing the highest possible development of the capabilities of all members of the society may be called social justice.

GREEK PERSPECTIVE: PLATONIC UNDERSTANDING OF JUSTICE

The question of justice has been central to every society, and in every age, it surrounds itself with debate. Justice has been the most critical part of a person's morality since time immemorial. Perhaps, it is for this reason that Plato, the ancient Greek philosopher, considered it crucial to reach a theory of justice. Since the tradition of Greek Philosophy considered ethics to be important, they believed that the state comes into existence for the sake of life and continues for the sake of a good life. Plato believed in the same dictum and held that the state exists to fulfil the necessities of human life. The origin of the state, therefore, owed its existence to the fulfilment of human needs, and the Greek philosophers saw society and state as the same.

Unlike other living beings, human beings do not merely seek survival but essentially want to live a good life. Justice is the essential requirement to lead a good life. One cannot lead a good life without meeting their needs, and it's possible to meet one's needs only in the presence of Justice. The Republic discusses Justice in the form of a dialogue. This methodology is known as Dialectical Method, which Plato borrowed from his mentor, Socrates. The dialogue takes place between Socrates, Glaucon, Adeimantus, Cephalus and Thrasymachus. The dialogue concluded that if one were allowed to suppress another, there would be complete anarchy, and it would be difficult to have any state of affairs. To save oneself from any such suffering and to prevent injustice, men enter into a contract to prevent injustice upon themselves or on others. That is also how laws came into existence to codify standard human conduct and bring a sense of Justice.[1]

Justice, according to Plato, is at once a part of human virtue and the bond, which joins man together in society. Justice is an order and duty of the parts of the soul, it is to the soul as health is to the body. Plato says that justice is not mere strength, but it is a harmonious strength. Justice is not the right of the stronger but the effective harmony of the whole. However, Plato's concept of justice depends on three metallic virtues of gold, silver and iron naturally found in human beings in form of reason, courage and appetite. Corresponding to these three elements in human nature there are three classes in the social Organism-Philosopher class or the ruling class which represents the reason; auxiliaries, a class of warriors or defenders of the country that is the representative of spirit; and the appetite instinct of the community which consists of farmers, artisans and are the lowest rung of the ladder. To Plato, justice is a mechanism of functional specialization. Plato asserts that functional specialization demands from every social class to specialize itself in the station of life allotted to it. Justice, therefore to Plato is like a manuscript which exists in two copies, and one of these is larger than the other. It exists both in the individual and the society. But it exists on a larger scale and in more visible form in the society. Individually "justice is a 'human virtue' that makes a man self-consistent and good: Socially, justice is a social consciousness that makes a society internally harmonious and good."

Justice is thus an another form of specialization. It is simply the will to fulfill the duties of one's station and not to meddle with the duties of another station, and its habitation is, therefore, in the mind of every citizen who does his duties in his appointed place. It is the original principle, laid down at the foundation of the State, "that one man should practice one thing only and that the thing to which his nature was best adopted". True justice to Plato, therefore, consists in the principle of non-interference. Though, the idea of three classes seems to be similar with the idea of *chaturvarna vyavstha* (the fourth fold stratification of the human beings based on work that later converted to birth based). However, Varna system was a vertical mechanism in which intermingling was prohibited but Plato's was horizontal in which all three classes were importantly required to establish a just society. In this way, Varna system lacked justice and it was anti forth category and promoted their exploitation. In varna system, up and down movement was not permitted whereas upward circulation was open for people of third class under platonic system and any competent person belonging to third class families could be included to ruling and defending classes. Here it is obvious to see that Plato stresses upon social harmony to construct a society based on justice. In other words, without social unity and harmony, it is difficult to establish a just society and social harmony can not be imagined in absence of social justice.

WESTERN PERSPECTIVE: JOHN RAWLS'S VIEWS ON SOCIAL JUSTICE

A Theory of Justice (1971) Rawls's theory of justice revolves around the adaptation of two fundamental principles of justice which would, in turn, guarantee a just and morally acceptable society. The first principle guarantees the right of each person to have the most extensive basic liberty compatible with the liberty of others. The second principle states that social and economic positions are to be (a) to everyone's advantage and (b) open to all.

A key problem for Rawls is to show how such principles would be universally adopted, and here the work borders on general ethical issues. He introduces a theoretical "veil of ignorance" in which all the "players" in the social game would be placed in a situation which is called the "original position." Having only a general knowledge about the facts of "life and society," each player is to make a "rationally prudential choice" concerning the kind of social institution they would enter into contract with. By denying the players any specific information about themselves it forces them to adopt a generalized point of view that bears a strong resemblance to the moral point of view. "Moral conclusions can be reached without abandoning the prudential standpoint and positing a moral outlook merely by pursuing one's own prudential reasoning under certain procedural bargaining and knowledge constraints."

John Rawls who was born on February 21, 1921, at Baltimore, Maryland, U.S and died on November 24, 2002, Lexington, Massachusetts has been American political and ethical philosopher, best known for his defense of egalitarian and liberal society in his major work, *A Theory of Justice* (1971). He is widely considered the most important political philosopher of the 20th century and his thoughts on justice are of great significance.

Rawls believed in fairness and he took justice as fairness. In his famous book, *A Theory of Justice*, Rawls defends a conception of "justice as fairness." He did not admit utilitarianism as a criteria of justice because greater happiness of a majority is achieved by neglecting the rights and interests of a minority. Reviving the notion of a social contract, Rawls argues that justice consists of the basic principles of government that free and rational individuals would agree to in a hypothetical situation of perfect equality. In order to ensure that the principles chosen are fair, Rawls imagines a group of individuals who have been made ignorant of the social, economic, and historical circumstances from which they come, as well as their basic values and goals, including their conception of what constitutes a "good life." Situated behind this "veil of ignorance," they could not be influenced by self-interested desires to benefit some social groups (i.e., the groups they belong to) at the expense of others. Thus they would not know any facts about their race, sex, age, religion, social or economic class, wealth, income, intelligence, abilities, talents, and so on.

In this "original position," as Rawls characterizes it, any group of individuals would be led by reason and self-interest to agree to the following principles:

(1) Each person is to have an equal right to the most extensive basic liberty compatible with a similar liberty for others.

(2) Social and economic inequalities are to be arranged so that they are both (a) to the greatest benefit of the least advantaged and (b) attached to offices and positions open to all under conditions of fair equality of opportunity.

First principle comprises most of the rights and liberties traditionally associated with liberalism and democracy. It advocates for freedom of thought and conscience, freedom of association, the right to representative government, the right to form and join political parties, the right to personal property, and the rights and liberties necessary to secure the rule of law. in other words, first principle given by Rawls emphasises on all political and civil rights necessary for development of the individual. Here, Rawls does not seem to see Economic rights and liberties, such as freedom of contract or the right to own means of production, among the basic liberties.

Clause *b* of the second principle provides that everyone has a fair and equal opportunity to compete for desirable public or private offices and positions. This entails that society must provide all citizens with the basic means necessary to participate in such competition, including appropriate education and health care. Clause *a* of principle 2 is known as the "difference principle": it requires that any unequal distribution of wealth and income be such that those who are worst off are better off than they would be under any other distribution consistent with principle 1, including an equal distribution. Here, it is necessary to understand that Rawls does not recommend for complete equality but he holds that some inequality of wealth and income is probably necessary in order to maintain high levels of productivity.[2]

As a great supporter of justice, Rawls outlined a just society too that according to him, would be a "property-owning democracy" in which ownership of the means of production is widely distributed and those who are worst off are prosperous enough to be economically independent. It is why because each can live a life of respect and dignity. In true sense, he provided a philosophical foundation for egalitarian liberalism. In *Political Liberalism* (1993), Rawls revised the argument for the two principles of justice by construing the contracting individuals as representatives of conflicting comprehensive worldviews in a pluralistic democracy.[3]

MARXIAN VIEW OF SOCIAL JUSTICE

Karl Marx had been a staunch critic of exploitation and subjugation of men by men. He hardly hit the capitalism and supported socialism and communism. His theories of class struggle and economic interpretation of history are the mirror of his thoughts. He was a stalwart of equality and social justice being a greatest supporter of labourers' rights and he wanted to establish the rule of proletariats. According to McCarthy, Marx views justice as a form of ethical community based on beneficence, equality, and freedom, which nurtures and enhances the function or end of humanity. This view of justice is applied to a variety of issues in Marx's writings: the self-realization and self-determination of human being; physical well-being and spiritual enlightenment; human creativity, virtue, and happiness in the workplace; a symbiotic balance between humanity and nature; the communal fulfilment of economic reciprocity and need; and, finally, the industrial democracy of producers' co-operatives and workers' communes, as well as the political democracy of human rights and emancipation. Marx "redesigns these issues in terms of natural law based on human nature (species being), human needs (self-realization and self-determination), the natural environment, and democracy (equality, freedom, and participation)".[4]

In my opinion, social justice is nothing but the absence of discrimination and inequality on the basis of birth, caste, race, religion and gender. It is fairness while providing opportunities of development and social, economic and political rights to all the citizens so that each may live a life of respect and dignity without any humiliation, oppression and subjugation. To take positive and necessary steps to uplift the weak, poor and the lagging behind in social, economic and political aspects is social justice. Social justice is the foundation which is necessary to build an egalitarian and inclusive society and a representative and responsible democracy. Social justice is the accommodation of social differences and preventing these differences from converting into social and political divisions. In short, social justice is the key not only to the social harmony but also to the national unity and integrity. Social justice curbs the chances of political divisions, violence, civil war and disintegration of the country. This book put light on the life and contribution of some of the great intellectuals, saints, philosophers, thinkers and leaders and their fight against caste discrimination, humiliation, untouchability, inequality and social injustice.

<u>**REFRENCE**</u>

1. source-https://www.drishtiias.com/blog/platos-theory-of-justice
2. https://www.britannica.com/biography/John-Rawls
3. https://www.britannica.com/biography/John-Rawls
4. https://mronline.org/2020/01/03/marx-and-social-justice-ethics-and-

   natural-law-in-the-critique-of-political-economy-reviewed-by-xuanpu-zhuang

CHAPTER TWO

VOICE FOR EQUALITY & SOCIAL JUSTICE

IN ANCIENT AND MEDIEVAL TIMES

INTRODUCTION

However, the history is witness to the caste based discrimination, cruelty and social injustice that became prevalent in post Mauryan period and continued till the British period. The Shudras mainly untouchables had to face caste based brutality and subjugation for many centuries. They were forced to live a life full of misery and humiliation. But, it's a matter of pleasure to the mankind that it has been obtaining precious gifts from nature in forms of great saints, Mahatmas, philosophers, thinkers, intellectuals and social reformers in all eras-ancient, middle and modern. They tried to echo voice against injustice mainly against social injustice and advocated for social equality and fraternity. They fought against the social inequality, exclusion and injustice and untouchability even in opposite circumstances.

In ancient period, the most enlightened intellectual, person of scientific temperament and a great philosopher was Mahatma Gautam Buddha who paved the path leading to social equality, social justice and inclusive society. As far as the efforts made by the Buddha for the reform of Hinduism and the abolition of caste are concerned, Tathagata Gautam Buddha who was a lover of peace, non-violence, equality, fraternity and justice played a vital role against the caste system and the high-low behaviour on the basis of caste. Buddha gave the message of social and religious equality, influenced by which millions of people expressed faith in Mahatma Buddha and they became his followers. The shackles of caste were definitely weakened by the efforts of Gautam Buddha, but could not be broken completely. However, he showed the path of Dhamma that paved the path of social equality and fraternity. Due to influence of the teachings of Mahatma Buddha, Mauryan Emperors ruled according the philosophy of Buddha and promoted equality and fraternity.

Inspired by the teachings of Tathagata Buddha, Mauryan emperor Ashoka the Great discouraged caste discrimination and high and low tendencies to a great extent by ending slavery and created an atmosphere of social harmony and fraternity. Emperor Ashoka adopted Dhamma-policy, which was also against all kinds of discrimination and based on the welfare of humanity. He was possibly the first indigenous thinker who talked about fraternity, social equality and justice. He not only criticized but also attacked the Brahmanical traditions and rituals which were hindrances in the path of equality, justice and human brotherhood. He established sangha and made it open to all without discrimination of caste. He taught the lesson of not only kindness, tolerance, forgiveness, love, truth and non-voilence but also of humanity, equality, justice and fraternity to the mankind. This chapter sheds light on the contribution and vibrant voices of Mahatma Gautam Buddha, Sant Kabir Das, Sant Ravidas and Mahatma Gandhi towards equality and social justice.

Let's learn about the life and contribution of above mentioned great intellectuals, saints, thinkers and leaders and their fight against caste discrimination, untouchability, inequality and injustice.

(PART – 1) MAHATMA GAUTAM BUDDH

https://www.youtube.com/watch?v=zOyF4s_pPiE

INTRODUCTION

Gautam Buddha who born in ancient period was certainly first stalwart of equality and social justice in India. He not only initiated the fight against caste based inequality, discrimination, humiliation, exploitation and subjugation but also showed the path to the future generations to fight. He was a great Saint, spiritual intellectual, philosopher, thinker and religious and social reformer. Gautama Buddha, popularly known as the Buddha (also known as Siddhartha Gotama or Buddha Shakyamuni), was a Śramaṇa who lived in ancient India (5th to 4th century BCE). Buddha was born into an aristocratic family in the Shakya clan but eventually renounced lay life. According to Buddhist tradition, after several years of mendicancy, meditation, and asceticism, he awakened to understand the mechanism which keeps people trapped in the cycle of rebirth. The Buddha then traveled throughout the Ganges plain teaching and building a religious community. The Buddha taught a middle way between sensual indulgence and the severe asceticism found in the Indian sramaṇa movement.[1] He taught a training of the mind that included ethical training, self-restraint, and meditative practices such as *jhana* and mindfulness. The Buddha also critiqued the practices of Brahmin priests, such as animal sacrifice and the caste system and paved the way for equality and social justice. Really, Buddha began the long journey of struggle against caste discrimination and inequality in India.

According to the Buddhist tradition, Gautama was born in Lumbini, now in modern-day Nepal, and nurtured in Kapilvastu, which may have been either in what is present-day Tilaurakot, Nepal or Piprahwa, India. According to Buddhist tradition, he obtained his enlightenment in Bodh Gaya, gave his first sermon in Sarnath, and died in Kushinagar. One of Gautama's usual names was "Sakamuni" or "Sakyamunī" ("Sage of the Shakyas"). This and the evidence of the early texts suggests that he was born into the Shakya clan, a community that was on the periphery, both geographically and culturally, of the eastern Indian subcontinent in the 5th century BCE. The community was either a small republic, or an oligarchy. His father was an elected chieftain, or oligarch.[2]

The Shakyas were an eastern sub-Himalayan ethnic group who were considered outside of the Āryāvarta and of 'mixed origin' (*saṃkīrṇa-yonayaḥ*, possibly part Aryan and part indigenous). The laws of Manu treats them as being non Aryan. This is confirmed by the *Ambaṭṭha Sutta*, where the Sakyans are said to be "rough-spoken", "of menial origin" and criticised because "they do not honour, respect, esteem, revere or pay homage to Brahmans." Some of the non-Vedic practices of this tribe included incest (marrying their sisters), the worship of trees, tree spirits and nagas.[3] According to Levman "while the Sakyans' rough speech and Munda ancestors do not prove that they spoke a non-Indo-Aryan language, there is a lot of other evidence suggesting that they were indeed a separate ethnic (and probably linguistic) group".[4]

Buddha's father Śuddhodana was a hereditary monarch of the Suryavansha (Solar dynasty) of *Ikṣvāku* (Pāli: Okkāka). This is unlikely however, as many scholars think that Śuddhodana was merely a Shakya aristocrat (*khattiya*), and that the Shakya republic was not a hereditary monarchy. Indeed, the more egalitarian *gana-sangha* form of government, as a political alternative to Indian monarchies, may have influenced the development of the śramanic Jain and Buddhist sanghas, where monarchies tended toward Vedic Brahmanism. The day of the Buddha's birth is widely celebrated in Theravada countries as Vesak. Buddha's Birthday is called *Buddha Purnima* in Nepal, Bangladesh, and India as he is believed to have been born on a full moon day. According to later biographical legends, during the birth celebrations, the hermit seer Asita journeyed from his mountain abode, analyzed the child for the "32 marks of a great man" and then announced that he would either become a great king (*chakravartin*) or a great religious leader. Suddhodana held a naming ceremony on the fifth day and invited eight Brahmin scholars to read the future. All gave similar predictions. Kondañña, the youngest, and later to be the first Arhat other than the Buddha, was reputed to be the only one who unequivocally predicted that Siddhartha would become a Buddha.[5]

BUDDHA AND HIS SRAMAṆA SCHOOLS OF THOUGHT

Apart from the Vedic Brahmins, the Buddha's lifetime coincided with the flourishing of influential Śramaṇa schools of thought like Ājīvika, Cārvāka, Jainism, and Ajñana. Brahmajala Sutta records sixty-two such schools of thought. In this context, a śramaṇa refers to one who labors, toils, or exerts themselves (for some higher or religious purpose). It was also the age of influential thinkers like Mahavira, Pūraṇa Kassapa, Makkhali Gosāla, Ajita Kesakambalī, Pakudha Kaccāyana, and Sañjaya Belaṭṭhaputta, as recorded in Samaññaphala Sutta, whose viewpoints the Buddha most certainly must have been acquainted with. Indeed, Sāriputra and Moggallāna, two of the foremost disciples of the Buddha, were formerly the foremost disciples of Sañjaya Belaṭṭhaputta, the sceptic and the Pali canon frequently depicts Buddha engaging in debate with the adherents of rival schools of thought. There is also philological evidence to suggest that the two masters, Alara Kalama and Uddaka Rāmaputta, were indeed historical figures and they most probably taught Buddha two different forms of meditative techniques. Thus, Buddha was just one of the many śramaṇa philosophers of that time. In an era where holiness of person was judged by their level of asceticism, Buddha was a reformist within the śramaṇa movement, rather than a reactionary against Vedic Brahmanism. "Sakamuni" is also mentioned in the reliefs of Bharhut, dated to c. 100 BCE, in relation with his illumination and the Bodhi tree, with the inscription *Bhagavato Sakamunino Bodho* (The illumination of the Blessed Sakamuni). (Wikipedia)

FORMATION OF SANGHA AND ACCEPTANCE OF ALL TO SANGHA

Buddha did a remarkable task towards equality and social justice when he formed the sangha (Buddhist association) and made it open to all without any social discrimination. Mahatma Buddha spent his first vassana (residing during rainy season) at Varanasi when the sangha was formed. According to the Pali texts, shortly after the formation of the sangha, the Buddha traveled to Rajagaha, capital of Magadha, and met with King Bimbisara, who gifted a bamboo grove park to the sangha. There was a complete equality in sangha. All people were allowed to enter sangha without any discrimination of caste and varna. It was a remarkable thing at that time which was varna based and in Brahmanical order, shudras were not permitted to perform religious activities and enter in temples. They were also deprived of right to education. They were not only deprived of education but also they were denied to listen to religious hymens. In that situation, Buddha did a revolutionary act by laying a foundation for an open religious system that later on led to an inclusive and egalitarian social order to emerge. The Buddha's sangha continued to grow during his initial travels in north India. The early texts tell the story of how the Buddha's chief disciples, Sāriputta and Mahāmoggallāna, who were both students of the skeptic sramana Sañjaya Belaṭṭhiputta, were converted by Assaji.

They also tell of how the Buddha's son, Rahula, joined his father as a bhikkhu when the Buddha visited his old home, Kapilavastu. Over time, other Shakyans joined the order as bhikkhus, such as Buddha's cousin Ananda, Anuruddha, Upali the barber, the Buddha's half-brother Nanda and Devadatta. Meanwhile, the Buddha's father Suddhodana heard his son's teaching, converted to Buddhism and became a stream-enterer.[6]

CRITIC OF BRAHMANISM AND `BRAHMANICAL SOCIAL ORDER

As a social and religious reformer, Mahatma Buddha believed in equality and humanity. Hence, he protested against the discriminatory and inequality based social and religious order. He attacked on the Brahmanical social order which was discriminatory and biased towards Shudras. In the early Buddhist texts, the Buddha critiques the Brahmanical religion and social system on certain key points. The Brahmin caste held that the Vedas were eternal revealed (*sruti*) texts. The Buddha, on the other hand, did not accept that these texts had any divine authority or value. The Buddha also did not see the Brahmanical rites and practices as useful for spiritual advancement. For example, in the Udāna, the Buddha points out that ritual bathing does not lead to purity, only "truth and morality" lead to purity. He especially critiqued animal sacrifice as taught in Vedas. The Buddha contrasted his teachings, which were taught openly to all people, with that of the Brahmins', who kept their mantras secret. He also critiqued numerous other Brahmanical practices, such astrology, divination, fortune-telling, and so on (as seen in the *Tevijja sutta* and the *Kutadanta sutta*). The Buddha also attacked the Brahmins' claims of superior birth and the idea that different castes and bloodlines were inherently pure or impure, noble or ignoble. In the *Vasettha sutta* the Buddha argues that the main difference among humans is not birth but their actions and occupations. Buddha did not accept the concept of caste based on birth. He rejected varna system that categorised people into three varnas and later on in different castes on the basis of birth. According to the Buddha, one is a "Brahmin" only to the extent that one has cultivated virtue. Because of this the early texts report that he proclaimed: "Not by birth one is a Brahman, not by birth one is a non-Brahman; - by moral action one is a Brahman".

According to Kancha Ilaiah, the Buddha posed the first contract theory of society. The Buddha's teaching then is a single universal moral law, one Dharma valid for everybody, which is opposed to the Brahmanic ethic founded on "one's own duty" (*svadharma*) which depends on caste. Because of this, all castes including untouchables were welcome in the Buddhist order and when someone joined, they abandoned all caste affiliation.[7]

BUDDHA'S SOCIO-POLITICAL TEACHINGS: INSISTED ON FREEDOM AND EQUALITY

Buddha was a great supporter of freedom and equality and he favoured the social and political orders which promote freedom and equality. The early texts depict the Buddha as giving a deflationary account of the importance of politics to human life. In the *Aggañña Sutta*, the Buddha teaches a history of how monarchy arose which according to Matthew J. Moore is "closely analogous to a social contract." The *Aggañña Sutta* also provides a social explanation of how different classes arose, in contrast to the Vedic views on social caste.

SUPPORTER OF EQUALITY BASED REPUBLICAN FORM OF GOVERNMENT

Mahatma Gautan Buddha valued for equality, fairness and justice. He was a great supporter of Republican Form of Government too. In the *Mahāparinibbāna Sutta,* the Buddha outlines several principles that he promoted among the Vajjian tribal federation, which had a quasi-republican form of government. He taught them to "hold regular and frequent assemblies", live in harmony and maintain their traditions. The Buddha then goes on to promote a similar kind of republican style of government among the Buddhist Sangha, where all monks had equal rights to attend open meetings and there would be no single leader, since The Buddha also chose not to appoint one. Some scholars have argued that this fact signals that the Buddha preferred a republican form of government, while others disagree with this position. In last, Buddhists believe that there is no fundamental difference between any human. **Every individual is valued and should be treated fairly and therefore with justice**. Mahayana Buddhists believe that everyone should be treated equally because we all have 'Buddha Nature', i.e. the ability to become enlightened. Here it is obvious to understand that all people are capable to be enlinghtened, if they are given opportunity and proper training.[8] Buddha gave respect to many people belonging to shudra varna like Upali (a barber), Sunil (a sweeper), Sopak and Suppiy (untouchables), Sumangal (a farmer) etc and included them in Bhikkhu Sangh without consideration of their castes.

MAIN FEATURES OF BUDDHA'S PHILOSOPHY

Mahatma Buddha was a great thinker and philosopher of ancient India who had immense concern for humanity and the welfare of people. His great ideas were *Pragya, Karuna, Sheel, Kshama, Satya, Ahinsa, Maitri* and *Bandhutva.* He strongly believed in equality, liberty, fraternity and justice. Buddha found the chaturvarna system unnatural as it was obligatory and absolute. It was like a society created by order of someone. Buddha gave priority to an open and free society against Brahmanical society based on chaturvarna. He wanted to create a world without sorrow through the education and enlightenment. He believed in inclusive society having no discrimination and attacked on inequality. The main characteristics of Buddha's philosophy were following-

1. Equal treatment with all
2. Right and of education to all
3. Freedom of profession to all
4. Equal Rights to women as compared with men[9]

Mahatma Gautam Buddha was really a true champion of equality and social justice. He echoed his vice for equality and humanity and showed his concern for the upliftment of the lagging behind people. His Dhamma was a path of humanity, equality, freedom, social justice, pity, kindness, pardon and nonviolence which leads the human beings to the humanity, progress and development through the logical and scientific thinking. His path of living (the Dhamma) connects the human beings with each other rathan than dividing them.

(PART – 2) SANT KABIR DAS

https://www.hindu-blog.com/2018/11/kabir-panth-sect-practicing-thoughts-and-ideas-kabir-das.html

INTRODUCTION

Kabir Das was a great saint belonging to Nirguna Sakha during medieval period (in the 15th century). He was regarded as a disciple of Saint Ramanad. He was not only a famous saint but also an intellectual, philosopher and thinker who criticized caste system and voiced for equality and social justice. He assaulted on caste based discrimination, inequality, superstition and religion based hypocrisy. He is known for being critical of religions promoting inequality, superstition and hypocrisy. He questioned meaningless and unethical practices of all religions primarily the wrong practices in Hindu and Muslim religion. During his lifetime, he was threatened by both Hindus and Muslims for his views. When he died, both Hindus and Muslims he had inspired claimed him as theirs. Kabir emphasised upon truth and suggested that Truth is with the person who is on the path of righteousness, considered everything, living and nonliving, as divine, and who is passively detached from the affairs of the world. To know the Truth, suggested Kabir to drop the "I" or the ego.

KABIR'S ATTACK ON CASTE SYSTEM AND LOVE FOR EQUALITY

Kabir is also known for attacking caste and caste system and echoed his voice for equality. This can be understood through the following lines said by Saint Kabir

JAATI NA POCHHO SAADHOO KI,
POOCHH LIJIYE GYAN;
MOL KARO TALAVAAR KA,
PARA RAHANE DO MYAAN.
Don't ask caste of a monk, ask for knowledge.
Buy Talwar, leave the sheath.

Kabir Das criticized the caste and preferred the knowledge and merit over caste. He taught the people not to ask caste of a gentle man and a meritorious one but to know his knowledge. A sword is valuable not the sheath as we use sword not the sheath. Similarly, we should know a person by his knowledge and merit not by his birth and caste. It is the knowledge which is significant not the caste.

KABIRA SOI PIR HAI,
JO JAANE PAR PIR;
JO PAR PIR N JAANAHI,
SO KA PIR MEIN PIR.
Kabir says he is the only sage who knows the pain of others.
One who does not know the pain of others is not a real sage.

Through these fantastic lines, Kabir Das ji wanted to say that a sage cannot be a real sage if he does not have pain and sympathy for others. Here, Kabir attacked the hypocrite people who want to be called sage and spiritual but don't have pain and mercy for the poor and weak people. Kabir was full of sympathy towards people victim of discrimination and sufferings. He wanted to remove their sufferings and make their lives full of happiness. In this way, Kabir Das advocated for love, respect and care for people in pain.

KABIR' STRESS UPON GOOD DEEDS RATHER THAN BIRTH

Kabir Saheb believed in good actions not in caste based superiority and inferiority. According to him, our actions determine our greatness and upper position in the society not our caste. He critised the Brahmins for setting up a discriminatory social order and focused on actions which make anyone upper and lower. Our actions should be humanistic and unoppressive to mankind. His love for good actions can be understood by his following verse.

OONCHE KUL KA JANMIYA,
KARNI OONCHI NA HOY;
SUVARN KALASH SURA BHARA,
SAADHOO NINDA HOY.
One does not become high by being born in a high family if his deeds are not high.
He is condemned like a golden jar full of wine.

Here, Kabir rejected the superiority of the individuals on the basis of birth. He emphatically, said that a person born in a so called upper caste or family cannot be high if his actions are mean and inferior. To prove his thoughts and arguments right, he gave the example of a golden pot full of wine. He meant to say that a golden pot is meaningless if it is full of wine. Any person can be high by his/her good actions not by taking birth in a high family. In this way, Kabir not only rejected the discrimination and unequal treatment on the basis of caste but also assaulted the caste based discrimination and social injustice.

KABIR'S CONTRIBUTION TO THE RE-CONSTRUCTION OF SOCIAL LIFE

The perennial contribution to the re-construction of social life of Kabir was so immense that it makes him a great stalwart of social harmony.

1. <u>**Kabir's Assault on Superstition and Illusion**</u>

Kabir belonged to the Julaha (weaver) community who supported himself and his family by hard work, and hence wasn't a traditional monk living at the mercy of others. Though he lived in Kashi, he had gone to Meghar towards the end of his life, in order to challenge the traditional belief that 'to die in Kashi would merit entry to heaven and to die in Meghar, would lead to hell'.

1. <u>**Kabir-A Revolutionary and Humanistic Thinker**</u>

Kabir was not scientifically educated but had wise insights and was of a revolutionary nature who seemed committed to bring social change. His thinking was practical as well as radical. He was saint, a poet, a mystic, a great thinker, a social reformer, and the like – all in one. Kabir was deeply involved in Indian Society and its issues. His heart and mind were fully alive to the spiritual, cultural, ideological and behavioral patterns of Indian Life. He was deeply committed to the diverse dimensions of the genius of Indian world-view, such as spiritual outlook, individual freedom, plurality, integration, philosophical concept, experiential approach, aesthetic attitude and poetic expression. According to him, their perennial value travels across the boundaries of caste, creed, profession, community and nationality. Kabir gave a powerful message of mutual love, cooperation, peace, humanity, equality and fraternity to the main-kind. Kabir could not close his eyes against the rampart forms of enslavement of human beings.

3. <u>**Critique of Caste and Religion Based Discrimination**</u>

As earlier, the era of Kabir had bondages of casteism, ritualism, fundamentalism, communalism, etc. Attitudinal form of slavery like prejudice, hatred, and ill feeling were strongly prevalent. Discrimination based on caste, class, sect, office or post, social status, profession, language, region, etc., was the most commonly found social malady. Kabir attempted a campaign of reformation with a view to freeing the humans from the clutches of diverse bondages. Kabir emphatically said that nothing else has divided the human society so appallingly as religion. The worst of the wars and tensions in the world have taken place in the name of religion. No doubt, it has facilitated the humans in the search of the Divine. But, Pseudo-orthodoxy and discriminatory attitudes based on caste, class, language, ideology, profession, sect, etc. gain undue power. It is obvious that the religious system failed to maintain the social equilibrium. Kabir was really an extra ordinary sant (sage). However, he was encircled by today's Hindu religion where his roots were in the discriminated section of the society. In that unbalanced social system, Kabir Das hit hard on the discriminatory caste system and echoed voice for equality and social justice.

4. <u>**Kabir's Emphasis on Equality**</u>

Kabir was of the opinion that all being share the same Creator and the same creation. All share the same water, the same light and the same air. It is indeed foolish for one to make difference between one another. Sorrows and joys, hopes and disappointments, suffering and struggles, successes and failures, dreams and achievements are a common experience for all. In fact, there is no reasonable ground for discrimination and unsocial behaviour with people belonging to deprived communities. The basic reality of life is just equal for all. The so-called religious and secular leaders of the society erected a system of classification of human beings, where they can satisfy their selfish interest. Kabir challenges the proponents of the caste system, who undervalue others and thus fall short of a social conduct which is humanly dignifying. He asks in an ironical tone, 'you Brahmin, why haven't taken another way to be born'? What he meant by this is that 'if both Brahmin and Sudra have taken the same way to be born into the world, then there is no difference between them. Both have blood of the same colour; both have hunger and thirst as well as needs and problems. One has to learn from nature, the lessons of equality and good behaviour. In this way, we can see sufficient space for social equality and justice in Kabir's thinking and philosophy.[10]

Hence, by standing with equality and opposing caste discrimination Sant Kabir Das ji not only opposed injustice but also he echoed vibrant vice for social justice. He used his vani (vice) as a strong and effective weapon against superstition, inequality and injustice.

(PART – 3) SANT SHIROMANI RAVIDAS

https://amritvichar.com/sant-ravidas-dedicated-his-life-to-end-casteism-untouchability-pm-modi/

INTRODUCTION

Guru Ravidas was one of the most influential spiritual critic of caste, humanistic poet and a saint of the Bhakti Movement during the 15th to 16th century. He was a powerful and influential voice and torch bearer for equality and social justice. He strongly responded to the caste inequality, discrimination and social exclusion. Every year on the day of the full moon, in the Magh month his birth anniversary is celebrated as Guru Ravidas Jayanti. Guru was born on Magh Purnima, the full moon day in the Magh month near Varanasi, Uttar Pradesh, India. His birthplace is now known as Shri Guru Ravidas Janam sthan. Guru Ravidas was born to Mata Ghurbinia and Raghuram. His family was considered schedule-caste because of his parents belonging to a leather-working Chamar community. The great saint is well-known by many other names such as Raidas, Rohidas, and Ruhidas. He was idolized as a teacher (GURU) in the region of Punjab, Uttar Pradesh, Rajasthan, Maharashtra, and Madhya Pradesh. He was a renowned poet-saint, social reformer, and a spiritual figure.[11]

Sant Ravidas was a spiritual poet, lover of humanity, sant of the Bhakti movement and founder of Ravidassia religion during the 15th to 16th century CE. He is acclaimed as a *guru* (teacher) in the region of Uttar Pradesh, Rajasthan, Gujarat, Maharashtra, Madhya Pradesh and mainly Punjab and Haryana. He was a poet-saint, social reformer and a spiritual figure. The life details of Ravidas are uncertain and contested. Ravidas was a humanistic philosopher and saint and whished for the welfare of all. His devotional Verses' inclusion in the Sikh scriptures known as *Guru Granth Sahib* proves it right that Sant Ravidas really was egalitarian thinker of medieval period. The *Panch Vani* text of the Dadupanthi tradition within Hinduism also includes numerous poems of Ravidas.[12] He taught removal of social divisions of caste and gender, and promoted unity in the pursuit of personal spirituous well known. Some Scholars state that he was born in 1388CE and died in 1518 CE.[13]

According to some other sources, Ravidas was also known as Raidas. He was born in the village of Seer Goverdhanpur, near Varanasi in what is now Uttar Pradesh. His birthplace is now known as Shri Guru Ravidas Janam sthan. Mata Kalsan was his mother, and his father was Santokh Dass. His parents belonged to a leather-working Chamar community making them an untouchable caste. While his original occupation was leather work, he began to spend most of his time in spiritual pursuits at the banks of the Ganges. Thereafter he spent most of his life in the company of Sufi saints, sadhus and ascetics.[14]

RAVIDAS'S ATTACK ON CASTEAND HIS ADVOCACY FOR SOCIAL EQUALITY

Ravidas was a staunch critic of caste and caste based discrimination and inequality. He defeated Brahmin scholars and intellectuals by his strong arguments based on logic and truth. He did not accept mechanism of caste based inequality and constantly echoed his voice against it. His attack on caste based discrimination and inequality can be understood from his literal works and lines given as under.

1. **RAVIDAAS JANM KE KAARANAI, HOT NA KOU NEECH,**

   NAR KO NEECH KAR DETEE HAI, OCHHE KARAM KEE KEECH .
   Ravidas stressfully says due to birth, no one is low, it is the sludge of low karma indeed that degrades the man. Here, Ravidas rejected the birth based superiority and valued the deeds. According to him, deeds make man up or low not the birth.

2. **JAATI-JAATI MEIN JAATI HAIN, JO KETAN KE PAAT,**

   RAIDAAS MAANAV NA JUD SAKE JAB TAK JAATI NA JAATEE.
   Ravidas admits that there is caste in the caste, like the leaf under the leaf and he further states human could not join till the caste did not end. In other words, Ravidas took the caste responsible for disunity among human beings in India. Caste prevented men to come closure to each other and it promoted inequality among them.

3. **JAAT JAAT KE PHER MEIN ULAJH RAHE SAB LOG .**

   MANUSHYATA KO KHA RAHA, RAIDAAS JAAT KA ROG
   All the people are getting entangled in the difference of caste.
   Raidas the disease of caste, eating humanity.
   Ravidas in this couplet, while criticizing the caste system created by Brahmins, Aryans, says that this poison of casteism created by Brahmins has failed in everyone. Whoever sees him is entangled in this disgusting swamp of caste. Raidas says that caste is a disease, it is a disease that is eating human beings and humanity, due to which the human inside is getting destroyed. Discrimination, untouchability, inequality exploitation, which has flourished from caste, has destroyed humanity itself.

RAVIDAS'S EMPHASIS ON RESPECT FOR VIRTUES

Sant Ravidas was a huge supporter of merit and meritorious persons cutting across the castes and religions. He insisted upon the respect and worship of a merits person without consideration of his caste and religion. His vision for respect for merit can be understood from the following couplet:

BRAHMAN MAT POOJIE, JO HOVE GUNAHEEN;

POOJIE CHARAN CHANDAAL KE, JO HOVE GUN PRAVEEN.

Ravidas stressfully advocated for not worshiping Brahmins who are without merit and worship or honour the feet of *Chandalas* who are full of virtues. Here again, Ravidas focused on merit not on caste and gave the message of respecting virtuous chandals (untouchables) rather than unmeritorious Brahmins. It was an immense attack on Brahmins and casteism.

HIS VISION FOR BEGHAMPURA, A STATE FREE OF SUFFERINGS

Ravidas was a visionary and dreamt of an egalitarian state based on equality and having no discrimination and humiliation of downtrodden. His views on a state having space for all cutting across caste and religion, can be understood from following verse.

AISA CHAHUN RAJ ME, MILE SABAN KU ANN;

CHOT-BADE SAB SAM BASE RVIDAS RAHE PRASANN.

Above doha (verse) highlights that Sant Ravidas was a champion of social justice as his words clearly shows that he believed in construction of a society and political order where all had enough food to eat and no one live in a starving condition. He wanted all people without any discrimination to live a poverty free life. Each individual could have equal rights and live a respectable life. He wanted to construct a society and social order where all people poor and rich live together harmoniously and happily.

Sant Ravidas was a philosopher who visioned for *Beghampura* and he wanted to set up a state free of sorrow and sufferings which he named as *Beghampura*. No doubt, he was the only thinker who dreamt of state where citizen will have no sorrow and suffering. He did not want anybody in agony and trouble. He wanted a discrimination free state where all live together without any feeling of superiority and inferiority. His focus was on construction a state and governing system where all could easily fulfil their needs and could live a life of respect.

In other words, Sant Ravidas led the fight against caste based discrimination during the medieval period and paved the path for equality and social justice to emerge. He stressfully attacked caste based inequality and caste based feeling of superiority and inferiority. His teachings and confrontations with Brahmin intellectuals echoed the voice for humanity, equality and social justice. He without fear strongly criticized caste based humiliation, exploitation, marginalistion and subjugation. However, most effective battle against caste and caste based discrimination and humiliation was fought and strong voice was echoed for equality and social justice during modern period under the leadership of Dr. Ambedkar, but we can find its roots in Sant Kabir Das and Sant Ravidas who began to challenge discriminatory Brahmanical social order.

(PART – 4) MAHATMA GANDHI

Enter Captionhttps://www.dailyexcelsior.com/the-amazing-story-of-mahatma-gandhi/

INTRODUCTION

Mahatma Gandhi was a prominent intellectual, social reformer, thinker and freedom fighter who locates himself as an insider to mainstream Hinduism and he claimed to follow the Sanatana Dharma. His full name was Mohandas Karam Chand Gandhi. He belonged to vaishya (third Varna) community of Porbandar (Gujrat). Gandhi does not reject, he simply affirms what he considers to be authentic, and allows the inauthentic to be marshed off. B.R. Nanda identifies a few fundamental beliefs in Gandhi's Hinduism: the reality of god, the unity of all life and the value of ahimsa (the desire not to harm) as love. His profound redefinition of Hinduism gave it a radically novel reorientation with his seva marg (the path of service), adding a new dimension to three margs of traditional Hinduism – jnana, karma and bhakti (path of knowledge, path of duties and path of devotion). Yet, Gandhi's Hinduism has a spiritual meaning beyond service, for Gandhi's seva marg is inspired by, and is a means to, moksha (world release). This is just one of his radical reinterpretations, as Bhikhu Parekh demonstrates.[15]

GANDHI'S OPPOSITION OF CASTE BUT SHOFT ATTITUDE TO VARNA SYSTEM

However, Mahatma Gandhi being a sanatani Hindu supported the Varna system but he was critic of, casteism and untouchability prevalent in the Hindu tradition. Later on, he also worked towards making public opinion against the same. Further, though Gandhi distinguished the caste system from the "chaturvarna," that is, the scriptural four fold Varna order of hereditary occupational divisions, his criticism with regards to the latter is scarcely addressed. Anil Nauriya observes that though he initially defended the Varna order, he later acknowledged the need to do away with the Varna system. However, this itself had a slow trajectory. In 1933, Gandhi thought of untouchability as the bigger evil, and felt it necessary to first abolish the caste system and "cross the other bridge later." For a long time, then, his fight was restricted to the caste system, though he did not rule out a later time to struggle against the Varna order. This later time came in 1947 when Gandhi began to directly speak out against the Varna system.

Gandhi had a contrary attitude on the issues of caste and Varna. He had not similar position as Dr. Ambedkar had on the issues of caste and Varna system. Dr. Ambedkar wanted to uproot the caste and Varna sytem as well. But Gandhi was not in favour of abolition of Varna sytem. On the one hand, Gandhi emphatically stated that "caste must go if Hinduism is to survive". On the other hand he also said, 'There was room for varna, as a duty.' According to him: 'This was true of all religions whether the name used was other than Varna. What was a Muslim 'maulvi' or a Christian priest but a Brahmin if he taught his flock its true duty, not for money but because he possessed the gift of interpretation? And this was true of the other divisions.' Significantly, the position of a maulvi in Islamic society does not indicate any inherent superiority and does not necessarily pass hereditarily. However, Gandhi assaulted untouchability and caste directly but he had not the same position on the Varna system. Arundhati Roy, however, argues that Gandhi, for all his claims of rejecting the caste system, was not in fact a denouncer of it, as one would think. Responding to Rajmohan Gandhi's critique of her "The Doctor and the Saint," where she accuses Gandhi of being casteist, Roy defends her assertions by observing that Gandhi (including, later, Rajmohan Gandhi) conflated the fight against untouchability with that against caste. It is exactly this nuance on which several Hindu reformers functioned, where they "cleverly narrowed" the question of caste to that of untouchability. Therefore, on deeper probing, Gandhi's apparent compassion and persistent campaigning against untouchability may not have been as genuine. Moreover, she underscores Gandhi's stance on the Varna system and how his lack of explicit disavowal of the same proves his rather superficial take on the subject. (https://en.wikipedia.org/wiki/Mahatma_Gandhi)

Keep in mind here that Gandhi did not want 'bhangis' (scavengers as he was fond of calling them) to amass wealth even from their supposedly divinely designated professional occupation of cleaning other people's shit, on the other hand he developed his famous doctrine of trusteeship: 'The rich man must be left in possession of his wealth...' The rich man, then as well as now, was and continues to be the Bania. Gandhi was certainly troubled by caste injustices, but not by caste itself. He never once denounced the caste system in clear uncertain terms. On the few occasions in the later years of his life when he did gently criticise it, he suggested it should be replaced by Varna—which Ambedkar described as the 'parent' of the caste system. Gandhi constantly reiterated his belief in the tradition of hereditary occupation. And since Rajmohan Gandhi offers us 'The Ideal Bhangi' with such approbation, should we assume that he agrees with his grandfather's views?[16]

OPPOSITION OF UNTOUCHABILITY

No doubt to say that Gandhi believed in Varna system and did not attack it but he strongly opposed the untouchability. Gandhi spoke out against untouchability early in his life.[17] Before 1932, he and his associates used the word *antyaja* for untouchables. Gandhi attacked on untouchability and considered it harmful to the society. In a major speech on untouchability at Nagpur in 1920, Gandhi called it a great evil in Hindu society but observed that it was not unique to Hinduism, having deeper roots, and stated that Europeans in South Africa treated "all of us, Hindus and Muslims, as untouchables; we may not reside in their midst, nor enjoy the rights which they do". Calling the doctrine of untouchability intolerable, he asserted that the practice could be eradicated, that Hinduism was flexible enough to allow eradication, and that a concerted effort was needed to persuade people of the wrong and to urge them to eradicate it.[18]

According to Christopher Jaffrelot, while Gandhi considered untouchability to be wrong and evil, he believed that caste or class is based on neither inequality nor inferiority.[19] Gandhi seemed to support inter-caste marriages. He believed that individuals should freely intermarry whomever they wish, but that no one should expect everyone to be his friend: every individual, regardless of background, has a right to choose whom he will welcome into his home, whom he will befriend, and whom he will spend time with.[20]

DR. AMBEDKAR'S INFLUENCE ON GANDHI AND HIS ACHOOTODDHAR PROGRAMS

As we know that in 1928, Simon Commission visited India and submitted its report to the British government. After study of the report British government decided to hold round table conferences in London where the several issues mainly the miserable plight of depressed castes was discussed. During the discussion, Gandhi's confrontation with Dr. Ambedkar on the issue of depressed castes in second Round Table Conference that held in 1931 in London heralded a new beginning. Gandhi had to take the notice of depressed community's miserable life and he had to adopt some steps to eradicate untouchability, however, he did not give attention to the problems of depressed people before conflict with Dr. Ambedkar and his efforts for upliftment of depressed people too were not genuine in the opinion of Dr. Ambedkar.

In 1932 after Poona Pact, Gandhi began a new campaign to improve the lives of the untouchables, whom he began to call *Harijans*, "the children of god".[21] On 8 May 1933, Gandhi began a 21-day fast of self-purification and launched a year-long campaign to help the *harijan* movement.[22] This campaign was not universally embraced by the Dalit community: Ambedkar and his allies felt Gandhi was being paternalistic and was undermining Dalit political rights. Ambedkar described him as "devious and untrustworthy".[23]

Dr. Ambedkar accused Gandhi as someone who wished to retain the caste system. Ambedkar and Gandhi debated their ideas and concerns, each trying to persuade the other.[24] It was during the Harijan tour that he faced the first assassination attempt. While in Poona, a bomb was thrown by an unidentified assailant (described only as a Sanatani in the press at a car belonging to his entourage but Gandhi and his family escaped as they were in the car that was following.[25] Gandhi later declared that he "cannot believe that any sane sanatanist could ever encourage the insane act. The sorrowful incident has undoubtedly advanced the Harijan cause. It is easy to see that causes prosper by the martyrdom of those who stand for them".[26] In 1935, Ambedkar made an announcement his intentions to leave Hinduism and join Buddhism*. According to Sankar Ghose, the announcement shook Gandhi, who reappraised his views and wrote many essays with his views on castes, intermarriage, and what Hinduism says on the subject. These views contrasted with those of Ambedkar.[27]

However, Dr. Ambedkar had worked with other Congress leaders through the 1940s and written large parts of India's constitution being a chsirmsn of Drafting Committee in the late 1940s. But he could not remain a Hindu by religion and converted to Buddhism in 1956 for which he had announced in 1935 that he would not like to die as a Hindu. Relationship between Gandhi and Dr. Ambedkar was not good as Dr. Ambedkar took Gandhi as a supporter of varna system. But when Gandhi was assassinated, he expressed sorrow and relief as well. "Even though Ambedkar was a party to Poona Pact, he was never reconciled to it. His contempt against Gandhi continued even after his assassination on January 30, 1948. On the death of Gandhi, he expressed, "My real enemy has gone; thank goodness the eclipse is over". He equated the assassination of Gandhi with that of Caesar and the remark of Cicero to the messenger – "Tell the Romans, your hour of liberty has come". He further remarked, "While one regrets the assassination of Mahatma Gandhi, one cannot help finding in his heart the echo of the sentiments expressed by Cicero on the assassination of Caesar".[28]

To conclude, it can be said that Gandhi took soft position towards removal of caste system and did not strongly criticized the Varna system. However, he was not a strong and serious critic of social inequality and injustice. E.V. Ramasami too had criticised Gandhi ji for his soft position on caste system. But his attack on untouchability makes Gandhi a supporter of social equality and social justice. Gandhi understood the importance of Dr. Ambedkar and his battle against caste system and untouchability and he began a new campaign to uplift the life of untouchables. However, it was, in the view of Dr. Ambedkar, a move of Gandhi to counter increasing popularity of Dr. Ambedkar among depressed castes and to establish himself as a true well-wisher of depressed people. More or least Gandhi by attacking untouchability and taking some steps for the welfare of depressed stood in favour of equality and social justice.

REFERENCE

*Nicholas B. Dirks (2011). *Castes of Mind: Colonialism and the Making of Modern India*. Princeton University Press. pp. 267–74. ISBN978-1-4008-4094-6.

1. Laumakis, Stephen (2008), *An Introduction to Buddhist philosophy*, Cambridge; New York: Cambridge University Press, ISBN978-0-521-85413-9

2. Tuladhar, Swoyambhu D. (November 2002), "The Ancient City of Kapilvastu – Revisited" (PDF), *Ancient Nepal* (151): 1–7

3. Huntington, John C. (September 1986), "Sowing the Seeds of the Lotus: A Journey to the Great Pilgrimage Sites of Buddhism, part V" (PDF), *Orientations*, **17** (9): 46–58, archived (PDF) from the original on 28 November 2014

4. Gombrich, Richard F. (1988), *Theravada Buddhism: A Social History from Ancient Benares to Modern Colombo*, Routledge and Kegan Paul

5. https://en.wikipedia.org/wiki/Gautama_Buddha)

6. https://en.wikipedia.org/wiki/Gautama_Buddha

7. https://en.wikipedia.org/wiki/Gautama_Buddha

8. https://en.wikipedia.org/wiki/Gautama_Buddha

9. Bodhisatva Babasaheb Dr. B.R. Ambedkar, *Bagwan Buddh aur unka Dhamm,* translated from *Buddha and his Dhamma* by Dr. Bhadant Anand Kausalyayan, Samyak Prakashan

10.http://mdthomas.in/publications/articles/ KABIR%20A%20PIONEER%20OF%20SOCIAL%20REFORM,%20LIBERA%20AND%20HARMO.pdf

11. https://www.yourselfquotes.com/guru-ravidas-jayanti-quotes/

12. James Lochtefeld (2002), The Illustrated Encyclopedia of Hinduism: N-Z, Rosen Publishing, ISBN978-0823931804, page 569

13. Arvind Sharma (2003).*The Study of Hinduism.* University of South Carolina Press. p. 229. ISBN978-1-57003-449-7.

14. Hardev Bahri. Harbans Singh; et al. (eds.).*"Ravidas". Encyclopaedia of Sikhism.* Punjabi University Patiala. Retrieved *11 February* 2017.

15. Wikipedia

16. Wikipedia

17. Coward, Harold G. (2003).*Indian Critiques of Gandhi.* SUNY Press. pp. 52–53. ISBN978-0-7914-5910 2.

18. Desai, Desai, Mahadev Haribhai (1930). *"Preface". Day-to-day with Gandhi: secretary's diary.* Hemantkumar Nilkanth (translation). Sarva Seva Sangh Prakashan. ISBN978-81-906237-2-8. pp. 230– 89.

19. Coward, Harold G. (2003).*Indian Critiques of Gandhi.* SUNY Press. pp. 52– 53. ISBN978-0-7914-5910-2.

20. Desai, Desai, Mahadev Haribhai (1930).*"Preface". Day-to-day with Gandhi: secretary's diary. Hemantkumar Nilkanth (translation).* Sarva Seva Sangh Prakashan. ISBN978-81-906237-2-8. pp. 230–89.

21. Roberts, Andrew (26 March 2011).*"Among the Hagiographers (A book review of "Great Soul: Mahatma Gandhi and His Struggle With India" by Joseph Lelyveld)". The Wall Street Journal.* Archived from the original on 3 January 2012. Retrieved 14 January 2012.

22. Nicholas B. Dirks (2011). *Castes of Mind: Colonialism and the Making of Modern India.* Princeton University Press. pp. 267–74. ISBN978-1-4008-4094-6.

23. Gandhi-Ambedkar correspondence Archived 9 January 2017 at the Wayback Machine, Mahatma Gandhi writings, An Archive

24. Rajmohan Gandhi (2006).*Gandhi: The Man, His People, and the Empire.* University of California Press. pp. 333–59. ISBN978-0-520-25570-8. Archived from the original on 22 February 2017.

25. Benjamin, N.; Narkulwad, Ganesh (2019).*"Gandhi's Links with Poona: An Overview"* (PDF). Gandhi Marg. 40 (3–4): 165–186.

26. Sankar Ghose (1991). *Mahatma Gandhi.* Allied Publishers. p. 236. ISBN978-81-7023-205-6.

27. Rajmohan Gandhi (2006). *Gandhi: The Man, His People, and the Empire.* University of California Press. p. 385. ISBN978-0-520-25570-8.

27. Laxman Kawale (2012), *Dalit's Social Transformation: Redefining the Social Justice*, ISRJ, Volume 1, Issue XII, page 3.

CHAPTER THREE

MAHATMA JYOTIBA PHULE AND

MATA SAVITRIBAI PHULE

https://thedailyvoice.in/heres-who-was-jyotiba-phule-the-mahatma-whom-babasaheb-ambedkar-considered-as-his-guru/

INTRODUCTION

Jyotirao Govindrao Phule was a prominent social reformer, philosopher, thinker and great warrior of equality and social justice of the nineteenth century India. He is also known as Jyotiba and Jotiba. However, Mahatma Gautam Buddha in ancient period and Sant Kabir Das and Sant Ravidas in mediaeval times condemned caste and caste based inequality before Jotiba. As far as the social reformers of modern India like Raja Ram Mohan Rai, Dayanand Saraswati, Ramkrishan Paramhans etcetera were concerned, they too had heralded the journey of social reform in modern India but their efforts remained very liberal when they attacked religious and social evils. No doubt, Ram Mohan Rai contributed to ban the Sati, a brutal tradition of burning the widow with the dead body of her husband. With the serious efforts of Ram Mohan Rai, British government banned Sati in 1829. But these social reformers could not fight hard against other social evils like caste discrimination, social exclusion and untouchability.

It is not exaggeration to state that it was Mahatma Jyotiba Phule who paved the path for equality and social justice in British India. He took revolutionary and historical steps against caste discrimination. He not only condemned caste system and discrimination but also led the movement to dismantle the prevailing caste-restrictions in India.

He highly opposed caste based discrimination and injustice originated and supported by Varna system in Indian society. He revolted against the domination of the Brahmins and struggled for the rights of peasants and other people declared as low-castes under the caste ridden social system. Jyotiba Phule was also a pioneer for women education in India and fought for education of girls throughout his life. He is believed to be the first Hindu to start an orphanage for the unfortunate children. Dhananjay Keer authored a biography of Jyotiba in 1974 titled, 'Mahatma Jyotibha Phule: Father of Our Social Revolution'

CHILDHOOD & EARLY LIFE

Jyotirao Govindrao Phule was born in Satara district of Maharastra in 1827. His father, Govindrao was a vegetable-vendor at Poona. Jyotirao's family belonged to 'mali' (vegetable and flower grower) caste and their original title was 'Gorhay'. Malis were considered as an inferior caste by the Brahmins and were shunned socially. Jyotirao's father and uncles served as florists, so the family came to be known as `Phule`. Jyotirao's mother passed away when he was just nine months old. Jyotirao was an intelligent boy but due to the poor financial condition at home, he had to stop his studies at an early age. He started helping his father by working on the family's farm. Recognising the talent of the child prodigy, a neighbour persuaded his father to send him to school. In 1841, Jyotirao got admission in the Scottish Mission's High School, Poona, and completed his education in 1847. There, he met Sadashiv Ballal Govande, a Brahmin, who remained his close friend throughout his life. At the age of just thirteen years, Jyotirao was married to Savitribai (Wikipedia).

JYOTIBA'S EXPERIENCE WITH CASTE DISCRIMINATION AND HIS MISSION AGAINST CASTE DISCRIMINATION AND INJUSTICE

Jyotiba Phule was a staunch critic of caste and caste based discrimination. An incident in 1848 made Jyotiba revolutionary against the social injustice and caste discrimination. After that incident, he incited a social revolution against caste discrimination in the Indian society. Jyotiba was invited to attend the wedding of one of his friends who belonged to an upper cast Brahmin family. But at the wedding the relatives of the bridegroom insulted and abused Jyotiba when they came to know about his origins. Jyotirao left the ceremony and made up his mind to challenge the prevailing caste-system and social restrictions. His experience with case discrimination proved turning point in his life. He made it his life's work to destroy the social majoritarian domination and aimed at emancipation of all human beings that were subjected to this social deprivation.

As he was an educated person, therefore Jyotiba Phule studied many western philosophers and thinkers. Thomas Paine's famous book 'The Rights of Man', greatly influenced Jyotiba and he was highly impressed with his ideas. He believed that enlightenment of the women and lower caste people was the only solution to combat the social evils. That is why, he worked hard throughout his life to uplift the downtrodden and women using the weapon of education.

STRUGGLE TOWARDS ELIMINATION OF CASTE DISCRIMINATION

Jyotiba struggled very hard to eliminate caste discrimination and his fight against caste discrimination and inequality made him crusader in favour of social justice. He attacked the orthodox Brahmins and other upper castes and termed them as "hypocrites". He campaigned against the authoritarianism of the upper caste people and urged the "peasants" and "proletariat" to defy the restrictions imposed upon them. He opened his home to people from all castes and backgrounds. He was a believer in gender equality and he exemplified his beliefs by involving his wife in all his social reform activities. He believed that religious icons are implemented by the Brahmin as a means for subjugating the lower caste.

Jyotiba Phule's open attack on caste system and traditions made the conservative Brahmins very angry. They blamed him for distorting the norms and regulations of the society. Many accused him of acting on behalf of the Christian Missionaries. But Jyotiba was firm and decided to continue the movement. Interestingly, Jyotiba was supported by some Brahmin friends who extended their support to make the movement successful. Without diverting his mind towards opposition of conservative Hindus, he continued movement against caste based inequality and discrimination. He penned an influential book *Ghulamgiri* and exposed the caste and religion based hypocrisy and continued to echo a strong voice for egalitarian society.

FOUNDATION OF *SATYA SHODHAK SAMAJ* AND ATTACK ON BRAHMANISM

In 1873, Jyotiba Phule founded the Satya Shodhak Samaj (Society of Seekers of Truth). He was firmly determined for deconstruction of existing beliefs and history, only to reconstruct an equality promoting version. Jyotiba vehemently condemned the Vedas, the ancient holy scriptures of the Hindus. He traced the history of Brahmanism through several other ancient texts and held the Brahmins responsible for framing the exploitative and inhuman laws in order to maintain their social superiority by suppressing the "shudras" and "atishudras" in the society. The purpose of the Satya Shodhak Samaj was to decontaminate the society from caste discrimination and liberate the oppressed lower-caste people from the stigmas inflicted by the Brahmins. Jyotirao Phule was the first person to coin the term 'Dalits' to apply to all people considered lower caste and untouchables by the Brahmins. Membership to the Samaj was open to all irrespective of caste and class. Some written records suggest that they even welcomed participation of Jews as members of the Samaj and by 1876 the 'Satya Shodhak Samaj' boasted of 316 members.

In 1868, Jyotiba decided to construct a common bathing tank outside his house to exhibit his embracing attitude towards all human beings and wished to dine with everyone, regardless of their caste. Jyotiba Phule devoted his entire life for the liberation of untouchables from the exploitation of Brahmins. Apart from being a social activist and reformer, he was also a businessman. He was also a cultivator and contractor for the Municipal Corporation. He served as Commissioner of the Poona Municipality between 1876 and 1883. Jyotiba suffered a stroke in 1888 and was rendered paralyzed. On 28 November, 1890, the great social reformer, Mahatma Jyotirao Phule, passed away. (Wikipedia)

GHULAGIRI ANDHIS ATTACK ON CASTE SYSTEM

Mahatma Phule, whom Dr. Ambedkar considered his guru, authored a famous book *Ghulamgiri* — one of the first critiques of the caste system. This piece takes stock of its major argument and its significance. Written in Marathi, with an English preface, the text has been translated into English as Slavery.Mahatma Jotiba Phule wrote *Gulamgiri* in 1873 ant it is considered one of the first tracts against the caste system. Published in 1885, it critiques the institution of caste through a 16-part essay and four poetic compositions, and it is written in the form of a dialogue between Jyotiba, and a character he calls Dhondiba. It proved a revolutionary book against caste based discrimination, inequality, exclusion, subjugation and social injustice.

Following are some excerpts from the preface of the book 'Ghulamgiri' by Mahatma Jotiba Phule:

For hundreds of years till today, the Shudra-Atishudra (untouchable) society has been subjected to constant oppression and exploitation ever since the Brahmins came to power in this country. These people are passing their days in all kinds of tortures and difficulties. Therefore, these people should pay attention to these things and think seriously. How can these people free themselves from the atrocities of Brahmin Panda priests, that is the most important question for us today. That is the purpose of this book. It is said that more than three thousand years must have passed since the Brahmin priests came to power in this country. They came here from abroad. They made these people their slaves by depriving them of their homes and properties, by barbaric attacks on the original inhabitants of this country. He had adopted an attitude of great inhumanity with them. Even after hundreds of years have passed, seeing that the memories of the past events are being refreshed in these people that the Brahmins have made the original residents their slaves by evicting the natives from their homes, land and property, the proofs of this fact have been Ruined by the Brahmin priests. They have destroyed and buried them.

In order to maintain their influence and their supremacy on the mind and heart of these people, those Brahmins used various methods to fulfill their selfishness and they all continued to be successful in them. Since at that time these people were already subjugated from the point of view of power and later Brahmin-Panda-priests had made them ignorant, the result of which was that the Brahmin-panda-priests' gimmicks, their forgery, any of these Couldn't even notice. The Brahmin priests succeeded in creating more than one fabricated texts, keeping only their personal interests in view, to keep them as their slaves forever and ever, to establish their supremacy over them.

(http://ndl.iitkgp.ac.in/document/
aXpRbGhuZTluMXBPcS92SlBNUzJXbjBxYmVXcU4vcXYyS1NCVVc2L05Mbz0)

The main thrust of Mahatma Phule's text is an inversion of the racial theory of caste. Here it is obvious to see a question to be raised, What is the racial theory of caste? According to this theory, a superior, foreign race invaded this land. They became what we know as Brahmins today. The lowly, indigenous people who were conquered became the shudras. That Mahatma Phule gave credence to the racial theory of caste at all, is sometimes considered a limitation of the text. What must be noted however, as Gail Omvedt does in *"Hinduism as Brahman Exploitation: Jotiba Phule"*, Phule takes an already existing discourse, and he inverts its moral logic. He accepts the facticity of the theory. He says, yes Brahmins are a different race. Yes, they invaded and conquered us. But he upturns its moral logic and says the invaders were actually corrupt, cruel and depraved. Superior they were definitely not. (https://feminisminindia.com/2017/04/14/jotiba-phule-gulamgiri/)

JYITIBA'S EFFORTS TOWARDS WOMEN EDUCATION AND EMPOWERMENT

Jyotiba was an immense supporter of girl education and women empowerment. he was fully committed to provide right to education to women. His quest regarding women education was supported by his wife Savitribai Phule. One of the few literate women of the time, Savitribai was taught by her husband Jyotirao at home. In 1851, Jyotiba established a girls' school and asked his wife to teach the girls in the school. Later, he opened two more schools for the girls and an indigenous school for the backward castes, especially for the Mahars and Mangs.

Jyotiba was very sympethetic towards women, widows in particular. He realised the pathetic conditions of widows and established an ashram for young widows and eventually became advocate of the idea of Widow Remarriage. Around his time, society was a patriarchal and the position of women was especially abysmal. Female infanticide was a common occurrence and so was child marriage, with children sometimes being married to men much older. These women often became widows before they even hit puberty and were left without any family support. Jyotiba was pained by their plight and established an orphanage in 1854 to shelter these unfortunate souls from perishing at the society's cruel hands. (https://feminisminindia.com/2017/04/14/jotiba-phule-gulamgiri/)

Here, no doubt to say that the biggest legacy of Mahatma Jyotiba Phule is the thought behind his everlasting fight against social discrimination and injustice. He was dedicated to bring social change for which he strongly echoed his voice in favour of equality and social justice. In the nineteenth century, people were used to accepting these discriminatory practices as social norm that needed to be enforced without question but Jyotiba challenged then prevalent social order and sought to change this discrimination based on caste, class, colour and gender. He was the harbinger of unheard ideas for social reforms. He started awareness campaigns that ultimately inspired many social activists particularly Dr. B.R. Ambedkar who was the stalwart to ensure equality and social justice in the country and who undertook major initiatives against caste discrimination later as a fighter and architect of Indian Constitution.

JYOTIBA PHULE IN MEMORY THROUGH BOOKS, MUSEUMS AND INSTITUTIONS

A biography of Jyotiba was penned by Dhananjay Keer in 1974 titled, 'Mahatma Jyotibha Phule: Father of Our Social Revolution'. The Mahatma Phule Museum in Pune was set-up in honour of the great reformer. The Government of Maharashtra introduced the Mahatma Jyotiba Phule Jeevandayeeni Yojana which is a cashless treatment scheme for poor. A number of statues of the Mahatma have been erected as well as several street names and educational institutes have been rechristened with his name eg. Crawford Market in Mumbai is rechristened as Mahatma Jyotiba Phule Mandai and the Maharashtra Krishi Vidyapeeth at Rahuri, Maharshtra was renamed Mahatma Phule Krishi Vidyapeeth.

Mayawati led BSP Uttar Pradesh government too gave honour to Jyotiba Phule by erecting his statues in Ambedkar parks along with all stalwarts who dedicated their lives for bettering the lives of the poor and social justice. The Rohilkhand University that was established in 1975, was renamed as Mahatma Jyotiba Phule Rohilkhand University in August 1997 in honour of social reformer and crusader of social justice Mahatma Jyotiba Phule. In 1997, Amroha district was renamed as Jyotiba Phule Nagar but it was reverted to as Amroha by Akhilesh Government in 2012. Indeed, Jyotiba was a true champion of equality and social justice and a crusader against superstition, hypocrisy, casteism, social discrimination and subjugation. He alone with his wife Mata Savitribai Phule heralded a new era of consciousness and struggle against caste discrimination in the modern India and later on Babasaheb Dr. Ambedkar considering him his guru followed his path to echo energetic voice for equality and social justice.

MATA SAVITRIBAI PHULE

Savitribai Phule (3 January 1831 – 10 March 1897) was an Indian social reformer, educationalist, women activist, feminist and poet from Maharashtra. She is regarded as the first female teacher of India. Along with her husband, Jyotiba Phule, she played an important and vital role in improving women's plight in India. She is regarded as the mother of Indian feminism. Phule and her husband founded one of the first Indian girls' school in Pune, at Bhidewada in 1848.* She worked to abolish the discrimination and unfair treatment of people based on caste and gender. She is regarded as an important figure of the social reform movement in Maharashtra.

"Go, get education" was Savitribai Phule's appeal to people from the backward castes particularly the women. She encouraged them to get education as a means to break the shackles of socially-constructed discriminatory practices. Really, she was true Saraswati who with the help of her husband Jyotiba opened schools for girls and did a revolutionary job to pave the path for girl education in India.

EARLY LIFEAND EDUCATION OF SAVITRIBAI PHULE

Savitribai Phule was born on 3 January 1831 in the village of Naigaon in Satara District, Maharashtra. Savitribai Phule was the eldest daughter of Lakshmi and Khandoji Nevase Patil who belonged to the Mali Community. Savitribai and Jotirao had no children of their own. It is said that they adopted Yashawantrao, a son born to a Brahmin widow. However, there is no original evidence available yet to support this.[1] As far her education was concerned, Savitribai was illiterate at the time of her marriage. Her hubband, Jyotiba educated Savitribai and Sagunabai Shirsagar, his cousin sister at their home along with working at their farm.[2] After completing her primary education with Jyotirao, her further education was the responsibility of his friends, Sakharam Yeshwant Paranjpe and Keshav Shivram Bhavalkar.[3] She also enrolled herself in two teacher's training programs. The first was at institution run by an American missionary, Cynthia Farrar, in Ahmednagar. The second course was at a Normal School in Pune.[4] Given her training, Savitribai may have been the first Indian woman teacher and headmistress.[5] Savitribai's birthdate, i.e. 3 January, is celebrated as Balika Din in the whole of Maharashtra, especially in girl's schools. From last few years, her birth day, 3rd january is also being as first women teacher day. The bahujan movement as started by Manyawar Kanshi Ram has proliferated their contribution to the common people.

HER CONTRIBUTION TO THE GIRL EDUCATION AND UPLIFTMENT OF THE WOMEN

After completing her teacher's education, Savitribai Phule started teaching girls at the Maharwada in Pune. She did so alongside Sagunabai who was a revolutionary feminist as well as a mentor to Jyotirao. Not long after beginning to teach with Sagunabai, Savitribai and Jyotirao Phule along with Sagunabai started their own school at Bhide Wada. Bhide Wada was the home of Tatya Saheb Bhide, who was inspired by the work that the trio was doing. The curriculum at Bhide Wada included traditional western curriculum of mathematics, science, and social studies. By the end of 1851, Savitribai and Jyotirao Phule were running three different schools for girls in Pune. Combined, the three schools had approximately one hundred and fifty students enrolled. Like the curriculum, the teaching methods employed by the three schools differed from those used in government schools. The author, Divya Kandukuri believes that the Phule methods were regarded as being superior to those used by government schools. As a result of this reputation, the number of girls receiving their education at the Phule's schools outnumbered the number of boys enrolled in government schools.[6]

FOR EDUCATING GIRLS, SAVITRIBAI FACED CONSERVATIVE OPPOSITION WITH STONES, DUNG, AND VERBAL ABUSE

Unfortunately, Savitribai and Jyotiba Phule's success came with much resistance from the local community with conservative mindset. Kandukuri states that Savitribai often travelled to her school carrying an extra sari because she would be assailed by her conservative opposition with stones, dung, and verbal abuse. The Phules faced such strong opposition because of the conservative (Brahmin) and marginalized caste to which they belonged. The Sudra community had been denied education for thousands of years. For this reason, many Brahmins began to oppose Jyotirao and Savitribai's work and labeled it as "evil". Up until 1849, Savitribai and Jyotirao Phule were living at Jyotirao's father's home. However, in 1849, Jyotirao's father asked the couple to leave his home because their work was considered a sin as per the Brahmanical texts.[7] After moving out of his own father's home, the Phule couple moved in with the family of one of Jyotirao's friend, Usman Sheikh. It was there that Savitribai met a soon to be close friend and colleague named Fatima Begum Sheikh. According to Nasreen Sayyed, a leading scholar on Sheikh,

"Fatima Sheikh knew how to read and write already, her brother Usman who was a friend of Jyotiba, had encouraged Fatima to take up the teacher training course. She went along with Savitribai to the Normal School and they both graduated together. Despite, inconducive circumstances, Mata Savitribai Phule continued her efforts to educate the girls. It shows her determination towards women empowerment through education.

EDUCATION TO CHILDREN OF DIFFERENT CASTES

Savitribai was very committed and determined to proliferate education among the poor, backwards and girls. She along with Fatima Sheikh opened a school in Usman Sheikh's home in 1849.[8] She was very devoted and enthusiastic to the education of girls and other children of different castes mainly the children of downtrodden.Along with her husband, she taught children from different castes and had opened a total of 18 schools.[9] The couple also opened a care centre called Balhatya Pratibandhak Griha[10] (literally, "Child-killing Prohibition Home") for pregnant rape victims and helped deliver and save their children.[11] In the 1850s, Savitribai and Jyotirao Phule established two educational trusts. They were entitled: The Native Female School, Pune and the Society for Promoting the Education of Mahars, Mangs, and Etcetera. These two trusts ended up encompassing many schools which were led by Savitribai Phule and later, Fatima Sheikh. Jyotiba was very impressed with his wife's role in improving the condition of women. He summarises Savitribai and his work in an interview given to the Christian missionary periodical, Dnyanodaya, on 15 September 1853, saying, "It did occur to me that the improvement that comes about in a child due to the mother is very important and good. So those who are concerned with the happiness and welfare of this country should definitely pay attention to the condition of women and make every effort to impart knowledge to them if they want the country to progress. With this thought, I started the school for girls first. But my caste brethren did not like that I was educating girls and my own father threw us out of the house. Nobody was ready to give space for the school nor did we have money to build it. People were not willing to send their children to school but Lahuji Ragh Raut Mang and Ranba Mahar convinced their caste brethren about the benefits of getting educated".[12]

Savitribai was very sensitive and careful to the people. With her adopted son, Yashwant, she opened a clinic to treat those affected by the worldwide Third Pandemic of the bubonic plague when it appeared in the area around Nalasopara in 1897.[13] The clinic was established at stern outskirts of Pune, in an area free of infection. Savitribai died a heroic death trying to save the son of Pandurang Babaji Gaekwad. Upon learning that Gaekwad's son had contracted the Plague in the Mahar settlement outside of Mundhwa, Savitribai Phule rushed to his side and carried him on her back to the hospital. In the process, Savitribai Phule caught the Plague and died at 9:00PM on 10 March 1897.[14]

SAVITRIBAI PHULE'S CONTRIBUTION TO SOCIAL JUSTICE AS A FEMINIST

Savitribai Phule being a prolific author and poet also published *Kavya Phule* in 1854 and *Bavan Kashi Subodh Ratnakar* in 1892, and also a poem entitled "Go, Get Education" in which she encouraged those who are oppressed to free themselves by obtaining an education. As a result of her experience and work, she became an ardent feminist. She established the Mahila Seva Mandal to raise awareness for issues concerning women's rights. She also called for a gathering place for women that was free of caste discrimination or differentiation of any kind. Symbolic of this was that all the women that attended were to sit on the same mat. She was also an anti-infanticide activist. She opened a women's shelter called the Home for the Prevention of Infanticide, where Brahmin widows could safely deliver their children and leave them there to be adopted if they so desired. She also campaigned against child marriage and was an advocate of widow remarriage.[15] Savitribai and Jyotirao strongly opposed Sati Pratha, and they started a home for widows and forlorn children. (Source- https://en.wikipedia.org/wiki/Savitribai_Phule)

Source**

MAA FATIMA SHEIKH

INTRODUCTION

The sparkling story of the contribution of Jyotiba Phule and Savitribai Phule is incomplete if we don't highlight the life and struggle of Fatima Sheikh. Nearly two centuries have passed since Fatima challenged the status quo to ensure that all children have access to education, no matter their caste, gender, or religion. It is a small consolation that some young children in Maharashtra today might stumble across her name in a textbook in school, and hopefully recognise the role she played in creating this present for them. Fatima Sheikh, however, is so unknown that even her date of birth (9 January) is debated. Fatima Sheikh was an Indian educator and social reformer, who was a colleague of the social reformers Jyotirao Phule and Savitribai Phule.[16]

Fatima Sheikh was the sister of Mian Usman Sheikh, in whose house Jyotiba and Savitribai Phule took up shelter. One of the first Muslim women teachers of modern India, she started educating Bahujan children in Phules' school. Jyotirao and Savitribai Phule along with Fatima Sheikh took charge of spreading education among the downtrodden communities. Sheikh met Savitribai Phule while both were enrolled at a teacher training institution run by Cynthia Farrar, an American missionary.[17] She taught at all five schools that the Phules went on to establish and she taught children of all religions and castes. Sheikh took part in the founding of two schools in Bombay in 1851.[18]

FATIMA'S SHELTER TO JYOTIBA PHULE AND SAVITRIBAI, A SHELTER TO GIRL EDUCATION WOMEN EMPOWERMENT

Due to the activities of Jyotiba, his father was not happy with him. Jyitiba challenged the then prevalent social and religious orders and found them against humanity. Jyotiba believed in equality and wanted egalitarian society. He wanted inclusive education system open to all including girls. His father took his activities against the social order and religion. Jyotiba's father had asked Jyotiba and Savitribai to vacate their ancestral house as his father was angry with the reform agenda of the couple. In the situation of homelessness, Fatima and her brother Usman Sheikh proved angel as they opened the doors of their house for the Phules. They gave shelter not only to the Phule couple but also shelter to the girl education. It was the same building in which Jyotiba with his wife started the girls' school. It wouldn't have been easy for them to do so, considering the fact that the social elite of the time were dead against the idea of girls going to school and that too from all castes and religions together. And yet, any mention of Fatima Sheikh is largely absent. By doing so, Fatima not only provided shelter to Jyotiba Phule and his wife but also to girl education as well. Indeed, her bold and cooperative decision opened the door for women empowerment because it is the education that is the most effective tool that can elevate anyone to the hights of success. Indeed, education is the first requirement of pregress of the individual.

IGNORANCE TO SAVITRIBAI AND FATIMA SHEIKH'S CONTRIBUTION

This is not to say that the glory came to Savitribai Phule easily. Mainstream historians were very cruel to her – while mentioning the Indian Renaissance, they talked of Ram Mohan Roy, Ishwar Chandra Vidyasagar, Swami Dayananda, Swami Vivekananda, or Mahadeo Govind Ranade. In early textbooks, even the name of Savitribai found no mention. It was only after decades of oblivion that Dalit and Bahujan activists started to write about her, and her pictures started appearing on the banners and posters of BAMCEF, an organisation started by Kanshi Ram, who later founded the Bahujan Samaj Party. In the last decade, with the advent of digital age, Savitribai's name and her contribution to society have reached millions through social media. Now Savitribai's contribition is in public domain but the situation is not so good. Yet, we need to work hard to bring her works and contribution in its full worth.But the same process has eluded Fatima Sheikh. Her contribution as an educator and social reformer was no less the Phules. Rather, she must have faced bigger hurdles. As her works are not documented, we can only assume how difficult it must have been for a Muslim woman to work for girls' education, which was considered irreligious at that time, especially in the Hindu-dominated Pune society. Some writers suggest she was opposed by both the Hindu and the Muslim community for what she was doing. Savitribai was fighting against the bigotry of Brahmanism. She was an insider, fighting against the ills of the system. Opening the gates of her schools for Dalits was her challenge to patriarchy and the caste system at the same time. Fatima Sheikh had a different proposition. Islam does not prohibit girls' education per se. So, being part of the anti-caste project started by Phule makes her more of a revolutionary. She was not fighting for her own community alone. Her efforts to introduce modern education to Muslim girls were not liked by the Muslim clergy. We know about some of these things because Savitribai, while writing letters to her husband, mentioned the contribution of Fatima Sheikh. A brief profile of Fatima Sheikh is now part of Maharashtra's Urdu school textbook.

CAUSES OF FATIMA SHEIKH'S OBSCURITY

Absence of Fatima Sheikh's writings on her life or work

Fatima Sheikh never wrote any treaties on her life or work, which is why we know so little about her. On the contrary, Savitribai and her husband Jyotirao Phule, wrote a lot. Although one can be deterministic, and blame the twice-born historians for ignoring anti-caste reformers like Fatima Sheikh, we must acknowledge the fact that there is not enough material available that can give us a clue about her life and contributions.

Dalit-Bahujan movement's Indifference towards Fatima Sheikh

Savitribai and Jyotirao Phule fit well in the anti-caste social movement narrative in Maharashtra. Their writings and works resonate with the Dalit-Bahujan movement. A range of scholars like Gail Omvedt and Rosalind O'Hanlon has documented their contribution in this sphere, and B. R . Ambedkar dedicated his book *Who were the Shudras* to *Jyotiba Phule*. On the contrary, the Dalit-Bahujan movement largely ignored the contribution of Fatima Sheikh. We don't know the reason for this. The Dalit movement effortlessly adopted non-Dalit 'backward class' icons like Phule, Shahuji Maharaj, Narayana Guru, Basavanna and others, but failed to acknowledge the likes of Fatima Sheikh. It is for the researchers to find out if this is due to the sectarianism of the anti-caste movement or some other reason.

Muslim scholars' Ignorance

Even Muslim scholars largely ignored the contributions of Fatima Sheikh. A Muslim woman, fighting for a casteless society and for modern education for girls probably does not gel with the dominant Muslim narratives. Fatima Sheikh and Savitribai established the school for girls in 1848. Sir Syed Ahmed Khan established Muhammadan Anglo-Oriental College in 1875, which later became Aligarh Muslim University. Khan is considered as one of the harbingers of modern education in India and rightfully so. But Fatima Sheikh was not accorded the same status despite doing equally pioneering work. Due to our ignorance to her contribution in the fight for social justice, Fatima Sheikh continues to fight for her rightful place in history. (https://theprint.in/opinion/why-indian-history-has-forgotten-fatima-sheikh-but-remembers-savitribai-phule/175208/) There is need of research on Fatima Seikh's life and contribution. Now, we need to make contribution of Savitribai Phule and Fatima Seikh part of curriculum in the schools.

NOTES AND REFERENCES

* American missionary Cynthia Farrar had started a girls' school in Bombay in 1829. In 1847, the Students' Literary and Scientific society started the Kamalabai High School for girls in the Girgaon neighborhood of Bombay. The school is still operational in 2016. Peary Charan Sarkar had started a school for girls called Kalikrishna Girls' High School in the Bengali town of Barasat in 1847.

** https://www.google.com/searchq=fatima+shaikh+hd+image&tbm=isch&chips=q:fatima+shaikh+image,online_chips:social+reformer:7Z9y1SFTtYQ%3D&rlz=1C1ONGR_enIN982IN982&hl=en&sa=X&ved=2ahUKEwjmuPLE1-76AhXsgGMGHe6zDjkQ4lYoBHoECAEQKw&biw=1899&bih=860

1. O'Hanlon, Rosalind (2002). Caste, Conflict and Ideology: Mahatma Jyotirao Phule and Low Caste Protest in Nineteenth-Century Western India (Revised ed.). Cambridge University Press. p. 135. ISBN978-0-521-52308-0.
2. Kandukuri, Divya (11 January 2019). "The life and times of Savitribai Phule". Mint. Retrieved 19 April 2019.
3. "Teachers' Day Special: The life of Savitribai Phule, India's first female educator". HinduTimes. 5 September 2019. Retrieved 16 June 2020.
4. O'Hanlon, Rosalind (2002). Caste, Conflict and Ideology: Mahatma Jyotirao Phule and Low Caste Protest in Nineteenth-Century Western India (Revised ed.). Cambridge University Press. p. 135. ISBN978-0-521-52308-0.
5. Sundararaman, T. (2009). Savitribai Phule first memorial lecture, [2008]. National Council of Educational Research and raining. ISBN9788174509499. OCLC693108733.
6. Kandukuri, Divya (11 January 2019). "The life and times of Savitribai Phule". Mint. Retrieved 19 April 2019.
7. Kandukuri, Divya (11 January 2019). "The life and times of Savitribai Phule". Mint. Retrieved 19 April 2019.
8. Kandukuri, Divya (11 January 2019). "The life and times of Savitribai Phule". Mint. Retrieved 19 April 2019.
9. Savitribai Phule Second Memorial Lecture, [2009]. National Council of Educational Research and Training. ISBN978-8-17450-931-4.
10. Sundararaman, T. (2009). Savitribai Phule first memorial lecture, [2008]. National Council of Educational Research and Training. ISBN9788174509499. OCLC693108733.
11. "Life Sketch of Savitribai Phule – Timeline". Velivada. 9 November 2017. Retrieved 16 June 2020.
12. Rege, Sharmila (2009). Savitribai Phule Second Memorial Lecture, [2009]. National Council of Educational Research and Training. ISBN978-8-17450-931-4.
13. O'Hanlon, Rosalind (2002). Caste, Conflict and Ideology: Mahatma Jyotirao Phule and Low Caste Protest in Nineteenth-Century Western India (Revised ed.). Cambridge University Press. p. 135. ISBN978-0-521-52308-0.
14. https://www.esakal.com/amp/saptarang/today-is-savitribai-phule-jayanti-the-indian-womens-liberation-tmb01
15. O'Hanlon, Rosalind (2002). Caste, Conflict and Ideology: Mahatma Jyotirao Phule and Low Caste Protest in Nineteenth-Century Western India (Revised ed.). Cambridge University Press. p. 135. ISBN978-0-521-52308-0.
16. Madhu Prasad (2019). "A strategy for exclusion". Elementary Education in India: Policy Shifts, Issues and Challenges. ISBN9781000586954.
17. Grey, Mary (2016). "Opposition to Untouchability: Gandhi and Ambedkar". A Cry for Dignity: Religion, Violence and the Struggle of Dalit Women in India. Taylor & Francis. p. 118. ISBN9781315478401. Retrieved 17 February 2021.
18. Tschurenev, Jana (2019). "Civil Society, Government, and Educational Institution-Building, Bombay Presidency, 1819-1882". Empire, Civil Society, and the Beginnings of Colonial Education in India. Cambridge University Press. p. 276. ISBN9781108656269. Retrieved 17 February 2021.

CHAPTER FOUR

CASTE DISCRIMINATION AND SOCIAL EXCLUSION:

HISTORICAL BACKGROUND

INTRODUCTION

The history is the witness to the fact that a large number of people have been facing discrimination, humiliation and social, economic and political exclusion in India for centuries. A big chunk of the population was deprived of all facilities and rights and they were forced to live a life of misery, humiliation and subjugation. Caste has been a peculiar attribute of Indian society for centuries and a decisive factor in Indian politics right since independence. While, heinous casteism already exists in form of caste-based discrimination and atrocities. Dalits and backward castes are being constantly humiliated, victimised and tortured. Youths are being killed for doing inter-caste marriages. Casteism seems to be prevalent until caste come to its ebb. For ensuring national integrity and unity, caste will have to be annihilated or a caste-less society should replace caste-ridden society to secure better future for the country.

However, the deprived people belonged to the glorious roots. Once upon they were rulers. Adi Hindus, today's Dalit, had kingdoms, capital cities, forts and a thriving civilization. But when Aryans invaded this country they conquered these Adi Hindus variously by brute force, repression and treachery. Being righteous good and free from deceit, the Adi Hindus were no match for the cunning Aryans, even though they were heroic and brave.[1]

According to the ideology of Adi-Hinduism, *bhakti* was religion of the ancient, pre-Aryan inhabitants and rulers of India, the Adi-Hindus from whom untouchables were supposed to have descended. Underlying the argument of Adi-Hindus, ancestry was the central assertion that the social division of labour based on caste status was forced on Indian society by the Aryan conquerors, who had subjugated the Adi Hindus as servile labourers.[2]

As far as the merit is concerned, they (the deprived) too have been meritorious and fully competent. But caste Hindus enslaved them and propagated them as unmeritorious. Later on, they declared them Shudras and untouchables under Varna system. Briggs in his work, *The Chamars,* says that he interviewed the people living in villages and towns, who are working as farmers, tanners, shoemakers, wizards, gurus and servants and his "single aim has been in all cases to record the Chamars point of view."[3] Robertson presented the Chamars, in his work, *The Mahar Folk*, not as mere object of scientific interest, but as a man possessing all the worth and dignity, and all the capacity for practical, intellectual and spiritual attainment, that are found in other members of God's great family".[4]

WHAT DOES CASTE MEAN?

Many scholars have expressed different views as far as the meaning of caste id concerned. They made their attempts to define the Caste. But no one could succeed in encompassing its various facets in a single definition. Most significant definitions given by the learned authorities are given as under:

Lundberg defined caste as "a rigid social class into which members are born and from which they can withdraw or escape only with extreme difficulty".

Lisley defined caste as "a collection of families or groups of families bearing a common name; claiming a common descent from a mythical ancestor, human or divine; professing to follow the same hereditary calling, and regarded by those who are competent to give an option as forming a single homogeneous community".

According to **Arnold Green**, "caste is a system of stratification in which mobility, up and down the status ladder, at least ideally may not occur".

Nesfield has defined caste as "a class of the community, which disowns any connection with any other class and can neither intermarry nor eat or drink with any but persons of their own community".

Ketkar says, " Caste is a social group having two characteristics: (i) membership is confined to those who are born of members and includes all persons so born; (ii) the members are forbidden by an inexorable social law to marry outside group".

Dr. B.R. Ambedkar has defined caste as "an artificial chipping off the population into fixed and definite units, each prevented from fusing into another through custom of endogamy". He further said that caste is not a division of labour but a division of labourers. It has been done to break the unity of labour class so that they cannot put a threat to the hegemony of few in future.

ORIGIN AND DEVELOPMENT OF CASTE AND CASTEISM

Now, a significant question, which needs a definite answer, is how caste has come into existence. Different intellectuals and scholars have contributed their theories to meet the question. Dr. Ambedkar had evolved a rational and convincing theory in this regard. It may be noted that all over the world exogamy had been practiced. In exogamy, there could be no place for castes. When endogamy is super positioned on exogamy, castes are created (Busi, 1997).

Caste is a centuries old phenomenon in Indian society. Its roots are very deep. However, the basis of Indian ancient society is the tribal system and caste seems to come into existence with the philosophy of Chaturvarna (four segments of human beings named as Brahmin, Kshatriya, Vaishya, and Shudra) propounded by Manu Maharaj in his Manusmriti. Through this idea, Manu Maharaj had bifurcated tribal masses into four segments - Brahmin, Kshatriya, Vaishya, and Shudra. In Chaturvarna system, Brahmins, Khatriyas and Vaishyas held first, second and third position respectively in social hierarchy of Hindu society. Shudras were placed at the bottom (fourth place) of the hierarchical system. Following triangular diagram pictures the structure of India's caste system.

In other words, people having learning and teaching capabilities were regarded as Brahmins. People having spirit or courage were leveled as Kshatriyas. People indulged in trading and other business activities were named as Vaishyas. Lastly, remaining individuals who were not doing these activities were regarded as Shudras which comprise the workers, artisans and peasants and they were supposed to do service of above mentioned three Varnas. In beginning, the Chaturvarna system was flexible and all respected each other. In this way, this classification of masses was based on Karma (deeds).

With the passage of time, Chaturvarna system converted into rigid caste system and many castes came into existence. People started to be known by their castes and it became hereditary system. Generations of Brahmin were regarded as Brahmin and Shudras' Shudra. Chaturvarna system became Panchvarna indeed as some castes seemed to be marginalised and degraded of human status. They have been regarded as Ati-shudras (Backward among Shudras) by the social scientists. They were treated worse than cattle too. In this way, such human beings were dubbed as outcastes, pollutants and finally untouchables. This led them to prohibition of using good food, clean water and splendid wearing like jewelry and clothes. They were strictly prohibited to mingle with the society and thrown outside the settlements. They were forced to live in separate settlements regarded as ghettos. In this way, casteism emerged in India and became an integral part of Hindu society.

DIFFERENT THEORIES REGARDING *VARNA* SYSTEM

There are different theories regarding emergence of varna system, which is the mother of caste system in India.

Theory of Mahabharata: In the Mahabharata, the origin of the Varna has been described from the various parts of the body of the creator. The Brahmana originated from the mouth of the Brahma or the creator, the Kshatriya from his arms, the Sudra-from his feet, the Brahmana was created to preserve the Vedas, the Kshatriya to rule the world and to protect it, the Vaishyas to support the other two Varnas and himself by agriculture, and the Sudras to serve the other three Varnas.

Theory of Manu: According to Manu Smiriti, the four Varnas have been created from the limbs of the creator. To protect the universe, different duties and occupations were assigned to the different Varnas. Brahmana Varna has been regarded as the supreme creation of God. Manu has asserted that the Brahmana, the Kshatriya, the Vaishya and the Sudra are the only in existence and there is no Pancham Varna.(http://www.yourarticlelibrary.com/sociology/ essay-on-varna-system-in-india-1513-words/ 4006**)**

According to G. S. Ghurye, Varna means distinction. In the beginning we find that there are two classes in Hindu society, the Aryas and the Dasas. Ghurye has written, "In the Rig Veda, the word Varna is never applied to any one of the classes (Brahmana, Kshatriya etc.). It is only the Arya Varna or the Aryan people that is contrasted with Dasa Varna. The Satapatha Brahmana, on the other hand, describes the four classes as four Varnas. Varna means colour and it is in this sense that the word seems to have been employed in contrasting the Arya and the Dasa, referring to their fair and dark colour respectively. He is of the opinion that the distinction between the Arya and Dasa was latter responsible for the distinction between Arya and Sudra. The term Varna has been used to denote the colour scheme of the different sections of the society. Since the Aryans came from outside India and conquered the indigenous population in India, they occupied a higher social status and the people who were defeated got the lowest position in the society. In this way, Ghurye has adopted the racial theory of the origin of the Varna system. (http://www.yourarticlelibrary.com/sociology/essay-on-varna-system-in-india-1513-words/4006).

In his book *Revolution and Counter-Revolution in India*, Dr. Ambedkar asserted that Manusmriti was written by a sage named Brigu during the times of Pushyamitra Sungha in connection with social pressures caused by the rise of Budhism (Walter Kaufmann, 1980). It is obvious to understand that there is no unanimity as far as the origin of varna system is concerned. Historically, it is difficult to find the originator of varna system. However, Hindu mythology is full of many theories in this regard. But the main credit of creating a stratified social order based on fourth fold division goes to Manusmriti that has been most significant book used to run the social, legal and political system in Hindu society for centuries. Manusmriti favoured an unequal social order that was mainly inclined towards top three varnas-Brahmans, Kshatriyas and Vaishyas. Out of these three varnas, Brahmans possessed privileges and much immunity.

VARNA VYAVASHTHA: ROOT CAUSE OF INEQUALITY, DISCRIMINATION AND SOCIAL INJUSTICE

Defined by various scholars and specialists as a system of elaborately stratified social hierarchy that distinguished India from all other societies, caste has achieved the same significance in the social, political, academic debate as race in the US, class in Britain and faction in Italy (Bayley, 1999)[5]. Here, it is natural for a question to rise, where did the caste come from? Or how caste has come into existence? Different scholars have contributed their theories in this regard. Dr. Ambedkar who is also known as the strong fighter against caste and caste system evolved a rational and convincing theory regarding caste. According to him, all over the world exogamy had been practiced. In exogamy, there could be no place for castes. When endogamy is super positioned on exogamy, castes are created.[6] Dr. Ambedkar criticised caste and defined it as "an artificial chipping off the population into fixed and definite unites, each prevented from fusing into another through custom of endogamy".[7]

Caste is a centuries old phenomenon in Indian society. Its roots are very deep. However, the basis of Indian ancient society is the tribal system and caste seems to come into existence with the philosophy of *Chaturvarna* (four segments of human beings named as Brahmin, Kshatriya, Vaishya and Shudra). In *Chaturvarna* system, Brahmins, Kshatriyas and Vaishyas held first, second and third position respectively in social hierarchy Hindu society. Shudras were placed at the bottom (fourth place) of the hierarchical system ... in beginning *Chaturvarna* system was flexible and all respected each other. With the passage of time *Chaturvarna* system converted into rigid caste system and many castes came into existence. People started to be known by their castes and it became a hereditary system[8].

EMERGENCE OF DEPRIVATION, UNTOCHABILITY AND EXCLUSION

The most negative impact of *Varna* system has been that it led a large section of the society to degradation, deprivation, injustice, untouchability and finally to exclusion. A portion of Shudras had been started to be regarded as Atishudras (Backwards among Shudras). In this way *Chaturvarna* emerged into *Panchvarna* indeed. These were treated worse and forced to live a degraded and disrespectful life. In this way, such human beings were dubbed as outcastes, pollutants and finally untouchables. This led them to prohibition of using good food, clean water and splendid wearing like jewelry and clothes. They were not permitted to enter temples and use public water bodies like wells and ponds. They were forcefully reduced in separate settlements regarded as ghettos to live a life of deprivation, marginalization, subjugation, disgrace and injustice in all fields of life. Varna system concreted the social, economic and political hegemony of few over more. They were not deprived of economic resources but also of respect and dignity. Their political and administrative rights were snatched. In brief, Shudras were reduced as socially inferior, economically poor and politically deprived of freedom and rights. They faced injustice throughout their life and this injustice continued from one generation to another for centuries. Ram Charan, an Adi Hindu leader, putting some light on the origin of the depressed people said in 1927, "They (untouchables) were made to do the most insulting and demeaning jobs, such as cleaning excreta and dirty clothes. They were repeatedly told that you are shudras and your only work to serve (*gulami*). Those who were thus made to serve, *gulam* or *dasa* were then called untouchables".[9] To sum up, it can be said that the *varna vyavashtha* and caste system were the root cause of inequality, social exclusion, discrimination, humiliation and social injustice. Caste system led a large chunk of population to inequality and untouchability that led them to social exclusion and injustice.

RELIGIOUS JUSTIFICATION OF INEQUALITY AND SOCIAL INJUSTICE

Some of the Hindu intellectuals too openly extended their support for inequality, discrimination and social injustice. They played their negative role in engulfing the gap between the forward and backward people. For instance, sant Tulsi Das, a famous Hindi poet of mediaeval era and author of *Ramcharit Manas,* had stated that

"Dhol, Ganwar, Shudra, Pashu, Nari;

Sakal Taadana Ke Adhikari."

It means, drum, cattle, fools, down-trodden people and women all deserve *tadna* i.e. to be beaten, reprimanded and kept away from the society. That statement of Maharishi Tulsi Das showed that most of the forward people and their intellectuals did not want to involve the oppressed people into the mainstream. Depressed people and women were kept in category of animals and fool fellows. Tulsi Das also emphatically stated,

Poojahi vipr sakal gun heena,

Shudra na poojahu ved praveena.

That meant worship a Brahmin (priest) though he is thoroughly meritless but do not worship a Shudra, a backward though he is meritorious.

This thinking heped to make depressed people not only disrespected but also humiliated. This not only deprived them from all opportunities to be respected but also blocked the path of development and progress to them. Such kind of discriminatory thinking promoted social injustice, which worsened the state or condition of the unassertive poor people and paved the way for the untouchability to emerge. Some of the Shudras (backwards and depressed people) started to be leveled as pollutants and untouchable. The respect and dignity of the untouchables lost its meaning. They didn't remain even as human beings in the sight of the other Hindus.

SOCIAL EXCLUSION AND CASTE-BASED ATROCITIES: CONTEMPORARY PERSPECTIVE

In contemporary India too, the deprived people particularly the Dalits are not as honoured as the upper caste Hindus, though they have prosperity and qualification. For example, Mr. H.K. Peepal an owner of Heritage Hospital situated at Agra, in Utttar Pradesh is a Dalit, Jatav by caste. He is an intellectual person having knowledge of six languages including English. But the Doctors belonging to upper castes do not greet him in whom hospital they are employed. According to Mr. Peepal, the upper caste Hindu doctors feel shame and inferiority in saluting him. But Mr. Peepal always greets them with the hope that one day they will learn a lesson of morality and etiquettes. Some upper caste Hindu doctors had left their job when they came to the fact that the owner of the hospital was a Dalit.[10]

Another incident is of Bhandara of Maharashtra where the well educated people, teacher by profession of the so-called upper castes still believe in untouchability. In their opinion, the presence of a Dalit headmistress had desecrated the entire school. Mrs. Tilottama Tembhurkar was a headmistress in a school of Surewada village near Bhandara town of Maharashtra. But as soon as she was transferred out, the caste Hindus conducted the processes of purification of the school by chanting mantras, conducting *pooja* and sprinkling cow-urine in the school premises. In their sight, the school had got desecrated and polluted due to the presence of a Dalit headmistress in the school.

For purifying it, they sprinkled cow-urine in the office used by a Dalit headmistress, furniture, class rooms and even upon the students. [11]

There are several questions about the social position or status of the depressed class' people, which have been answered by several intellectuals and scholars. A famous novelist, Mulk Raj Anand had put some light on the social position of the down-trodden through his novel, *Untouchability* published in 1935. The story of this novel moves round the characters like Lakha and Bakha. The novelist shows how were the depressed people down-trodden in particular treated by the caste Hindus? How were they made physically and mentally weak and helpless? According to the story of novel, Bakha had inherited from his forefathers: the weakness of the down-trodden, the helplessness of the poor. Bakha was highly insulted and abused when he walking along a footpath touched by mistake an upper caste person. Bakha was sad and angry but helpless. His father Lakha, hearing of the incident reacts in the following words:

'My son', said Lakha, with a forced mixture of anger and kindliness, didn't you give a warning of your approach? "They would ill-treat us, even if we shouted. They think we are mere dirt, because we clean their dirt. Lakha reminds an episode that he was insulted and scolded by all upper caste persons when he entered in a clinic of a village doctor. They called him *"Bhangi, Bhangi"*.[12] Unfortunately, it is also happening even today in some parts of India particularly in villages. It is a bitter truth that the economic growth of marginalized people is a social crime in the sight of the developed castes or the cow headed tigers.[13]

The ongoing incidents of caste discrimination and atrocities show the attitude of the caste Hindus towards the Dalit community who feel proud to be called as Hindu and are dedicated to this religion loyally and honestly. On the contrary, the caste Hindus had not given the status of Hindu to the downtrodden people for centuries. The history shows that the Dalits have been regarded as outcastes and untouchables in the past. They were not allowed to read and listen to vaids and other religious ethics and even to enter into temples. Unfortunately, such things are still going on in our country at present, which is an era of liberalization, multi-culturalism and constitutionalism. This era talks about democracy, humanism, human rights, rule of law, etc. Indeed, such incidents are stigma on us. But it is a matter of concern that the serious efforts have not been made by the religious leaders to end the caste and untouchabilty. Is this all not a mater of shame and concern for us being a nation, a largest democracy in the world? But we are crying against reservation in spite of being serious to eradicate social and religious atrocities against the deprived people. These pictures of the contemporary India show how are Dalits even today struggling for self-respectin many parts of the country?

In other words, the status of human being too was snatched from the down-trodden. They had been deprived of all rights and facilities. They were deprived of right to education and all possibilities of their progress had been washed off. Even right to water was not permitted to the untouchables. In addition, the castist people justified this inequality, discrimination, social injustice and humiliation of the deprived people by evolving the theories of *punrjanma* (re-carnation) and *bhagyavad* (fortunism). This all too remained them silent and non-violent. The non-violent nature and non-assertiveness of the depressed people were considered as their stupidity or mindlessness. The castiest forces continued discrimination and humiliation with the Shudras specially untouchables. They closed all doors leading to social justice and commited hienious brutality to them. This horrible and paiful condition led some intellectuals and thinkers to raise voice against social injustice and caste based discrimination. Though the caste based discrimination has weakened as compared to the past but it still exists in its changed form. Contemporary times too are full of incidents of caste discrimination and atrocities. Still, Dalits are facing cruelty of caste in form of untouchability. Hower, untouchability has dwindled in cities but it is still found in rural India. Every day, news of caste discrimination are reported. Incidents of Hathras (UP) and Jalaur (Rajasthan) are few samples of caste atrocities.

<u>REFERENCES</u>

1. Nadani Gooptu (2006): "Swami Acchutanand & the Adi Hindu Movement", Cambridge University Press, p.19.
2. Nandini Gooptu, Ibid, p.10.

3. Briggs, Geo. W. (1920): *The Chamars,* Calcutta, P. 38.

4. Alexander Robertson (1938): *The Mahar Folk*, Calcutta, P. XII (forward)

5. Bayly, S. (1999): *Caste, Society and Politics in India*, Cambridge University Press.

6. Busi, S. N. (1997): *Mahatma Gandhi and Babasaheb Ambedkar-Crusaders Against Caste and Untouchability,* Saroj Publications, Hyderabad, Andhra Pradesh, p.1.

7. Ambedkar, B.R. (1977) *Caste in India: Their Mechanism, Genesis and Development*,Bheem Patrika Publication, Jallandhar, p.5 also see

8. Singh, Kuldeep (2007): "Reservation: An Issue of Controversy in Contemporary India" in *Punjab Journal of Politics*, Amritsar, Punjab.

9. Nadani Gooptu (2006): "Swami Acchutanand & the Adi Hindu Movement", Cambridge University Press, p.19

10. "Harijan se Dalit", Vishesh, *Reported on NDTV*, December 05, 2006

11. Tribune News Service, "Teachers suspended for 'purifying' school headed by Dalit", *The Tribune*, New Delhi, April 23, 2007.

12. Mulk Raj Anand, *Untouchable,* Banglore, First Published in 1935 (revised in 1981), p. 20. also see in James Massey, *Dalits in India: Religion as ...*, opcit, p.109.

13. Kusuma Dharmanna, "Samyavadanni Sahinchani Hinduism, Presidential Address", Act-Andhra conference at Vizianagaram, 1936, (Reprinted in Nalupu, Nov. 1992-Jan., 1993) in 3 parts.

CHAPTER FIVE

CHATRAPATI SHAHUJI MAHARAJ

Source*

INTRODUCTION

Shahuji Maharaj was a liberal and egalitarian ruler, welfare supporter, social reformer and a visionary as well. He seemed committed towards equality and social justice. He was also known as Rajarishi. Truly, he was a warrior of social justice who was driven towards the development of his people and the betterment of the socially deprived sections. He strongly believed in equality amongst all members of the society. He was the greatest king of that time, Maharaja of Kolhapur. His personality was very attractive he had solid body yet he was simple and ground to earth king. Shahu Maharaj was so close to his fellow peoples. In his rule, he initiated many revolutionary schemes in the caste discriminating system to promote equality. He also initiated compulsory free primary education in all his states. Rajarshri Shahu Maharaj was a man of strong will. He had a vision and mission of betterment and upliftment of the socially deprived sections. He dedicated his life to this objective and worked tirelessly for the same. He initiated the first known reservation system to abolish the system of caste segregation and the exploitation of the lower castes. He was influenced by the two great freedom fighters, mahatma Jyotiba Phule and Agarkar. In his work the influence of modernity and foresight is always seen. From the coronation to the present state of affairs and social affairs, Maharaj made many bold decisions, and brought them too.

"I want to point out to all the leader of the community that it is desirable to break apart the caste discrimination, it is of course, keeping the caste is sin, this is a barrier in the path of patriotism, efforts should be made to overcome this, keeping this awareness in mind. Therefore, it is noteworthy that such councils should not be affected due to the increase in casteism, intensification of caste system.[1]

EARLY LIFE

Shahu Maharaj was born on 26 June 1874 in the Ghatge family of Kagal. His original name was Yashwantrao, his father's name was Jaysingrao and his mother's name was Radhabai. After the death of Shivaji Maharaj IV, King of Kolhapur, his wife Anandibai adopted Yashwantrao on 17 March 1884, naming him Shahu. During the period of four years from 1889 to 1893, Shahu Maharaj underwent educational and physical development at Dharwad. Maharaj's education took place at Rajkot and Dharwad. Arrangements were made in the palace for his higher education. The responsibility of his education was given to a British officer Sir Stuart Fraser. While studying, Shahu married Lakshmi Bai, daughter of Gunajirao Khanvilkar of Baroda on April 1st, 1891. He was 17 years old at the time of marriage and Lakshmibai was less than 12 years old. During 1889 to 1893 he studied English, World history and polity. He became ruler in April 1894 at the age of 20. After his coronation till 1922, he was the king of Kolhapur for 28 years. (Wikipedia)

EMPHASIS ON SPREADING EDUCATION AMOUNG BACKWARDS AND WOMEN AND ERADICATION OF UNTOUCHABILITY

Shahuji was a strong supporter of education of the backward people to make their life worthy and repectful. During the British rule, Shahuji Maharaj worked tirelessly to bring justice to the common people and to the overall social upliftment of the backward people, accelerating social change. Despite the opposition of the Sanatani class, he played an important role in the development of the Dalit (untouchable) and backward classes.

Shahu Maharaj laid special emphasis on spreading education in the Bahujan Samaj. The Shahu Maharaj were passionate about the education of the Bahujans. So Kolhapur enacted the law of compulsory free education. He also set up schools in villages with a population of 500 to 1000. Parents who do not send their children to school will be charged Rupee 1 per month. Made a legal provision to levy fines. He made primary education compulsory and free.

He made primary education compulsory and free in Kolhapur. He issued a royal decree to spread women's education. He was an immense supporter of education to all. He also wanted to uproot the untouchabilty. In 1919, with a view to eradicating untouchability, he abolished the practice of setting up separate schools for upper castes and untouchables. Shahuji was a strong supporter of equality and social inclusion and believed in the mingling of all people. He wanted to see the untouchables also read and write and progress along with other people. Therefore, in 1919, he put an end to the practice of setting up separate schools for upper castes and untouchables with a view to eradicating untouchability.

RECOGNITION TO INTER-CASTE MARRIAGE

Shahuji believed in social equality and was an immense supporter of social justice. For bringing equality, it was necessary to dismantle the rigidity of caste. Therefore, to eliminate caste discrimination, he enacted a law recognizing inter-caste marriage in his state. In 1917, he passed the Remarriage Act, which legalized widowhood. He established the Deccan Rayat Association at Nipani in 1916 to involve the Bahujan Samaj in the political decision-making process. The Vedokta affair over the right to chant the Vedokta mantra took place during the reign of Shahu Maharaj. He was educated by Fraser, a British officer. Further education took place at Rajkumar College, Rajkot and at Dharwad. Shahuraj's personality was developed due to the knowledge gained through study and educational trip.

HIS VISION FOR SOCIAL JUSTICE AS A SOCIAL REFORMER

Shahu Maharaj was not only a king but also a great social reformer who was fully committed to bring social change in the society. For his liberal and welfaristic attitude he was given the title 'Rajarshi' by the Kurmi Kshatriya community of Kanpur. Many years before independence, Shahu Maharaj implemented the principles of equality, brotherhood, secularism, equal opportunity for development for all. That is why he is glorified as 'Maharaj's Maharaj' all over the country. Shahu worked to give rights and justice to the people of Rayat and the neglected community.

Throughout his life's work, he exercised his power to ensure justice and rights for the masses in the society, which is why he became a public welfare ruler. Maharaj ruled for about 28 years.

Shahu Maharaj wanted untouchables to live a good life. Therefore, he decided to make the untouchables self-reliant with the aim of improving the economic condition of the untouchables. It encouraged the untouchables to run their own businesses, set up shops and hotels, and offered financial assistance. He encouraged untouchables to run their own businesses by providing sewing machines. He started sewing clothes from the palace. Gangadhar Kamble removed the man from a tea shop in Kolhapur. In order to give prestige to the untouchables in the society, he conferred the titles of Mahar Palawan to Palawan Chambar, Sardar Abhang to Pandit, appointed untouchable educated youth as Talathi. With a view to eradicating untouchability. The practice of filling separate schools for the untouchables was discontinued in 1919. He also implemented Patil schools, vocational schools, technical and skill teaching schools for the betterment of the village. [2]

SAHUJI WAS A STRONG ADVOCATE OF EQUALITY AND HE PROMOTED BACKWARDS IN HIS ADMINISTRATION

Sahuji was a strong advocate of equality among all stratas of society and treated all equally. He viewed Brahmins such as other human beings and refused to give them any special status. He removed Brahmins from the post of Royal Religious advisers when they refused to perform religious rites for non-Brahmins. He appointed a young Maratha scholar in the post and bestowed him the title of `Kshatra Jagadguru' (the world teacher of the Kshatriyas). This incident together with Shahu's encouragement of the non-Brahmins to read and recite the Vedas led to the Vedokta controversy in Maharashtra. This dispute brought a storm of protest from the elite strata of society and vicious opposition to his rule. He established the Deccan Rayat Association in Nipani during 1916. The association sought to secure political rights for non-Brahmins and invite their equal participation in politics. Shahu was influenced by the works of Jyotiba Phule, and long patronized the Satya Shodhak Samaj, formed by Phule.

FINNACIAL ASSISTENCE TO DR. AMBEDKAR FOR HIS EDUCATION

As a visionary, he not only promoted education of backwards and downtrodden but also financially assisted Babasaheb Dr. Ambedkar for his education. He helped him for the Mooknayak newspaper as well. Shahuji financially assisted Dr. Ambedkar when On 4th September 1921, Dr. Ambedkar wrote a letter to Shahuji Maharaj seeking financial assistance to overcome his difficulties, which is given as under

My Dear Maharaja Saheb,

As directed by Mr. Dalvi I am placing my financial difficulties before you in the hope of getting some relief. But I am sorry to have to approach you but thinking that as you had been pleased to regard me as your friend you would do something to enable me to tide over my difficulties. They have chiefly arisen through the fall in the Indian exchange on London. When I left India I had calculated the total expenses I would have to incur for my two years' stay in London and according to then prevailing rate of exchange I found that I had sufficient funds for my purposes. But as the funds had been invested by a friend with whom I had deposited them, I was not able to transfer them to London at the time when I left India. Last year in the month of December when the funds were sent to me I found that owing to the low rate of exchange the funds realized a sum in London which fell short of the required amount by nearly £ 150. I have to pay £100 for my Law fees and need about another £100 for my return passage to India. In all therefore I need about £200 to tide over my difficulties. I would be very much obliged if Your Highness can see your way to help me with a loan of that amount. I will repay it with interest when I return. The matter is so urgent and I know so few people that I ventured to sound the matter by first approaching Mr. Dalvi and as Your Highness desired me through him, to write directly I feel sure that hopes are not misplaced.

I hope Your Highness is enjoying good health. We need you ever so much for you are the pillar of that great movement towards social democracy which is making its headway in India.

Awaiting the favour of an early reply I am yours sincerely.[3]

FATHER OF RESERVATION SYSTEM IN INDIA

At present, the reservation system in India is a constitutional system which is being disputed for a long time because it is such a system which ensures participation in education and employment and political representation of socially and educationally backward classes and deprived. But most of the people of the general class are unable to digest this system which ensures social justice and they openly oppose it and promote it as compromise with merit. Some advocate reservation on economic basis. The many constitutional amendments allowing reservations on economic grounds always generate much interest, but the quota system in India is much older than you think. Way before it was enshrined in the Indian Constitution, this policy was first implemented by a young raja who was outraged at being misled by palace priests during religious rituals. 26th July (1902) in Dalit History – Chhatrapati Shahuji Maharaj of Kolhapur issued orders for reservation of 50% posts in the state services for the backward classes. This farsighted ruler was Chhatrapati Shahu of the princely state of Kolhapur who started the reservation system in India. Issuing an order for reservation to non-Brahmans, Shahuji Maharaj became the father of reservation system in India. An administrative order was passed in the Kolhapur State Gazette that sent shockwaves across British India. It stated:

'His Highness is pleased to direct that from the date of this order, 50% of the vacancies that may occur shall be fixed by recruits from among the backward classes. In all offices in which the proportion of officers of the backward classes is at present less than 50%, the next appointment shall be given to a member of those classes.[4]

UPLIFTMENT OF FARMERS - CONCRETE STEP TPWARDS SOCIAL JUSTICE

Rajarshri Shahu Maharaj believed in upliftment and welfare of all including farmers. He had true concerns for welfare of farmers. Therefore, he took adequate and sustainable measures to improve the conditions of the *Rayyats* (farmers). During the drought of 1902, he recognized the hardship of the farmers' community and made honest attempts to solve the problems in agricultural activities. He introduced the "Mass Irrigation Policy" in the same year. For this policy, he appointed irrigation officers who investigated every village in his province and arranged irrigation fund for the villages according to the severity of the drought condition. He also initiated the construction of the Radhanagari Dam on February 18, 1907, in the Kolhapur city to solve the problems of irrigation. The project was completed in 1935. The dam stands proof to Chhatrapati Shahu's vision towards the welfare of his subjects and made Kolhapur self-sufficient in water.

During the famine of 1896 and the ensuing plague, he was put to the test and completely overcome. The people feel that there is no such thing as 'becoming a king' in view of drought, distribution of food, cheap grain shops, establishment of destitute ashrams. He was instrumental in establishing Shahu Chhatrapati Spinning and Weaving Mill, Shahupuri Trade Center, Farmers' Cooperative Society, King Edward Agricultural Institute for Agricultural Technology Research in Kolhapur. He also paid attention to agricultural development through the construction of Radhanagari Dam and providing loans to farmers. He was not only king he was a social reformer. His steps for upliftment and welfare of poor and farmers were concrete steps towards social justice as well.

Not only he made efforts to provide irrigation to the farmers, but he also made credits accessible to farmers looking to buy technical equipment. He also established the King Edward Agricultural Institution to teach farmers modern techniques to increase their crop yield and different farming methods. He introduced numerous projects that enable the citizens of his kingdom to develop self-sustaining business such as The Shahu Chhatrapati Spinning and Weaving Mill,dedicated marketplaces for farmers and cooperative society for farmers to eliminate the involvement of middlemen in trading. He always strived to build an environment of growth and development for his subject.[5]

To sum up it can be said that Shahuji Maharaj not only worked his way for the social justice but also he promoted it from the deep of his heart. Being a King, he took very bold decisions and launched several policies to uplift the backwards and downtrodden people. He not only provided financial help to Babsaheb to complete his studies but also initiated reservation policy to ensure inclusion of backwards in administration and the social justice during British India. As the father of reservation policy, he laid a strong foundation for the welfare of the oppressed, downtrodden and backward by taking a unique initiative towards building equality, social justice and inclusive society in India, on which Babasaheb Dr. Bhimrao Ambedkar later built a grand building of social justice. constructed. Inspired by his movements and ideology of equality, liberty, fraternity and justice, he not only provided all social, economic, political and religious rights to the underprivileged, backward and women through the Constitution of India, but also by arranging reservation for their empowerment and education, It also paved the way for employment and their appointment to political and constitutional posts. In fact, Dr. Ambedkar fulfilled his objective by taking inspiration from Shahuji Maharaj and other architects of social justice. Undoubtedly, Shahuji Maharaj was a great warrior and a supporter of equality and social justice. Really, he was a great champion of equality and social justice.

REFRENCES

*https://www.google.com/searchq=shahuji+maharaj+hd+image&tbm=isch&ved=2ahUKEwiRwYK
Rlu76AhUL8jgGHYB6BSgQ2cCegQIABAA&oq=shahuji+maharaj+hd+image&gs_lcp=CgNpbWc
QAzoECCMQJzoGCAAQBxAeOgcIABCABBAYOgQIABAeOgYIABAFEB46CQgAEIAEEAoQG
FCQD1j2J2CIN2gAcAB4AIABjQGIAYoKkgEEMC4xMJgBAKABAaoBC2d3cy13aXotaW1
nwAEB&sclient=img&ei=telQY9GSKovk4EPgPWVwAI&bih=625&biw=1366&rlz=1C1CHBF_
enIN880IN880#imgrc=1qSw7uZ5walAmM

1. http://aissms.org/rajarshri-shahu-maharaj-a-visionary-and-social-reformist/
2. http://aissms.org/rajarshri-shahu-maharaj-a-visionary-and-social-reformist/
3. https://velivada.com/2011/06/27/when-babasaheb-sought-shahu-maharajas-financial-support/
4. https://www.livehistoryindia.com/story/people/the-first-reservations-in-india
5. https://en.wikipedia.org/wiki/Shahu_of_Kolhapur

CHAPTER SIX

SREE NARAYANA GURU

https://www.news18.com/news/lifestyle/sree-narayana-guru-jayanthi-2022-who-was-sree-narayana-guru-and-what-were-his-contributions-to-the-society-5922733.html

EARLY LIFE AND EDUCATION OF NARAYANA GURU

Sree Narayana Guru has been a renowned champion of equality and social justice in south India. His messages of liberation through education and empowerment through organization clearly echo Dr. Ambedkar's slogan 'educate, organize and agitate'. His belief was that caste is the evil that annihilates the human and prevents the making of an egalitarian society, writes Ajay S. Sekher.*

One of the great stalwart of equality and social justice, Narayana Guru was born on 20 August 1856 in the village of Chempazhanty near Thiruvananthapuram, in the erstwhile state of Travancore, in Britih India. His parents were Sh. Madan Asan and Smt. Kuttiyamma who belonged to the Ezhava caste. His early education was in the Gurukul way under Chempazhanthi Mootha Pillai. He faced mental sufferings from childhood. He lost his mother when he was 15 year old. At the age of 21, he went to central Travancore to learn from Raman Pillai Asan, a Sanskrit scholar who taught him Vedas, Upanishads and the literature and logical rhetoric of Sanskrit. He returned to his village in 1881 when his father was seriously ill, and started a village school where he taught local children which earned him the name *Nanu Asan*. A year later, he married Kaliamma but soon disassociated himself from the marriage to commence his public life as a social reformer.[1]

FOUNDATION OF EZHAVA SHIVA TEMPLE AT ARUVIPPURAM

He had interset in sprotuality and for religious reasons, he visited many places. Leaving home, Sree Narayana Guru traveled through Kerala and Tamil Nadu and it was during these journeys, he met Chattampi Swamikal, a social and religious reformer, who introduced Guru to Ayyavu Swamikal from whom he learned meditation and yoga.[2] Later, he reached the Pillathadam cave at Maruthwamala where he set up an hermitage and practiced meditation and yoga for the next eight years. In 1888, he visited Arruvippuram where he meditated for a while and during his stay there, he consecrated a piece of rock taken from the river, as the idol of Shiva, which has since become the Aruvippuram Shiva Temple.[3] His act regarding *Aruvipuram Pratishta* created a social commotion among the upper caste Brahmins who questioned Guru's right to consecrate the idol.[4] He replied that "This is not a Brahmin Shiva but an Ezhava Shiva"[5] His reply to them later became a famous quote, used against casteist.[6]

OPENING OF A SCHOOL FOR THE CHILDREN OF MARGINALISED SECTIONS

Narayana Guru was very anxious for the upliftment and development of poor and depressed people. He believed in education of all including the downtrodden and backwards. Education for all was his vision. Narayana Guru shifted his base from Aruvippuram to Sivagiri, near Varkala in 1904 where he opened a school for children to poor and marginalised sections of the society. Due his anti-casteism nature, he provided free education to the children without considering their caste. However, he built a temple there, the Sarada Mutt in 1912. He had faith in progressive religion not in conservative one and he also built temples in other places such as Thrissur, Kannur, Anchuthengu, Thalassery, Kozhikode, and Mangalore. Soon after the meeting at Pallathuruthy, which was the last public function he attended, Narayana Guru became ill and underwent treatment at places such as Aluva, Thrissur, Palakkad, and finally to Chennai. He returned to Sarada Mutt and died on 20 September 1928, at the age of 72.[7 .]

PLURALISTIC, SECULAR AND HUMANISTIC PHILOSOPHER

Narayana Guru was a pluralist, secular and humanist philosopher and activist. His thinking seemed to be influence by Mahatma Buddha. His *Panchasudhi* concept is a regional re-rendering of Buddha's *Panchaseela* (five principles). He advised Sahodaran to develop Christ like patience when Sahodaran met him at Aluva after the 1917 Cherai inter-caste dining. In his later philosophical works, he also wrote on Prophet Mohammad and Christ, comparing them to Buddha. It is true that he wrote about the Hindu gods and the pantheon in his early devotional works or *Stotra Kritis*, but this was part of his traditional Kudipallykoodam education in Sanskrit and Bhasha in his early devotional developmental phase, in which he was called Nanu Bhaktan (Nanu the devotee) or Nanu Asan (Nanu the teacher) (Shekher 2016: 20-27). In his later dialogues, writings and acts, a clear polyphonic, pluralistic and secular legacy and ethical, humanist philosophy is evident. He never celebrated the Vedas or the Gita, the iconic texts of Varnasramadharma. In fact, he mercilessly ridiculed the Rigvedic creation story in *Purushasukta*: "Is it something like the tree putting out leaves that the Virat Brahmapurusha or the cosmic Man is said to have given birth to the four Varnas through his body organs?"[7A]

NARAYANA GURU'S FIGHT AGAINST CASTEISM

Narayana Guru was a strong fighter against casteism and social discrimination. He was a spiritual leader, philosopher, and social reformer who led the anti-caste movement in Kerala in the 19th Century. Casteism was practised in Kerala during the 19th and early 20th centuries and the lower caste people such as Ezhavas and the untouchable castes like Paraiyars, tribals and Pulayars had to suffer discrimination from the upper caste community[8] However, Guru had performed his first major public act, the consecration of Siva idol at Aruvippuram against caste discrimination in 1888. He continued to construct temples and overall, he sanctified forty-five temples across Kerala and Tamil Nadu. His consecrations were not necessarily conventional deities; a slab inscribed with the words, *Truth, Ethics, Compassion, Love,*[9] a vegetarian Shiva, a mirror and a sculpture by an Italian sculptor were among the various consecrations made by him.[10] He propagated the ideals of compassion and religious tolerance and one of his noted works, *Anukampadasakam*, extols various religious figures such as Krishna, The Buddha, Adi Shankara, Jesus Christ[11]

VAIKOM SATYAGRAHA - AN AGITATION AGAINST UNTOUCHABILITY

Narayana Guuru protested against caste discrimination and untouchability. Personally, he faced caste discrimination that led him to launch Vaikom Satyagrah. The social protest of Vaikom Satyagraha was an agitation by the lower caste against untouchability in Hindu society of Travancore.[12] It was reported that the trigger for the protest was an incident when Narayana Guru was stopped from passing through a road leading to Vaikom Temple by an upper caste person. It prompted Kumaran Asan and Muloor S.Padmanabha Panicker, both disciples of Guru, to compose poems in protest of the incident. T. K. Madhavan, another disciple, petitioned the Sree Moolam Popular Assembly in 1918 for rights to enter the temple and worship, regardless of the caste. A host of people including K. Kelappan and K. P. Kesava Menon, formed a committee and announced Kerala Paryatanam movement and with the support of Mahatma Gandhi, the agitation developed into a mass movement which resulted in the opening of the temple as well as three roads leading to it to people of all castes.[13] Vaikom Satyagrah under the leadership of Sree Narayana Guru proved fruitful. The protest also influenced the Temple Entry Proclamation of 1936.[14]

EQUALITY IN HIS WRITINGS AND PHILOSOPHY

Sree Narayana Guru was a good writer and philosopher too. He not only fought for equality and social justice, he echoed his loud voice for equality through his writings also. He published 45 works in Malayalam, Sanskrit and Tamil languages which include Atmopadesa Śatakam, a hundred-verse spiritual poem and Daiva Dasakam, a universal prayer in ten verses.[15] He also translated three major texts, Thirukural of Valluvar, Ishavasya Upanishad and Ozhivil Odukkam of Kannudaiya Vallalaar.[16] It was he who propagated the motto, One Caste, One Religion, One God for All (Oru Jathi, Oru Matham, Oru Daivam, Manushyanu) which has become popular as a saying in Kerala. He furthered the non-dualistic philosophy of Adi Sankara by bringing it into practice by adding the concepts of social equality and universal brotherhood.[17]

POPULARITY OF NARAYANA GURU AS A CRUSADER AGAINST UNTOUCHABILITY AND A WARRIOR OF SOCIAL JUSTICE

The life and contribution of Sree Narayana Guru has been portrayed in a number of movies starting with the 1986 film Sree Narayana Guru, made by award-winning director P. A. Backer. Swamy Sreenarayana Guru, an Indian Malayalam-language film directed by Krishnaswamy, released the same year. Some other movies too have been screened on his life. Really, Sree Narayana Guru earned a grave popularity as a great crusader against inequality and caste discrimination and a strong warrior for social justice. He himself launched many styagrahas and movements to uproot the social inequality and exclusion of untouchables. He also inspired number of supporters of social justice to echo their vehement voice in favour of equality and social justice. His most effective movement was Vaikom movement that was against the cruelty of untouchability and atrocities against the untouchables. His contribution indeed is of great value as far as social justice is concerned. He not only fought against social discrimination but also echoed vibrant voice in favour of equality and social justice. He was really a path exhibitor to other warriors of social justice.

<u>REFERENCES</u>

Source-Wikipedia

*(https://www.forwardpress.in/2020/10/narayana-guru-was-modern-like-ambedkar-and-anti-caste-unlike-gandhi/)

1. "Sree Narayana Guru, Varkala, Thiruvananthapuram, Kerala". Kerala Tourism - Varkala. Retrieved 1 March 2021.
2. Younger, Paul (2002). Playing host to deity : festival religion in the South Indian tradition. New York: Oxford University Press. p. <u>127</u>. <u>ISBN0-19-514044-3</u>.
3. Staff Reporter (24 December 2012). "125 years of Aruvippuram temple". The Hindu. Retrieved 1 April 2019.
4. "125 years of Aruvipuram Pratishta". The New Indian Express. Retrieved 1 April 2019.
5. <u>"Sree Narayana Guru in a new light"</u>. 13 November 2013. Archived from <u>the original</u> on 13 November 2013. Retrieved 1 April 2019.
6. A. Sreedhara Menon (4 March 2011). Kerala History and its Makers. DC Books. pp. 205–. <u>ISBN978-81-264-3782-5</u>.
7. "Sree Narayana Guru, Varkala, Thiruvananthapuram, Kerala". Kerala Tourism - Varkala. Retrieved 1 March 2021.
   7A. (https://www.forwardpress.in/2020/10/narayana-guru-was-modern-like-ambedkar-and-anti-caste-unlike-gandhi/)

8. "Guru-varsham 150: The year of Sree Narayana Guru". www.rediff.com. Retrieved 1 April 2019.

9. "TKMM College". tkmmcollege.org. 2 April 2019. Retrieved 2 April 2019.

10. "These places were a part of Sree Narayana Guru's life". OnManorama. Retrieved 2 April 2019.

11. Sekher, Dr Ajay (6 September 2017). "Guru who made Kerala fit to bear 'god's own' label". Deccan Chronicle. Retrieved 2 April 2019.

12. "Extreme injustice led to Vaikom Satyagraha, says Romila Thapar". The Hindu. 22 July 2009. Retrieved 1 April 2019.

13. "Vaikom: A Story of Courage & The Extraordinary Movement That Changed India!". The Better India. 30 October 2018. Retrieved 1 April 2019.

14. Mahadevan, G. (12 November 2011). "Temple Entry Proclamation the greatest act of moral freedom: Uthradom Tirunal". The Hindu. Retrieved 1 April 2019.

15. Staff Reporter (7 October 2009). "Kerala recommends national prayer song to Centre". The Hindu. Retrieved 1 April 2019.

16. "Writings of Sree Narayana Guru". www.sndp.org. Retrieved 1 April 2019.

17. Diane P. Mines; Sarah Lamb; Sarah E. Lamb (2010). Everyday Life in South Asia. Indiana University Press. pp. 209–. ISBN 978-0-253-35473-0.

CHAPTER SEVEN

SWAMI ACHHOOTANAND

Source**

INTRODUCTION

Though, the Indian society was filled with huge inequality, discrimination and social injustice but many warriors continued to be born here from time to time to echo the voice for social justice. One of those crusaders for social justice wasSwami Achhootanand. When Babasaheb was fighting in Maharashtra, Swamy Achhootanand was echoing his vibrant voice in favour of social justice in North India mainly in today's Uttar Pradesh. Known as "Swami Achutanand or Swami Hariharanand" also, he was a poet, critic, dramatist, historian, social reformer, former Arya Samajist and founder of the Adi Hindu movement.[1] Swami Achhootanand was born to Moti Ram and Ram Piari into Chamar caste and were followers of Kabir panth. His father and uncles, Kalu Ram and Subedar Mathura Prasad and elder brother, Subedar Bant Lal, all of them were in the Brtish Indian Army.[2] Swami Acchutanand was born on 6 May, 1879 in a Chamar family in Farrukhabad district (now his village is a part of district Kannauj) Uttar Pradesh and later his family shifted to Mainpuri UP. He died on 20 July 1933 in Kanpur, Uttar Pradesh.

EARLY LIFE AND EDUCATION

As far as the education of Swami Achhootanand was concerned, he was very learned personality. He studied in the town of Nasirabad and was well versed in eight languages – Urdu, English, Hindi, Sanskrit, Persian, Marathi, Bengali, and Punjabi. He was married at a young age to Hira Bai or Durga Bai.[3] He had interest in sprituality and joined a group of sadhus. He left for a pilgrimage and lived with Sadhus for 10 years. Thereafter, he came under the influence of Swami Sachitanand of Arya Smaj and joined him. After joining he changed his name to "Swami Hariharanand" and read Vedas and Satyarth Prakash. After a series of incidents he understood Arya Smaj's influence fizzled out, after death of many Arya samajist.[4] But Arya Samaj didn't prove helpful in eradication of caste. Therefore, he made distance from Arya Samaj and tried his own ways to fight against caste cruelty. His main contribution towards the eradication of caste and social justice and creating an egalitarian society can be understood from the following discussion.

FOUNDATION AND EMERGENCE OF ADI HINDU MOVEMENT

Swami Achhootanand had been a part of Arya Samaj too. But after some time working for removal of caste under Arya Samaj, he got disillusioned of Arya Samaj. He found Arya Samaj's efforts for removal of caste insufficient. He decided to distance from the Arya Samaj movement and started campaigning against them by his writings and protests. He was invited to Delhi and successfully debated with Arya Samaji leader, Swami Akhilanand over scriptures.[5] He then laid the foundation of "Jati Sudhar Achhoot Sabha'" and was conferred the title of "Shri 108" by proposal of Arya preacher, Pandit Ramchandra & Naubat Singh, the minister of Shahdara Samaj in Delhi.[6]

To strengthen the fight for equality and social justice, he decided to launch a new movement. He wanted to establish an egalitarian society free of caste based discrimination. Therefore, in 1922, he founded Adi Hindu Movement and pioneered the first social reform movement for Dalits in Hindi belt.[7] He advocated that Dalits to be the original inhabitants of India and later, he came to be known as "Swami Achhootanand". Swami became one of the revolutionaries in Adi movements of India and stood in row with its founders – Gopal Baba Walangkar, Bhagya ReddyVerma, B. Shyam Sunder and Mangu Ram Mugowalia.[8]

ADI HINDUISM: A VOICE AGAINST SOCIAL EXCLUSION AND FOR RESTORATION OF RIGHTS

The message of Adi Hinduism was predominantly twofold.

First, it attempted to dissociate low-caste status from menial occupations. Adi Hinduism challenged the imposition of specific 'low' social roles on untouchables based on their ritual status. In this, Adi Hinduism was a direct response to the exclusions that untouchables encountered in urban society, especially in the sphere work and labour. Its emphasis was less on caste oppression and exploitation, which might have been the chief concern if the movement had emerged in rural areas, and more on ritual exclusion, which was directly relevant to the urban untouchables.

Second, Adi Hindu movement challenged the exclusion of untouchables. The Adi Hindu leaders not only argued for caste equality but also highlighted a view that the untouchables had become deprived of their original rights through force and political machinations by the higher castes, and that their rights should be restored. Arising from this, the second focus of Adi Hinduism was the notion that the untouchables were the past rulers of India. Through this generalised assertion, Adi Hindu leaders also attempted to fortify the claims of the untouchables to rights and opportunities.

ACHHOOTANAND PROCLAIMED AN AUTONOMOUS IDENTITY TO THE UNTOUCHABLES THROUGH INTROSPECTIVE SPRITUALISM

Achhootanand announced an autonomous identity to the untouchables through *Bhakti* orintrospective spiritualism. Bhakti is based on the idea of direct and personal communion with God, through devotion, meditation and spiritual introspection. Achhootanand, decidedly highlighted the introspective dimension of bhakti (atmavad) and gave this religious concept a new social significance. *Atma-anubhav* (Spiritual introspection) was accorded supreme importance as the only way to arrive at true knowledge or sadgyan and to evolve one's own world-view. Introspection, it was held, would lead to self-realisation or selt-knowledge (atmagyan). This would, in turn, facilitate the articulation of an autonomous value system that was not derived from or imposed by the higher castes. The concept of introspective self-realisation (atmavad) was, thus, propounded not simply as a way of worshipping but more importantly to stimulate 'thinking-for-oneself' without reference to received notions and religious prescriptions from higher castes. Achhootanand thus urged, "Do not follow any ideology (mat) because you have been hearing it for a long time, or because it is held by some great (bade, literally big, implies a socially superior person of upper class or caste) person or because it is the view held by any cult or sect. Accept only an ideology that you have arrived at yourself". This cultivation of atmagyan would finally enable one to express an independent self-identity (swatantra satta). By deploying the concept of introspective spiritualism and atmavad, therefore, Achhootanand proclaimed an autonomous identity tor the untouchables. The realisation of true knowledge and independent thinking through atmavad was above all seen as the key which would help to discern the difference between truth and falsity. It would then crucially reveal the irrelevance and falsity of one's low status in society. Achhootanand, at a session of religious catechism with an audience of untouchables, in reply to the question, what is atma-anubhav? said: "Real knowledge is the knowledge gained through introspection and which you have understood and realised on your own".* In other words, it can be said that Swami Achhootanand adopted the way of meditation that Mahatma Buddha, Sant Kabir and Snt Ravidas had showed to the humanity. He focused upon experience and knowledge. This was an attempt to give Dalits or untouchables a separate identity so that they could live a life of dignity and respect.

CONVENTIONS OF ADI HINDU MOVEMENT

The Adi Hindu movement organised several conventions from time to time to educate the untouchables. The first national Adi Hindu convention was held at Delhi in 1923 followed by Nagpur in 1924, Hyderabad in 1925, Madras in 1926, Allahabad in 1927, Bombay in 1928, Amravati in 1929 and Allahabad in 1930 with several provincial and special conventions also held at different places. (Wikipedia)

SWAMI ACHHOOTANAND'S SUPPORT TO DR. AMBEDKAR

Swami Achhootanand was aware about Dr. Ambedkar and his stuggle against caste discrimination and social injustice. He seemed to be a true and serious supporter of Babasaheb Dr. Ambedkar and supported him at several occasions. He welcomed King Edward VII, the Prince of Wales and even demanded proposals for Depressed classes which was going to be submitted before Simon Commission.[9]Later, he met Dr. Ambedkar in Adi Hindu Conference at Bombay and then supported Simon Commission at Lucknow. He also supported Dr. Ambedkar through telegram during Round Table Conferrence held in London. Like Dr. Ambedkar, he strongly opposed the term 'Harijan' referring to untouchables which was coined by Mahatma Gandhi.[10]

SWAMI ACHHOOTANAND: A GREAT WARRIOR OF SOCIAL JUSTICE

To bring a new awareness among the Depressed Classes Swami Achhootanand started his own publications and used to publish his poetry under his pen name "Harihar". Swamiji was one of the "Pioneer of <u>Dalit Literature</u>" in Hindi. In 1922, he started his first monthly paper "Achhut", from Delhi but closed down in 1923 and again he started "Prachin Hindu" but that too closed within a year. There upon, he established, Adi Hindu Press and started publishing his journal *The Adi-Hindu Journal* from Kanpur between 1924–32.[11]

He was a philosopher-poet and also a playwright. He wrote six books in Hindi - "Shambuk Balidan (Drama), Achhut Pukar - Religious songs, Mayanand Balidan (biography), Pakhand Khandani, Adi-Vansh Ka Danka," etc. In brief, Swami Achhootanand was a great warrior of social justice in North India who led the struggle against the social discrimination, inequality and injustice. he not only challenged the prevalent caste order but also connected the downtrodden to the glorious roots and depicted them as former rulers. by doing so, he craeted confidence and enthusiasm in the depressed people. He supported Dr. Ambedkar too in his fight against the enemies of social justice. He attempted to dissociate low-caste status from menial occupations. He launched Adi Hinduism that challenged the imposition of specific 'low' social roles on untouchables based on their ritual status. Adi Hinduism was a direct response to the exclusions that untouchables encountered in urban society, especially in the sphere work and labour. Its emphasis was less on caste oppression and exploitation, which might have been the chief concern if the movement had emerged in rural areas, and more on ritual exclusion, which was directly relevant to the urban untouchables.

REFERENCES

**https://www.google.com/searchq=achhootanand&rlz=1C1ONGR_enIN982IN982&sxsrf=ALiCzsYtX0SCr6B4uZ37gErK9oxg1sQJg:1665831319324&source=lnms&tbm=isch&sa=X&ved=2ahUKEwiw4qygieL6AhWG6jgGHa9cAZAQ_AUoAXoECAIQAw&biw=1920&bih=860&dpr=1#imgrc=axoHJ57l8sUjM&imgdii=DJkVqpY4d275ZM

#Wikipedia

*Gooptu, Nandini (2006). Swami Acchutanand & the Adi Hindu Movement, Cambridge University Press, Critical Quest, New Delhi.

1. Service, Tribune News. "Saga of Dalits' assertion". Tribune India News Service. Retrieved 26 May 2020.
2. Narayan, Badri (18 April 2014). Kanshiram: Leader of the Dalits. Penguin UK. ISBN978-93-5118-670-0.
3. Raj Bahadur (13 September 2016). "Swami Achhootanand: Progenitor of North India's Dalit movement". Forward Press. Retrieved 11 December 2019.
4. https://www.alislam.org/articles/death-of-lekh-ram-a-sign-for-the-people-of-india/
5. https://indianexpress.com/article/explained/explained-who-was-swami-shraddhanand-who-fell-to-bullets-in-december-1926-6188039/
6. "Swami Acchutanand and Adi-Hindu Movement". Velivada. 9 May 2020. Retrieved 26 May 2020.
7. Narayan, Badri (15 May 2019). "The Bahujan movement needs to reinvent itself". The Hindu. ISSN0971-751X. Retrieved 26 May 2020.
8. "Caste and other demons". www.telegraphindia.com. Retrieved 26 May2020.
9. Kshīrasāgara, Rāmacandra (1994). Dalit Movement in India and Its Leaders, 1857-1956. M.D. Publications Pvt. Ltd. ISBN978-81-85880-43-3.
10. Kanwal bharti (8 February 2019). "Swami Achhootanand 'Harihar': A profile". Forward Press. Retrieved 26 May 2020.
11. Kshīrasāgara, Rāmacandra (1994). Dalit Movement in India and Its Leaders, 1857-1956. M.D. Publications Pvt. Ltd. ISBN978-81-85880-43-3.

E.V. RAMASAMY NEIKER (PERIYAR)

SOURCE*

EARLY LIFE OF E.V. RAMASAMY NAICKER (PERIYAR)

E.V. Ramasamy no doubt to state that was an influential and charismatic crusader and warrior against caste inequalities and caste based discrimination and injustice. He was a strong voice in favour of equality and social justice. E.V. Ramasamy's father, Venkata Naicker at his initial stage worked as an assistant to a stone mason. In due course by dint of his ability he became a fairly rich merchant. His wife Chinnathayamma contributed her share of industry for the income of the family. When her husband worked as an assistant to a stone-mason, she carried head loads of bricks from the yards to building spots. Later when Venkata Naicker started a shop, she was selling hand-pound rice at home. She stopped her rice business only when her husband became a wholesale merchant and commission agent. While E.V.R was born, his father was a reputed merchant in Erode locality. E.V. Ramasamy was the fourth son of his parents. E.V. Ramasamy was born on 17th September, 1879.[1]

EDUCATION OF E.V. RAMASAMY

The young E.V. Ramasamy was naughty and mischievous from childhood. He was of independent nature and due to of his independent nature, he had freely mingled with the low caste boys in school. However, his parents had not liked his such nature and they felt worried about the way the boy was growing up. His father brought him back to his home and sent him to school. The boy attended school for six years, but learnt very little. When he was twelve, his father took him to his shop. There, to the astonishment of everybody, he showed keen interest in business and learnt its techniques within a few years. Very soon, he acquired efficiency in in running a business successfully. His interest in business made Venkata Naicker, his father a happy man. Ramasamy was not enthusiastic to religious discourses and he seemed much keen to excel business tactics. However, he appeared to be dull in studies but proved to be extra cute in reasoning.

Ramasamy was not enthusiastic about sermons and was very keen on perfecting the business strategy. Although, he seemed to be slow in studies but proved to be extra sweet in reasoning. However, Ramasamy's family was very religiously conservative. His parents had deep faith in the Vaishnava system of Hinduism. Vedic pundits and shastris used to visit his home and often receive lavish gifts for worships and yagyas. But Ramasamy was not interested in religion and religious activities. He openly ridiculed the pundits who gave religious discourses by highlighting the contradictions in the statements and also their incredible exaggeration. Ramasamy was married with Nagammai to whom Ramasamy was familiar for some years and both were actually in love with each other. Nagammai was not only an ideal wife but also very cooperative with her husband. She took participation in all his later public activities and agitations. Two years after marriage, this couple got a girl child which lived only for five months, and thereafter they had no children.[2]

PERIYAR'S ENTRY IN POLITICAL LIFE

Initially, Periyar showed interest and sympathy with the political views of Indian National Congress. He started attending the Congress conferences from 1908 onwards. Having spontaneous sense of logical reasoning from childhood, he was capable of making rational enquiries about whatever he heard from others like religious preachers and learned visitors. Being engaged in business from the very early age he had learnt the art of conversing with others. His exposure to worldly affairs helped him to acquire a vast fund of knowledge. These qualities, later on, groomed him into a powerful speaker and effective leader. Between 1914 and 1918 E.V. Ramasamy held several powerful and honorary posts. During this period, he convened many conferences of the Indian National Congress in Tamil Nadu. He served as the president of the Erode Registered Merchants Association. He was the member of the Administrative Council of the South Indian Merchants' Association. The Government of India constituted the five districts Income Tax Tribunal and appointed E.V.R as one of the three commissioners.[3]

E. V. Ramasamy acted as the Secretary of the Erode Town Reading Room, the Erode Alumnae Association and the High School Board. Later on he rose to the position of President of the same High School Board. He served as the Secretary of the Coimbatore District Congress Conference. E.V.R had been functioning as Honorary Magistrate for 10 years.[4] He was the president of Erode Taluk Board and Chairman of the Erode Municipality for many years. During his tenure in Erode Municipality E.V.R worked effectively for drinking water supply and provision of Health facilities to the people.[5] He was very committed towards the service and welfare of the common people mainly backwards and depressed. He wanted to make their life easier and ful of respect. Serving on many administrate positions, he tried to give maximum advantage to the poor and backward people.

PERIYAR' SUPPORT FOR REPRESENTATION TO NON-BRAHMINS

E.V. Ramasamy or Periyar was a great supporeter of an inclusive social and political order and wanted to secure representation to all even in Indian National Congress. Influential leader of Congress, C. Rajagopalachari. and E.V. Ramasamy were fast friends. But when he was enrolled in Congress in 1919, then the Congress showed agreement with the principle of communal representation advocated by the Non Brahmin Movement. Further, he was led to believe that 50% of the Government jobs would be set apart for Non-Brahmins and that the Congress had no intention of contesting the general election. E.V. Ramasamy fully believed in these assurances and went on pressing for acceptance of his resolutions on communal representation at various committee meetings and conference of the Congress held every year, at Tiruchirapally in 1922, Madras in 1923, Thiruvannamalai in 1924 without avail.[6]

Finally, Ramasamy attended the Tamil Nadu Congress Committee convention in Kancheepuram in 1925, ready to perform along with the Brahmins. In this conference, he presented two resolutions recognizing the principle of communal representation for non-Brahmins in public services and representative bodies. These proposals were rejected on the ground that they had already been rejected by the Committee of Subjects. On this occasion E.V. Ramasamy and many other non-Brahmins walked out in the conference. As far as social justice was concerned, he soon became disillusioned with the functioning of the Congress Party and left the Congress in 1925 and freed himself to start his own organisation.

EARLY MOVEMENTS LED BY PERIYAR

Toddy Shop agitation

In 1921, E.V. Ramasamy (Periyar) led a mass movement against the Toddy Shops in Tamil Nadu. It was called the famous "Kallukadai Mariyal", in support of prohibition. During this period E.V. Ramasamy launched Khadhar propaganda programme throughout the state.[7] In the year 1922, Periyar engaged in Toddy Shop agitation. He was arrested and imprisoned.

Vaikom Temple Agitation

Vaikom Temple agitation has been a famous movement of Periyar. In 1923, Periyar was elected president of the Tamil Nadu Congress Committee. In Kerala, there were strict laws regarding crossing roads by untouchables. Untouchables were also not allowed to enter temples. In Vaikom too, a small town in Kerala state, then Travancore, there were strict laws of untouchability in and around the temple area. Dalits, also known as Harijans, were not allowed into the close streets around and leading to the temple, let alone inside it. In 1924, a conflict arose over the question of untouchables using certain roads outside a temple in Vaikom in Travancore State. E.V. Ramaswamy along with his wife arrived in Vaikom on April 13 but he arrested and was imprisoned for a month in Travancore. After his release he began the agitation, again he was arrested and this got him a sentence of six months. Finally, the prohibitory order was removed by the Travancore Durbar. E.V. Ramaswamy got a lot of acclaim and was given the title, *Vaikom Veeran,* "The Hero of Vaikom".[8]

Self-Respect Movement

Self-Respect movement was the most popular and effective movement of Periyar. He was also involved in the agitation against the separate dining enforced for Brahmin students at the Gurukulam in Shermadevi, Thirunelveli District, established in December 1922, by V.V.S. Iyer. As a result of Non-Brahmin pressure, V.V.S. Iyer resigned the post as the Head of the Gurukulam in May 1925.[9] E.V. Ramasamy was committed to anihilate caste system and for this purpose he founded the Self-Respect Movement in 1925 after his exit from the Congress Party. In 1926, he condemned the Hindi imposition policy of the Government. He convened the First Non-Brahmin state conference in Madurai. Periyar opposed the introduction of compulsory Hindi in schools by C. Rajagopala Achariyar. While launching that agitation Periyar announced that C.N. Annadurai (Former Chief Minister of Tamil Nadu) would be the First General in leading the picketing against Hindi. The Self-Respect Movement and Justice Party ran on parallel lines, for both worked for the upliftment of Non-Brahmins. The first Self-Respect Conference was held at Chengleput in 1929. The Justice Party leaders participated actively in it. The conference heralded the formal inauguration of the Self Respect Movement, although it originated as soon as E.V. Ramaswamy came out of the Congress in 1925. The Resolution passed guaranteed social equality and freedom from economic exploitation to all castes and creeds.[10]

PERIYAR'S SUPPORT FOR EQUALITY AND WOMEN RIGHTS

E.V. Ramaswamy (Periyar) was an egalitarian thinker and agitator and was a staunch opponent of caste inequality. He was inclined towards Buddhism too. Therefore, from 1927 onwards, he interested himself in propagating the tenets of Buddhism and in expounding the teachings of Thirukkural. He was also a forerunner in the advocacy of women's education and championing the cause of women for equal rights.[11] E.V. Ramaswamy was attracted by the Bolshevik, revolution of Russia and its beneficial effects on the Proletariat. From 1931 he frequently wrote in Kudiarasu about this social revolution. In 1931 he visited Greece, Turkey, Africa, Germany, France, Portugal, England

and Ceylon. In Russia he attended the May Day Celebration of 1932 and was introduced as the leader of atheistic thought from India.[12] On his return from Russia he busied himself with meetings with workers of the Self-Respect Movement, and explained to them the novel features of the Socialist State. In this M. Singaravelu, the first communist in South India was of great help to him. E.V. Ramaswamy had also supported the Railway workers' strike in 1927 - 1928. Singaravelu helped in opening the eyes of several Self - Respect workers to a wide horizon and to a New Order in which the toiling people's- liberation would guarantee the abolishing of all social injustices and establish a society without the horrors of caste in social administration. Singaravelu gave the opening address in the conference of Self Respecters in Madras in December 1931. He told the Self-Respecters that only a Socialist society can be free from caste, religious distinction, and economic disparity. Further, Singaravelu wrote a series of articles in Kudiarasu on Socialism, Science and on Moral belief. These articles gave him a high standing among the Self - Respect workers.[13] The first Dravida Nadu Separation Day was celebrated on 1 July 1939. EV Ramaswamy was imprisoned for two years. While serving his sentence, he was elected the leader of the Justice Party.[14]

PERIYAR'S 14 POINT PROGRAM

Having an inclination towards socialism, Periyar went to Soviet Russia after traveling to various countries of Europe and stayed there for several days. Being the first nation of Karl Marx's communism founded by the great leader Lenin, the former Soviet Union captivated Periyar's heart.[15] In Russia (formerly Soviet Union) his stay was extended for a lengthy period of three months because he was invited to address many workers' meetings. Being the First Nation of Karl Marx's communism, established by the great leader Lenin, the former Soviet Union captivated very much the heart of Periyar. In 1932, November 11 he returned to Erode after completing the European journey via Colombo, the Capital of Ceylon.[16] Death of Nagammaiyar in 1933, May 11 his beloved wife E.V.R. Nagammal passed away and the burial took place the very next day.

After returning from the Soviet Union, he was fully convinced that materialism was the answer to India's problems and openly advocated mass revolution and the overthrow of the government. Somewhat angered by imprisonment for treason in 1933–34, he indicated his desire to join one of the major parties on a conditional basis.[17] He devised a fourteen-point program and passed it on to both the Congress and the Justice Party. submitted for their approval. This was completely unacceptable to Congress, but the Justice Party, which was rapidly going downhill, approved.

HIS EFFORTS FOR DRAVID NADU - AN EGALITARIAN STATE

In 1944, the Justice Party was recognized as the "Dravida Kazhagam" or "Dravidian Union" under Periyar's guidance and, at the Salem Conference, appeared to assume the character of a highly extremist mass organisation. The Justice Party was renamed as 'Dravida Kazhagam' on 27 August 1944 at the Provincial Justice Party Conference held at Salem as a purely social revolutionary movement for the liberation of the Dravidian caste oppressed by Brahmins. The object of the Dravida Kazhagam was proclaimed to be the achievement of a Sovereign Independent Dravidian republic, which would be federal in nature with four units corresponding to the linguistic divisions each having residuary power and autonomy of integral administration. It would be a "casteless society" an egalitarian "Dravida Nadu" to which the depressed and downtrodden could get allegiance.[18]

E.V. RAMASAMY AND SELF RESPECT MOVEMENT

Self-Respect movement was not a pre - planned one. It was purely accidental. E.V. Ramasamy's activities during 1925 to 1929, would prove that he adopted the line of action to sheer force of circumstances. Many of his colleagues including Rajaji wanted him to be in the Congress and fight for the cause of Non-Brahmins. But he did not like that idea. In this circumstance he was left with two alternatives. Either as suggested by Tiru. Vi. Ka and other non-Brahmin leaders, he could have continued with the Tamilnad Congress and strengthened the hands of the progressive elements both in the Brahmin and non-Brahmin groups in their attempts to eradicate social inequalities, or he could have inaugurated a new organization specifically to fight the then prevailing sectarian social practices.[19]

As he believed the first alternative was impossible in his lifetime, he chose the second and founded a new organization.[20] E.V.R. cut off from the Congress and gravitating towards the Justice, he was laying the foundation of a dynamic social movement that has come to be styled as the Self-Respect Movement. Self-Respect Movement was not a mere social reformist movement. It aimed at destroying the existing Hindu social order in its totality and creating a new, rational society without caste, religion and God. So it was considered a socially revolutionary movement which had been destroying and creating, i.e., creative destruction or creation through destruction.[21] E.V.R had fully explained the meaning of Self-Respect and the reasons for its emergence. "The Self-Respect Movement was inaugurated not for talking ill of a particular community or sect, but to destroy the social evils as a whole"[31] According to E.V.R even Brahma Samaj and Arya Samaj were established by the Brahmins only to safeguard their own self-respect. So the non-Brahmins, had a right to start counter associations to avoid those practices which were against their Self-Respect.[22]

MOTIVE AND OBJECTIVES OF THE SELF RESPECT MOVEMENT

The motive behind inauguration of the Self-Respect Movement was nothing but E.V. Ramasamy's contempt for caste system and its evils. His bitter experiences in the Congress were also responsible for its emergence. E.V.R.'s breaks with Congress in 1925 came essentially as a result of his show down with the Brahmin Leaders who were opposed to reforms. The Self-Respect Movement was dedicated to the goal of giving non-Brahmins a sense of pride based on their Dravidian past which also meant denial of the superiority of the Brahmins whom he described as representative of the Aryans. Unlike the Justice Party, the Self-Respect Movement was popular in its appeal. Though it began as a social reform movement its effects were felt in the political field also.[23]

The objectives of the Self-Respect Movement have been outlined and stated in two pamphlets Namathu Kurikkol and Tiravitakkalaka Lateiyam.

a) This movement aims to do away with such social structure of the society where one class of people claim to be superior to others and some men claim to be of higher birth than others.

b) It aims to work for getting equal opportunities for all people, irrespective of their communities it will strive to secure equal status for women along with men in life and according to law.

c) All people should be given equal opportunities for growth and development.

d) Friendship and fellow feeling should be natural among all the people.

e) It aims to completely eradicate untouchability and to establish a united society based on brotherhood and sisterhood.

f) To establish and maintain homes for orphans and widows and to run educative institutions. g) To discourage people from building new temples, mutts, chlorites or Vedic Schools. People should drop the caste titles in their names. Common funds should be utilized for educational purpose and for creating employment opportunities for the unemployed.[24]

The aims and resolutions were recommended for the careful scrutiny and guidance of all the people in Tamil Nadu, after the first Self Respect Conference which was held at Chegalpattu on 17 and 18 February 1929. More than six thousand people attended this great conference. About half of them were ordinary people who had come from distant places in the hope of getting sound advice on social equality, social evils and the ways of overcoming the forces of exploitation. The next Self-Respect Conference was held at Erode on 10 May 1930, under the chairmanship of the Guest National leader M.R. Jayakar. This conference took a bolder step than the previous one and discouraged idol worship in strong terms. At the Self-Respect Conference held at Virudhunagar in August 1931 under the president-ship of Sri Kanchi K. Shanmugam, all the progressive ideas were emphasized, in addition to these, strongly worded resolutions against untouchability and for the encouragement of inter-caste marriages were passed.[25]

CONTROVERSY REGARDING FOUNDER OF SEL RESPECT MOVEMENT

Beside the controversy regarding the foundation of Self Respect Movement, E.V.R. himself declared in 1930 that he was the founder of the Movement.[26] In his weekly Kudi Arasu, he had referred to the Self-Respect Movement in several articles as "the Movement of mine" and "the movement which was started by me".[27] All these facts go to prove that E.V.R was the sole architect to the Self-Respect Movement. Self Respect movement under, Periyar gave launched some operational programs.

Operational Programs:

To reform the society, the Self-Respect movement had the following operational programs:

1. It wanted to remove practices of using caste marks, caste costumes and caste names.

2. It aimed at the elimination of employing Brahmin priests to officiate at marriages and other ceremonies of the society.

3. It also favoured the simplifying of laws relating to divorce, widow remarriage and inter - caste marriage.[28]

SELF-RESPECT MOVEMENT: ROLE OF JUSTICE PARTY

E.V.R decided to fight against social injustice in an organized way and made use of the Justice Party's platform and newspapers for popularizing his creed. This movement was a crusade against superstitions, rituals and temple worship. It might be defined as a socio-organization whose aim is to reconstruct society on a human and rational basis and to destroy caste-root and branch and ultimately destroy religion as popularly understood and practiced. There was understanding and mutual co-operation between the Justice Party and Self-Respect Movement. In the election of 1926, the Justice Party was defeated and most of the leaders of Justice Party thought that their political life had come to an end. But, E.V.R made an attempt to give a new life and spirit to Justice Party. The Justicites also recognized his leadership. Thus, these two parties maintained a close contact among themselves and the people believed that the Self-respect Movement carried on the traditions of the Justice Party. E.V.R. who was not an admirer of the political aspirations of the Justice Party supported their efforts to improve the general status of the non-Brahmins. He utilized these opportunities to keep the spirit of the non- Brahmin leaders.[29]

The Justice Conference was held at Mayavaram in Tanjore district in May 1927 and it was named as Self-Respect Conference. E.V.R himself moved a resolution that clearly enunciated the aims of his Self-Respect Movement namely to discontinue the observance of caste distinctions, not to employ Brahmin priests for officiating marriage and other ceremonies and throwing open the temples and public roads, tanks and wells to all persons.[30] E.V.R. attended the Justice Special Conference held at Coimbatore in July 1927.[31] E.V.R who was very outspoken made a strong speech condemning the Governor of Madras for appointing C.P. Ramasami Iyer, a Brahmin as law member of the Executive Council; he even sought to introduce a resolution urging the recall of the Governor, but friends prevailed upon him to tone down his language and to withdraw the recall motion.[32] The happenings in the above conference did not satisfy E.V.R. They were concerned more with drawing up of plans to recapture political power after their election defeat than with indulging in politics against Brahmins. E.V.R. had understood the prevailing mood in the Justice Party and decided not to join forces with that party as they would obstruct his own plans of bringing about social changes in the Tamil Society.

OPPOSITION TO HINDUISM AND BRAHMINISM

Periyar and Self-Respect Movement were highly opponent of caste system and Brahmanical social order due to their discriminatory characters. He held religion responsible for exploitation of the downtrodden. He was an athiest and attacked on the religion and the authority of God as well. He called God creation of the men and it was done to establish the hegemony of few over all. According to the Self-Respect Movement, the root of all social evils can be found in religion. It believed that without destroying the superstitions based upon religion and tradition, it could not affect any social change. In its opinion, the caste system was closely intervened with the Hindu religion. So, in order to reform the society, it felt that there was a dire need for changing some of the basic practices in the religion.[33] E.V.R. stated, 'Man is disgraced by caste and the caste is disgraced by the religion. How can we destroy one, keeping the other alive?[34] He observed that religion was a disease and the society was affected with this disease. E.V.R. wanted not only to cure the society of its disease but he also washout to destroy the root of the disease - The Hindu religion.

Since the Brahmins were regarded as the custodians of Hinduism as they were highborn people according to Hindu Philosophy, the Self - Respect Movement segregated the Brahmins from the rest of the society and fixed the responsibility on them for all the social evils. The movement firmly believed that Brahmins used religion for dominating others because the rituals that gave religious purity had led to social supremacy and socio-political domination of the Brahmins.[35] The Self-Respect Movement wanted to replace Hindu religion with rationalism. It equated Hinduism with Brahmanism and maintained that it was the source of all irrational beliefs. In brief, it can be said that the Self-Respect movement propagated the policy of atheism.

CASTE ERADICATION MOVEMENT

Caste eradication movement adopted many programs as discussed under.

<u>Boycott of Brahmins through Conducting Self Respect Marriages</u> - Self-Respect movement wanted to establish a casteless society, for that purpose the movement advocated the boycott of Brahmin priests in conducting all ceremonies.[36] As a result of the movement's incessant preaching, some non-Brahmins started conducting their marriages without Brahmin priests. E.V.R. himself conducted several such marriages, which were popularly known as 'Self Respect Marriages'. Marriages styled as Self-Respect Marriages carried a threefold significance:

- Replacement of Purohits
- Inter-Caste Equality
- Man-Woman equality

<u>Inter Caste Marriages</u> - Periyar had regarded that the then conventional marriages were mere financial arrangements and often caused great debt through dowry. Self-Respect marriages encouraged inter-caste marriages and arranged marriages to be replaced by love marriages.[37] It was argued by the proponents of self-respect marriage that the then conventional marriages were officiated by Brahmins, who has to be paid for and also the marriage ceremony was in Sanskrit which most people did not understand, and hence were ritual and practices based on blind adherence. To E.V.R., marriage is a mutual agreement, co-operative enterprise, a deal, an order of Nature and not a one-sided contract in which a woman accepts a subdued role.[38]

<u>Removal of Caste Marks and Caste Names</u> - In its caste eradication programme, the movement insisted on the removal of caste marks and caste names. No one in the movement was allowed to wear the sectarian caste marks of faith on his forehead. The propaganda of the Self - Respect Movement against the practice of using caste names such as Pillai, Gounder, Naidu and Mudaliar resulted in the discontinuance of such proceedings among the educated and enlightened people.[39]

DIFFRENCES WITH GANDHI ON THE ISSUE OF CASTE

However, believed in Varna system but he was not in favour of brutality of casteism and untouchability. But there were huge differences between Gandhi and Periyar on the issue of abolition of caste system. In the <u>Vaikom Satyagraha</u> of 1924, Ramasamy and Gandhi both cooperated and confronted each other in <u>socio-political</u> action. Ramasamy and his followers emphasised the difference in point of view between Gandhi and himself on the <u>social issues</u>, such as fighting the Untouchability Laws and eradication of the caste system. According to the booklet "Gandhi and Periyar", Ramasamy wrote in his paper *Kudi Arasu* in 1925, reporting on the fact that Gandhi was ousted from the <u>Mahasabha</u> because he opposed resolutions for the maintaining of caste and Untouchability Laws which would spoil his efforts to bring about <u>Hindu-Muslim unity</u>. From this, Gandhi learned the need for pleasing the Brahmins if anything was to be achieved.

Periyar in his references to Gandhi used opportunities to present Gandhi as, on principle, serving the interests of the Brahmins. In 1927, Ramasamy and Gandhi met at <u>Bangalore</u> to discuss this matter. The main difference between them came out when Ramasamy stood for the total eradication of Hinduism to which Gandhi objected saying that Hinduism is not fixed in doctrines but can be changed. In the *Kudi Arasu*, Ramasamy explained that: "With all his good qualities, Gandhi did not bring the people forward from foolish and evil ways. His murderer was an educated man. Therefore, nobody can say this is a time of high culture. If you eat poison, you will die. If electricity hits the body, you will die. If you oppose the Brahmin, you will die. Gandhi did not advocate the eradication of *Varnasrama* Dharma structure, but sees in it a task for the humanisation of society and social change possible within its structure. The consequence of this would be continued high-caste leadership. Gandhi adapted Brahmins to social change without depriving them of their leadership".

Gandhi believed in *karma and* accepted it in the sense that "the *Untouchables* reap the reward of their *karma*, but was against discrimination against them using the revaluing term *Harijans*. As shown in the negotiations at Vaikom his methods for abolishing discrimination were: to stress on end of the <u>orthodox</u>, <u>inhumane</u> treatment of *Untouchables*; to secure voluntary lifting of the ban by changing the hearts of caste Hindus; and to work within a Hindu framework of ideas.

There were sharp differences between Periyar and Gandhi on the issue of temple entry. On the Temple Entry issue, Gandhi never advocated the opening of *Garbha Griha* to *Harijans* in consequence of his Hindu belief. These sources which can be labelled "pro-Periyar" with the exception of M. Mahar and D.S. Sharma, clearly show that Ramasamy and his followers emphasised that Ramasamy was the real fighter for the removal of Untouchability and the true upliftment of Harijans, whereas Gandhi was not. This did not prevent Ramasamy from having faith in Gandhi on certain matters.[40]

IMPACT AND ACHIEVEMENTS OF SELF-RESPECT MOVEMENT

Impact and achievements of Self-Respect Movement were comprehensive and fabulous as far as the voice for equality and social justice was concerned. Caste system and caste based hegemony suffered a lot due to the Self-Respect movement and it strengthened the voice for social justice not only in south India but also in north India. This movement showed a path of democratic fight against inequality and social injustice. The monopoly of power and influence enjoyed by the Brahmins was slowly lost due to E.V.R.'s unceasing propaganda against orthodoxy. It filled with the sense of self-respect and above all self-confidence, to fight against social injustice perpetrated by the Brahmins of the day. The practice of having separate dining places for Brahmins in every hotel or earmarking separate eating places in public feasts was slowly given up owing to the agitation of the volunteers of the movement. It was due to their relentless fight that the name boards of the hotels were changed from "Brahmins Hotel" into mere "Vegetarian Hotel".[41]

There was a system of allotting separate places for Harijan members in the Municipal Councils. Self-Respect movement under Periyar oppsed it and the opposition proved fruitfull and system of allotting separate places for Harijan members in the Municipal Councils was discontinued. The Self-Respect Movement played a significant role in the political, social and religious life of the people of South India. It was largely responsible for making an effective change in the social life of the vast majority of people through its ceaseless propaganda against superstitious beliefs, based upon religious traditions. It popularized and perpetuated the assumption that the non-Brahmans were of Dravidian origin and the original inhabitants of South India and the Brahmins were Aryan invaders from the North. Thus, it was instrumental in non-Brahmin communities of Tamil Nadu to create awareness amongst themselves, as one community. The Self-Respect movement brought the message of the Tamil Nationalism to the masses. In short, Self-Respect Movement may be defined as a social organization whose aim was to reconstruct society on a human and rational basis and to destroy caste - root and branch and ultimately destroy Hindu religion as popularly understood and practised.[42] In 1944, Justice Party was rechristened as Dravida Kazhagam. The Self-Respect Movement and Dravida Kazhagam since 1944 became one and the same. During the last days of E.V.R., he struggled hard for the abolition of caste system. After Self Respect Movement he conducted number of Movements to reform the society till his death.[43]

HOW RAMASAMY GOT TITLE OF PERIYAR

The title "Periyar" was conferred on him by Tamil Nadu Women Conference held in Madras on 13.11.1938 under the president ship of Neelambigai Ammaiyaar daughter of Mariamalai Adigal a veteran pure Tamil Scholar. The UNESCO, an international branch organization of the United Nations, conferred on Periyar a glorious title, the citation of which read as "Periyar the Prophet of New Age, Socrates of South East Asia, Father of the Social Reform Movement, and Arch enemy of ignorance, superstitions, meaningless customs, and baseless manners" - UNESCO, 27.06.1970. The award was presented by the Union Education Minister Trigunasen under the president-ship of Chief Minister Kalaingar M. Karunanidi.[44] In his last meeting at Thiagaraya Nagar, Chennai on 19th December 1973, Periyar gave an inspiring clarion call for action to gain social equality and dignified way of life. He fell ill on the next day and breathed his last on 24th December 1973.[45]

E.V. RAMASAMY AS A CHAMPION OF EQUALITY AND SOCIAL JUSTICE

Of course, E.V. Ramasamy was an influential and charismatic warrior against caste inequalities and caste based discrimination and injustice. He was a strong voice in favor of equality and social justice. As a founder of the self-respect movement, he contributed a lot in building an egalitarian society. Periyar made a strong attack on caste and religion to eradicate caste discrimination and also conducted many important and decisive movements to achieve the objective of social justice. He wanted to establish a casteless society, so he called for boycott of Brahmin priests in organizing all functions with the aim of bringing about social change. For this purpose, Periyar hit hard both the social and religious orders. He not only echoed his loud voice against caste discrimination but also brutally condemned superstition and hypocrisy. He held religion responsible for caste based discrimination and exploitation. As a result, some non-Brahmins started getting married without Brahmin priests. The Self-Respect movement led by Periyar brought about many changes in the caste-ridden society in South India. The system of allotment of separate seats for Harijans members in city councils was also stopped. Due to its influence, many people gave up their titles and took pride in publishing their names in Kudi Arasu. The Self-Respect movement played a role in bringing about significant changes in the political, social and religious life of the people of South India. The Self-Respect movement led by Ramasamy Nayakar (Periyar) was largely responsible for bringing about an effective change in the social life of a large number of people through its relentless propaganda against superstitions based on religious traditions. UNESCO, an international arm of the United Nations, honored "Periyar the Prophet of the New Age, Socrates of Southeast Asia, the father of the social reform movement and a staunch enemy of ignorance, superstition, meaningless customs and baseless etiquette. " Undoubtedly, Periyar will always be remembered as an advocate of egalitarian society and social justice and as a bitter critic of ignorance, hypocrisy and superstition. Really. Periyar was a great warrior of equality, social justice and social change.

REFERENCES

Wikipedia

*https://www.google.com/searchq=periyar&rlz=1C1ONGR_enIN982IN982&sxsrf=ALiCzsZV6XMpi41Q5rc7gFqnLWDa4Nw:1665831589576&source=lnms&tbm=isch&sa=X&ved=2ahUKEwjdxZuhiuL6AhX2zTgGSJwBIgAUoAXoECAIQAw&biw=1920&bih=860&dpr=1#imgrc=S8xB5InXqI4qcM

1. Gopalakrishnan, M.D. (1991). Periyar Father of the Tamil Race, Madras, p. 36
2. Veeramani, K., op.cit., p.3.
3. Anai Muthu, V. (1974). Periyar E.Ve. Ra Chinthanaigal, Vol.III (Tamil), Trichy, p.8. 40
4. Sarkar, Sumit; Sarkar, Tanika (2008). Women and Social Reform in Modern India: A Reader. Indiana University Press. p. 401. ISBN9780253352699.
5. Anai Muthu, V., opcit., p.8.
6. Veeramani, K., opcit, pp.11-13.
7. Viswanathan, E. Sa., The Political Career of E.V. Ramaswamy Naicker, A Study of the Politics of Tamil Nadu, 1920-1949, Ravi & Vasant Publisers, Madras, p.61.
8. Kent, David. "Periyar". ACA. Archived from the original on 15 June 2010.
9. Gopalakrishnan, p. 3.
10. Rajadurai, S.V., and Geetha, V., Periyar Suyamariyathai Samatharmam, Kovai, 1999, p.2.
11. Veeramani, K., Gurukula Porattam varalatrusuvadugal (Tamil), Chennai, 2002, p.134.
12. Saraswathi, p. 6.
13. Anaimuthu, V., op.cit., p.XXXIV.
14. Murugesan, K., op.cit., p.123.
15. Viswanathan, E. Sa., op.cit., p.236.
16. Veeramani 1992, Introduction – xi.
17. Saraswathi, S. (2004). Towards Self Respect, Chennai, p.54.
18. Kudi Arasu, 29 August, 1926, p.1 & 3. 178
19. Mehta, Vrajendra Raj; Thomas Pantham (2006). Political Ideas in Modern India: thematic explorations. Sage Publications: Thousand Oaks. p. 48. ISBN978-0-7619-3420-2.
20. Arora, N.D.; S.S. Awasthy (2007). Political Theory and Political Thought. Har-Anand Publications: New Delhi. p. 425. ISBN978-81-241-1164-2.
21. Thakurta, Paranjoy Guha; Shankar Raghuraman (2004). A Time of Coalitions: Divided We Stand. Sage Publications. New Delhi. p. 230. ISBN0-7619-3237-2.

22. E. Sa. Viswanathan, The Political career of E.V. Ramasami Naicker: A Study in the Politics of Tamilnad 1920-1949; unpublished Ph.D. Thesis, Canberra, 1973. Also see Thandavan, R., The Dravidian Movement, Chennai, 2001, p.9.

23. Kandasamy, W.B. Vansantha; Florentin Smarandache; K. Kandasamy (2005). Fuzzy and Neutrosophic Analysis of E.V. Ramasamy's Views on Untouchability. HEXIS: Phoenix. p. 106. ISBN978-1-931233-00-2

24. Engene F. Irschick, Politics and Social Conflict in South India, Bombay, 1969, p.330.

25. "As Tamil Nadu celebrated Periyar's birthday on September 17, we recall the impact of his foreign trips". G Olivannan. The Times of India. 20 September 2016. Retrieved 4 September 2020.

26. Subramanian, Ajantha (2019). The Caste of Merit: Engineering Education in India. Harvard University Press. p. 100. ISBN9780674987883.

27. Mahapatra, Subhasini (2001). Women and Politics. Rajat Publications. p. 211. ISBN9788178800233.

28. Kudi Arasu, 18 August, 1929, p.2.

29. Swaminathan, S. (1974). Karunanidhi - Man of Destiny, New Delhi; p.73.

30. Gopalakrishnan, pp. 50, 52.

31. Saraswathi, p. 6.

32. "Periyar.org". periyar.org. Archived from the original on 20 December 2014.

33. Navasakthi, 6 July 1927, p.3.

34. Jeyaraman, B. (2013). Periyar: A Political Biography of E.V. Ramaswamy. Rupa Publications India Pvt. Ltd. ISBN9788129132260.

35. "Tamil pride: What?s that? - Hindustan Times". hindustantimes.com. Archived from the original on 29 September 2014. Retrieved 4 January 2015.

36. Bent Smidt Hansen 1974). In respect of Periyar Ramasami in Janardhanam, Madras, p.18. also see Anita Diehl, Periyar E.V. Ramasami, Madras, 1979, p.26.

37. "About Periyar: Revolutionary Sayings". Dravidar Kazhagam. Archived from the original on 26 December 2008.

38. Anita Diehl, op.cit., p.6.

39. Veeramani 1992, Introduction – xi.

40. Anita Diehl, pp. 86–88

41. "Biography of Periyar E.V. Ramasami (1879–1973)". Barathidasan University. Archived from the original on 14 June 2007. Retrieved 6 September 2008.

42. Anita Dehil, op.cit., p.52.

43. Swaminathan, S., op.cit., p.73.

44. Anita Deihl, op.cit., p.12. 40 Ibid., p.48.

45. Velusamy (1999). Periyar - The Social Scientist, Salem, p.79.

Source- http://hdl.handle.net/10603/131208

CHAPTER NINE

SHAHEED-E- AZAM BHAGAT SINGH

https://www.google.com/searchq=bhagat+singh&rlz=1C1ONGR_enIN982IN982&oq=
bhagat+singh&aqs=chrome..69i57.9037j0j15&sourceid=chrome&ie=UTF-8#imgrc=KtiB36ypQdFHfM

ITRODUCTION

Shaheed-E-Azam Bhagat Singh was not only a freedom fighter and Charismatic revolutionary but also a humanistic thinker and great champion of equality and social justice. Being a revolutionary, he had enough concern for social justice too. He wanted to remove poverty and caste discrimination as well. Like other warriors of social justice, Shaheede Azam Bhagat Singh too echoed his vice for social justice but he could not live long. If he had lived some time more, he could take concrete steps for the empowerment of poor and deprived sections of the society.

He participated in the mistaken murder of a junior British police officer in what was to be retaliation for the death of an Indian nationalist, Lala Lajpat Rai who was injured in a police lathicharge at Lahore in 1928 during a protest of Simon Commission. He executed a largely symbolic bombing in the Central Legislative Assembly in Delhi. After his execution at age 23 into a martyr, Bhagat Singh emerged as a folk hero in Northern India.[1] Getting influenced with ideas from Bolshevism and anarchism, he electrified a growing militancy in India in the 1930s.[2]

In December 1928, Bhagat Singh and an associate, Shivaram Rajguru, both members of a small revolutionary group, the Hindustan Socialist Republican Association (HSRA), shot dead a 21-year-old British police officer, John Saunders, in Lahore (Punjab) what is today Pakistan, mistaking Saunders, who was still on probation, for the British senior police superintendent, James Scott, whom they had intended to assassinate.[3] They held Scott responsible for the death of a popular Indian nationalist leader Lal Lajpat Rai for having ordered a lathi (baton) charge in which Rai was injured and two weeks thereafter died of a heart attack. As Saunders exited a police station on a motorcycle, he was felled by a single bullet fired from across the street by Rajguru, a marksman.[4]

Bhagat Singh was convicted of the murder of John Saunders and Channan Singh, and hanged in March 1931, aged 23. He became a popular folk hero after his death. Jawaharlal Nehru wrote about him: "Bhagat Singh did not become popular because of his act of terrorism but because he seemed to vindicate, for the moment, the honour of Lala Lajpat Rai, and through him of the nation. He became a symbol; the act was forgotten, the symbol remained, and within a few months each town and village of the Punjab, and to a lesser extent in the rest of northern India, resounded with his name".[5] In still later years, Singh, an atheist and socialist in adulthood, won admirers in India from among a political spectrum that included both communists and right-wing Hindu nationalists. Although many of Singh's associates, as well as many Indian anti-colonial revolutionaries, were also involved in daring acts and were either executed or died violent deaths, few came to be lionised in popular art and literature as did Singh, who is sometimes referred to as the Shaheed-e-Azam ("Great martyr" in Urdu and Punjabi).[6]

EARLY LIFE AND EDUCATION

Bhagat Singh was born on 27 September 1907 in the village of Banga in the Lyallpur district of the Punjab in what was then British India and is today Pakistan; he was the second of seven children—four sons, and three daughters—born to Vidyavati and her husband Kishan Singh Sandhu. Bhagat Singh's father and his uncle Ajit Singh were active in progressive politics, taking part in the agitation around the Canal Colonization Bill in 1907, and later the Ghadar Movement of 1914–1915. After being sent to the village school in Banga for a few years, Bhagat Singh was enrolled in the Dayanand Anglo-Vedic School in Lahore. In 1923, he joined the National College in Lahore, founded two years earlier by Lala Lajpat Rai in response to Mahatma Gandhi's non-cooperation movement (NCM), which urged Indian students to shun schools and colleges subsidized by the British Indian government.[7]

Bhagat Singh influenced a large number of people mainly the youth. Singh's influence on youths made police's concern and police arrested him in May 1927 on the pretext that he had been involved in a bombing that had taken place in Lahore in October 1926. He was released on a surety of Rs. 60,000 five weeks after his arrest.[8] He was very keen and committed towards freedom of the country and started to fight not only physically but also with the strongest weapon, the pen. He wrote for, and edited, Urdu and Punjabi newspapers, published in Amritsar[9] and also contributed to low-priced pamphlets published by the Naujawan Bharat Sabha that excoriated the British.[10] He also wrote for *Kirti*, the journal of the Kirti Kisan Party ("Workers and Peasants Party") and briefly for the *Veer Arjun* newspaper, published in Delhi.[11]

BHAGAT SINGH'S IDEALS AND OPINIONS: SUPPORT TO SOCIAL JUSTICE THROUGH COMMUNISM

No doubt Bhagat singh is famous as a great revolutionary of India who sacrificed his life for the freedom of the country. He fought against British government to liberate India but beside patriotic feelings he had concern for the liberation of deprived and untouchables too as Dr. Ambedkar had in his heart. He was highly influenced with communism and believed to eradicate the poverty adopting communist approach. He attacked exploitation of poor by rich. Bhagat Singh regarded Kartar Singh Sarabha, the founding-member of the Ghadar Party as his hero. Bhagat was also inspired by Bhai Parmanand, another founding-member of the Ghadar Party.[12] In the age of 23, he had studied many foreign thinkers and philosophers who highly influenced him. He was an avid reader of the teachings of Mikhail Bakunin and also read Karl Marx, Vladimir Lenin and Leon Trotsky.[13] In his last testament, "To Young

Political Workers", he declares his ideal as the "Social reconstruction on new, i.e., Marxist, basis".[14] Singh did not believe in the Gandhian ideology – which advocated Satyagraha and other forms of non-violent resistance, and felt that such politics would replace one set of exploiters with another.[15]

Communism had great influence on Bhagat Singh and rampantly echoed his voice for socialism. He wanted death of capitalism and imperialism. On 21 January 1930, during the trial of the Lahore Conspiracy Case, Bhagat Singh and his HSRA comrades, appeared in the court wearing red scarves. When the magistrate took his chair, they raised slogans "Long Live Socialist Revolution", "Long Live Communist International", "Long Live People" "Lenin's Name Will Never Die", and "Down with Imperialism". Bhagat Singh then read the text of a telegram in the court and asked the magistrate to send it to the Third International. The telegram stated: "On Lenin day we send harty greetings to all who are doing something for carrying forward the ideas of the great Lenin. We wish success to the great experiment Russia is carrying out. We join our voice to that of the international working class movement. The proletariat will win. Capitalism will be defeated. Death to Imperialism".[16]

Bhagat Singh had a huge belief in Marxism and Leninism. Being a supporter of Marxism, he believed in eradication of exploitation and poverty. Historian K. N. Panikkar has described him as one of the early Marxists in India.[17] According to Jason Adams, a political theorist, he was more enamoured with Lenin than with Marx. From 1926 onward, he studied the history of the revolutionary movements in India and abroad. In his prison notebooks, he not only quoted Lenin in reference to imperialism and capitalism but also the revolutionary thoughts of Trotsky.

On the day of his execution, Bhagat Singh was reading the book, *Reminiscences of Lenin*, authored by Clara Zetkin, a German Marxist.[18] When asked what his last wish was, Singh replied that he was studying the life of Lenin and he wanted to finish it before his death.[19] In this way, Bhagat Singh wanted to eradicate economic inequality and exploitation of poor by rich. He believed in socialism and wanted an egalitarian society for Indians in which all have their share in progress and resources. This was a strong vice for justice indeed.

BHAGAT SINGH'S ATHEISM- A REVOLT AGAINST CULTURAL HEGEMONY

Bhagat Singh was an atheist and do not believe in the authority of God. He was a strong critic of oppression, exploitation and subjugation of poor by rich. Indeed, his atheism was a revolt against religion and cultural hegemony, which are foundations of inequality, discrimination, marginalistion, subjugation and social injustice. He began to question religious ideologies after witnessing the Hindu–Muslim riots that broke out after Gandhi disbanded the Non-Cooperation Movement. He did not understand how members of these two groups, initially united in fighting against the British, could be at each other's throats because of their religious differences.[20] At this point, Singh dropped his religious beliefs, since he believed religion hindered the revolutionaries' struggle for independence, and began studying the works of Bakunin, Lenin, Trotsky – all atheist revolutionaries. He also took an interest in Soham Swami's book *Common Sense*.[21]

While in prison in 1930–31, Bhagat Singh was approached by Randhir Singh, a fellow inmate, and a Sikh leader who would later found the Akhand Kirtani Jatha. According to Bhagat Singh's close associate Shiva Verma, who later compiled and edited his writings, Randhir Singh tried to convince Bhagat Singh of the existence of God, and upon failing berated him: "You are giddy with fame and have developed an ego that is standing like a black curtain between you and God".[22] In response, Bhagat Singh wrote an essay entitled "**Why I am an Atheist**" to address the question of whether his atheism was born out of vanity. In the essay, he defended his own beliefs and said that he used to be a firm believer in the Almighty, but could not bring himself to believe the myths and beliefs that others held close to their hearts.[23] He acknowledged the fact that religion made death easier, but also said that unproven philosophy is a sign of human weakness. In this context, he noted: As regard the origin of God, my thought is that man created God in his imagination when he realised his weaknesses, limitations and shortcomings. In this way he got the courage to face all the trying circumstances and to meet all dangers that might occur in his life and also to restrain his outbursts in prosperity and affluence. God, with his whimsical laws and parental generosity was painted with variegated colours of imagination. He was used as a deterrent factor when his fury and his laws were repeatedly propagated so that man might not become a danger to society. He was the cry of the distressed soul for he was believed to stand as father and mother, sister and brother, brother and friend when in time of distress a man was left alone and helpless. He was Almighty and could do anything. The idea of God is helpful to a man in distress.

Towards the end of the essay, Bhagat Singh wrote:

"Let us see how steadfast I am. One of my friends asked me to pray. When informed of my atheism, he said, "When your last days come, you will begin to believe." I said, "No, dear sir, never shall it happen. I consider it to be an act of degradation and demoralisation. For such petty selfish motives, I shall never pray." Reader and friends, is it vanity? If it is, I stand for it".24

BHAGAT SINGH'S EXPERIENCE WITH UNTOUCHABILITY AND HE DECIDED TO FIGHT FOR UNTOUCHABLES

Undoubtedly, Bhagat Singh was fully enthusiastic to liberate the country from the clutches of slavery. But possibly he was unaware of another slavery being carried by the untouchables in the country. The untouchables were people living in the slavery of Indians. They were slaves of slaves indeed. Once Bhagat Singh was going somewhere by train and the train stopped at a station, the train had to wait for a long time, then Bhagat Singh got down to drink water. Went to a well nearby, and drank water, then his eyes fell on a man standing some distance away, who was standing bare body in the sun and also carrying a very heavy weight on his shoulder. Looking at the water with yearning eyes, I was thinking in my mind, let me get some water to drink. Bhagat Singh went to him, and started asking who are you and why have you lifted such a heavy weight in the sun. So he fearfully said, sir, you stay away from me or else you will become untouchable because I am an unlucky untouchable. Bhagat Singh said that you must be thirsty, first take off this weight and I will bring water. You drink water He was very happy with this behavior of Bhagat Singh. Bhagat Singh made him drink water and then asked why do you call yourself untouchable, then he answered daringly. I do not say untouchable, so people of a particular class call me untouchable and tell me that you people are untouchables. Touching you will corrupt religion and treat me like a human. You have given me water, otherwise I do not have the right to drink water, nor do I have the right to stand in the shade, nor do I have the right to drink water from a public well.

Then Bhagat Singh realized that I have been told since childhood that the country is slave to the British, but this picture scares something else. The country is a slave to a particular class of religious people, who are fooling India in the name of religion, only then Bhagat Singh started thinking that the country would remain a slave even after being independent from the British, because who would liberate these untouchables, then Bhagat Singh said about Baba Saheb. Knowing (at that time Baba Saheb was abroad) then Bhagat Singh studied about this matter and then started thinking how did his condition happen.

Bhagat Singh had commitment to echo vice for social justice and he wanted to cut the shackles of caste discrimination. He got shocked when he came in the contact of an untouchable who was living an inhuman life. He has written in the book Why I am an atheist, I was fighting with fake enemies, the real enemies are in my country, against whom Baba Saheb Dr. Bhim Rao Ambedkar is fighting alone. If I am released from jail, I will fight for the freedom of these untouchable Indians while living with Baba Saheb for life. Reference - Bhagat Singh's Jail Diary25 Bhagat Singh's concern for poor and untouchables shows that he was a really a champion of social justice and we should give respect to him not only as a revolutionary against British rule but also a revolutionary against social inequality and injustice.

EXECUTION OF BHAGAT SINGH WAS AN EFFORT OF "KILLING HIS IDEAS"

Bhagat Singh seemed to be a man of ideas and he loved ideas as true weapon to bring change. In the leaflet he threw in the Central Assembly on 8 April 1929, he stated: "It is easy to kill individuals but you cannot kill the ideas. Great empires crumbled, while the ideas survived." 26 While in prison, Singh and two others had written a letter to Lord Irwin, wherein they asked to be treated as prisoners of war and consequently to be executed by firing squad and not by hanging.27 Prannath Mehta, Singh's friend, visited him in the jail on 20 March, three days before his execution, with a draft letter for clemency, but he declined to sign it.28 Really, Singh Sahab was a true warrior against slavery and kept his values up till death. He was a true champion of freedom and social justice as well. He lived for his humanistic values and patriotic ideas. Indeed, execution of Bhagat Singh was an effort of "killing his ideas". However, Mahatma Gandhi condemned the act of violence but he still considered Bhagat Singh to be a great patriot and martyr. All Indians love his patriotism and salute his bravery. He was not only a brave revolutionary but also a staunch critic of caste based discrimination and untouchabiity. He will always remain a stalwart of patriotism and valuable warrior of social justice. No doubt to say that if he had lived for some more years, he lived against exploitation, deprivation, subjugation and untouchability. Undoubtedly, he could speed up the battle against discrimination and echo his vibrant voice for social justice.

<u>**REFERENCES**</u>

Wikipedia

1. Maclean, Kama (2016), "The Art of Panicking Quietly: British Expatriate Responses", in Fischer-Tine, Harald (ed.), Anxieties, Fear and Panic in Colonial Settings: Empires on the verge of a Nervous Breakdown, Cambridge Imperial and Post-Colonial Studies, Palgrave Macmillan, p. 154, <u>ISBN978-3-319-45136-7</u>,

2. Jaffrelot, Christophe (22 September 2017), "The Making of Indian Revolutionaries (1885–1931)", in Bozarsian, Hamit; Batallion, Gilles; Jaffrelot, Christophe (eds.), Revolutionary Passions: Latin America, Middle East and India, Routledge, p. 122, <u>ISBN</u> 978-1-351-37809-3

3. Moffat 2016, pp. 83, 89.

4. Maclean & Elam 2016, p. 28.

5. Mittal & Habib (1982)

6. Raza, Ali (2020), Revolutionary Pasts: Communist Internationalism in Colonial India, Cambridge University Press, p. 107, <u>ISBN</u> 978-1-108-48184-7, Deol, Jeevan Singh (2004). "Singh, Bhagat [known as Bhagat Singh Sandhu". Oxford Dictionary of National Biography (online ed.). Oxford University Press.

7. Wikipedia

8. Singh & Hooja (2007), p. 16

9. "Sardar Bhagat Singh (1907–1931)". Research Reference and Training Division, Ministry of Information & Broadcasting, Government of India. Government of India. Archived from the original on 30 September 2015.

10. Gaur (2008), pp. 99–100

11. Gupta (1997)

12. Puri, Harish K. (2008). "The Influence of Ghadar Movement on Bhagat Singh's Thought and Action" (PDF). Journal of Pakistan Vision. 9 (2). Archived from <u>the </u>original (PDF) on 30 September 2015.

13. Adams, Jason (2005), Asian Anarchism: China, Korea, Japan & India, Raforum.info, archived from the original on 1 October 2015.

14. Singh, Bhagat. "To Young Political Workers". Marxists.org. Archived from the original on 1 October 2015.

15. "Bhagat Singh an early Marxist, says Panikkar". The Hindu. Chennai, India. 14 October 2007. Archived from the original on 15 January 2008.

16. "How Russian Revolution Inspired Undivided India's Literary, Political Figures". NewsClick. 7 November 2019.

17. "Bhagat Singh an early Marxist, says Panikkar". The Hindu. Chennai, India. 14 October 2007. Archived from the original on 15 January 2008.

18. "Understanding Bhagat Singh, one writing at a time". The Week. Retrieved 6 October 2020.

19. Chinmohan Sehanavis. "Impact of Lenin on Bhagat Singh's Life". Mainstream Weekly. Archived from <u>the original</u> on 30 September 2015.

20. <u>Nayar (2000)</u>, p. 26.

21. <u>Nayar (2000)</u>, p. 27.

22. <u>Singh & Hooja (2007)</u>, pp. 166–177, Louis E. Fenech; <u>W. H. </u>McLeod (2014). <u>Historical Dictionary of Sikhism</u>. Rowman & Littlefield Publishers. p. 64. <u>ISBN978-1-4422-3601-1</u>.

23. On Bhagat Singh's death anniversary: 'Why I am an atheist'. scroll.in (23 March 2015)

24. Singh & Hooja (2007), pp. 166–177

25.<u>http://www.tpsgnews.com/%E0%A4%93%E0%A4%B6%E0%A5%80%E0%A4%A8%E0%A4%87%E0%A4%A8%E0%A4%AC%E0%A5%89%E0%A5%8D%E0%A4%B8-</u>/Bhagat-Singh's-jail-diary/8/2388

26. India Today Web Desk (28 September 2016). <u>"Remembering Bhagat Singh:</u> 14 facts on the revolutionary who ascended the gallows laughing". <u>India Today </u>(TV channel). <u>Archived</u> from the original on 31 October 2020.

27. Philipose, Pamela (10 September 2011). "Is this real justice?". The Hindu. Chennai, India. Archived from the original on 1 October 2015.

28. Rana (2005b), p. 65

CHAPTER TEN

BABASAHEB DR. BHIMRAO AMBEDKAR

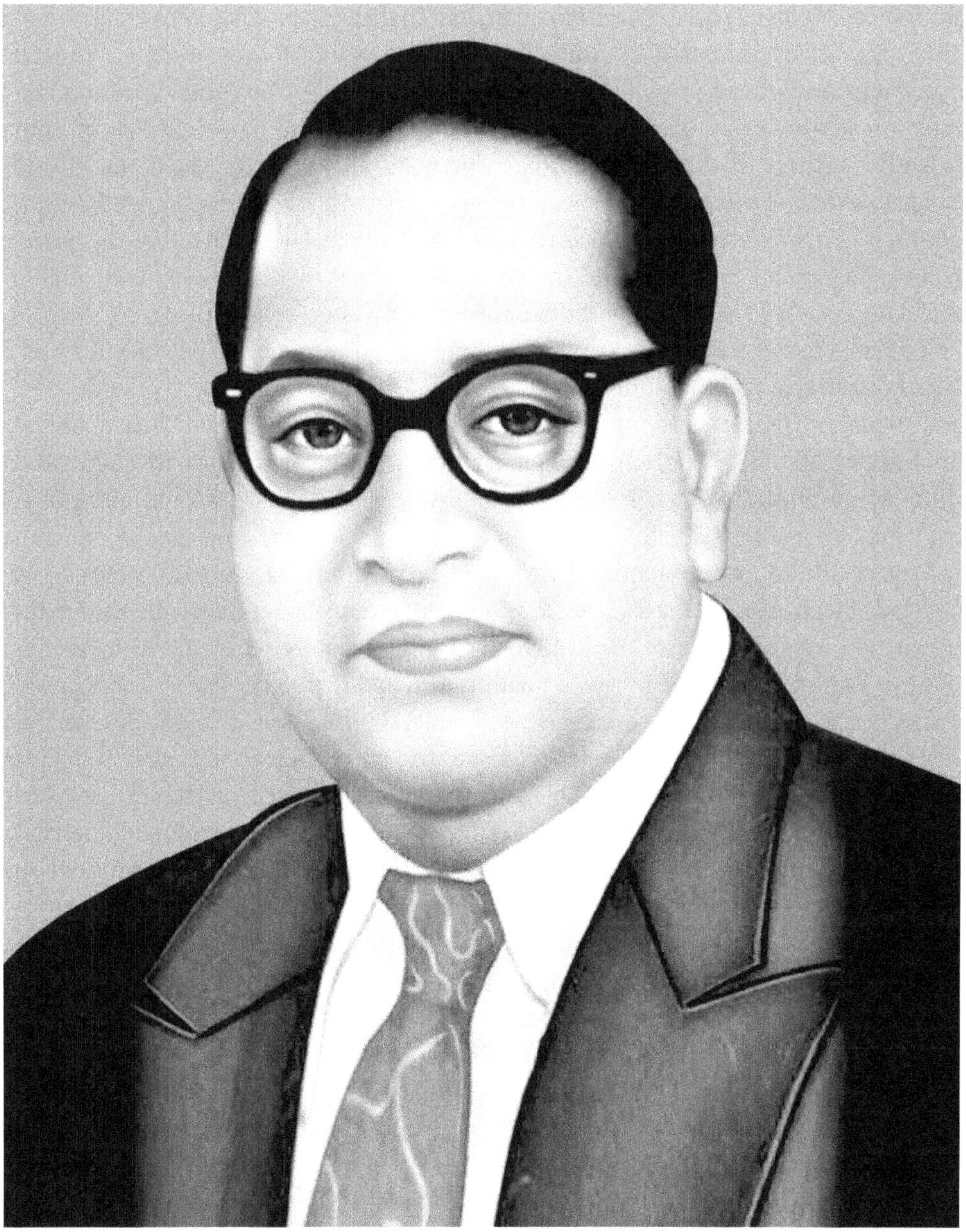

Source*

EARLY LIFE AND EDUCATION

Undoubtedly, many warriors of equality and social justice were born in India from time to time and they tendered the remarkable and worthy contribution to fight against social inequality, discrimination, exclusion, subjugation and injustice. But out of them, Dr. Ambedkar emerged as a most influential and effective fighter and he fought the decisive battle against social injustice. As a great scholar and a distinguished expert of law, he became the messiah of the downtrodden, women, backwards, exploited and deprived people of the country. Really, he was very special contributor towards social equality and justice. No doubt to say that he was an huge supporter of political democracy but more than this he was a supporter of social and economic democracy.

Ambedkar was born on 14 April 1891 in the town and military cantonment of Mhow (now officially known as Dr. Ambedkar Nagar) in the Central Province (now in Madhya Pradesh).[1] He was the 14th and last child of Ramji Maloji Sakpal, an army officer who held the rank of Subedar, and Bhimabai Sakpal, daughter of Laxman Murbadkar.[2] His family was of Marathi background from the town of Ambadawe (Mandangad taluka) in Ratnagiri district of modern-day Maharashtra. Ambedkar was born into a Mahar (dalit) caste, who were treated as untouchables and subjected to socio-economic discrimination.[3] Ambedkar's ancestors had long worked for the army of the British East India Company, and his father served in the British Indian Army at the Mhow cantonment.[4] Ambedkar face heinious discrimination and exclusion right from his childhood. Even in the school, he was brutally treated not only by students but also by teachers. He and other untouchable children were segregated and given little attention or help by teachers. They were not allowed to sit inside the class. When they needed to drink water, someone from a higher caste had to pour that water from a height as they were not allowed to touch either the water or the vessel that contained it. This task was usually performed for the young Ambedkar by the school peon, and if the peon was not available then he had to go without water; he described the situation later in his writings as *"No peon, No Water"*.[5] He had been highly humiliated in the office and sitting arrangements too were not respectable for him at office.

Dr. Ambedkar's Educational Qualifications

Of his brothers - Balaram and Anandrao and two sisters – Ganga, Manjula and Tulasa, only Ambedkar passed his pre-high school examinations and only Ambedkar could go to high school. Apart from two masters and Bar-at-Law, he had **four doctoral degrees** and he knew several European languages (and quite few Indian languages including Sanskrit). He also wrote the Pali language dictionary and was the first person from South Asia to have been conferred a Degree of Ph.D. in Economics. Dr. Ambedkar was only 24 years old when he wrote his paper on "Castes in India – Their Mechanism, Genesis, and Development". In his paper, he challenged many well established scholars who had already written on caste. He belonged to a poor family which faced hardships even to arrange for their bread but was richest as far as educational qualification and mental ability was concerned. Dr. Ambedkar's education was extra ordinary. Due to his great love for education, he was a highly learned personality having much knowledge of economics, law, political science, sociology, anthropology, different reliogious texts, different constitutions, journalism etc. It is almost impossible to state his extraordinarily vast educational experience. For his deep and vast knowledge, Columbia University honoured him giving a title the "Symbol of knowledge". He remained very keen and attentive to the education throughout his whole life. His thrust and hunger for education was so acute. Really, he was a lover and devotee of education. He earned following educational qualifications.

1. Elementary Education, 1902 Satara, Maharashtra
2. Matriculation, 1907, Elphinstone High School, Bombay Persian etc.,
3. Inter 1909, Elphinstone College, Bombay Persian and English
4. B.A, 1913, Elphinstone College, Bombay, University of Bombay, Economics & Political Science
5. M.A, 1915 Majoring in Economics with Sociology, History Philosophy, Anthropology and Politics
6. Ph.D., 1917, Columbia University conferred a Degree of Ph.D.
7. M.Sc. 1921 June, London School of Economics, London. Thesis – 'Provincial Decentralization of Imperial Finance in British India'

8. Barrister-at- Law 30-9-1920 Gray's Inn, London
9. (1922-23, Spent some time reading economics in the University of Bonn in Germany.)
10. D. SC Nov 1923, London School of Economics, London 'The Problem of the Rupee – Its origin and its solution' was accepted for the degree in Economics
11. L.L.D (Honoris Causa) 5-6-1952 Columbia University, New York For his achievements, Leadership and authoring the Constitution of India
12. D.Litt. (Honoris Causa) 12-1-1953 Osmania University, Hyderabad For his achievements, Leadership and writing the Constitution of India (*ambedkaritetoday.com*)[6]

Ramji Sakpal retired in 1894 and the family moved to Satara two years later. Shortly after their move, Ambedkar's mother died. The children were cared for by their paternal aunt and lived in difficult circumstances. His original surname was *Sakpal* but his father registered his name as *Ambadawekar* in school, meaning he comes from his native village 'Ambadawe' in Ratnagiri district. His Devrukhe Brahmin teacher, Krishnaji Keshav Ambedkar, changed his surname from 'Ambadawekar' to his own surname 'Ambedkar' in school records.[7]

Dr. Ambedkar had been invited to testify before the Southborough Committee, which was preparing the Government of India Act 1919. At this hearing, Ambedkar argued for creating separate electorates and reservations for untouchables and other religious communities.[7A] In 1920, he began the publication of the weekly *Mooknayak* (*Leader of the Silent*) in Mumbai with the help of Shahu of Kolhapur i.e. Shahu IV (1874–1922).[8]

CONTRIBUTION OF HIS FAMILY IN FIGHT AGAINST SOCIAL INJUSTICE

BABA RAMJI SAKPAL

Ramji Sakpal was the father of Babasaheb Ambedkar. He served as a Subedar in British Army and retired in 1894. Sakpal with his family moved to Satara two years later. He was a very progressive person and a man of high thoughts and confidence. He himself suffered from caste discrimination and humiliation from his childhood such as his forefathers did. He struggled hard and labored hard in his life but he never gave up to heinous caste cruelty. He loved his all children and never discriminated with anyone including his daughters. He did not want his children to leg behind in life. He had high aspirations for his children mainly Bhim Rao Ambedkar. He was very enthusiastic towards the education of his children and wanted to make them highly educated. He wanted to provide education to his daughters too but girl education was against traditions and religion at that time therefore he could not admit them in the school. Yet, he himself taught them at home.

He was much aspirational for his youngest son, Bhim Rao as he was very talented and brilliant from his childhood. Bhim Rao himself was so keen and passionate to studies that he wanted to earn more and more education. But he had to face a drastic protest and torture of the so called upper caste people who tried their best to deprive Bhim Rao from formal education. However, Ramji Sakpal always stood for the help and protection for Bhim Rao and his studies. From school to college (Satara to Bombay), Sakpal ji always proved a helping hand to Bhim Rao and groomed him to face the situation whatever it was. No doubt, when we honour Babasaheb for his struggle and contribution, we should not forget Ramji Sakpal and his struggle and commitment to the education of Babasaheb. Family faced severe poverty and a miserable circumstance but it was Ramji Sakpal and his confidence that always stood with Dr. Ambedkar like a strong rock. Sakpal felt very upset whenever any hurdle took place in the way of Bhim Rao. He had kicked away his pension for the education of his son, Bhim Rao. He was very angry and disappointed when Bhim Rao had accepted his job as a sweeper under Bombay municipality. (Mahanayak Serial &TV, 30 December, 2021)[9] Ramji Sakpal really played a huge and great role to turn Bhim Rao into Dr. Ambedkar. He had dreamt of equality, rights and respect to the downtrodden people, which could be fulfilled by Bhim Rao in his opinion and for this he was very confident. Finally, Dr. Ambedkar succeeded to be what his father had dreamt of. Indeed, Ramji Sakpal was also a champion of equality and social justice who himself fought against discrimination, inequality and injustice but prepared Dr. Ambedkar as well to fight against inequality and caste brutalities.

MATA BHIMA BAI

Bhima Bai was the mother of Babasaheb who nurtured him with love and care. However, she could live long with him and died when Bhim Rao was ten-year-old. She was sick and could not get treatment due to poverty. But she always supported him for his education. She also wanted Bhim Rao to become the champion of downtrodden who could give them salvation from discrimination, humiliation, marginalistion and subjugation. Before her death, she used to motivate Bhim Rao to higher studies. She also deserves our full respect.

MATA RAMABAI AMBEDKAR

Ramabai was Dr. Ambedkar's wife and she along with him and his family proved to be Babasaheb's true companion in the fight against poverty and cruelty of caste-ridden society. In fact, she was a supportive and devoted co-warrior with Babasaheb. Despite being illiterate, he understood the importance of education and always supported and encouraged Babasaheb in the fight against caste discrimination and cruelty. She helped Babasaheb not only as a wife but also as a true friend. She was much younger than him but she had enough understanding. Being an uneducated woman, she not only understood her husband's passion for education but also fully supported him and remained a strong fighter during his struggle and through caste discrimination, social exclusion and social injustice. To ensure Babasaheb's proper and uninterrupted education, he himself worked as a labourer. She used to do household chores and did not hesitate to wash dishes in other houses. He protected Babasahed many times from casteist enemies and fanatics. In fact, Mata Ramabai also contributed a lot in building a society based on equality and social justice. (Mahanayak Serial &TV, 30 December, 2021)[10]

WAITING FOR A VISA HIGHLIGHTS UNTOUCHABILITY FACED BY BABASAHEB

Waiting for A Visa an autobiography of Dr. Ambedkar reveals about the discrimination and brutality faced by him and his struggle. As Dr. Ambedkar was helped with fund for his education by the Princely State of Baroda, he was bound to serve it. He was appointed Military Secretary to the Gaikwad but had to quit the post in a short time. He described the incident in his autobiography, *Waiting for a Visa*.[11] Thereafter, he tried to find ways to make a living for his growing family. He worked as a private tutor, as an accountant, and established an investment consulting business, but it failed when his clients had learned that he was an untouchable.[12] In 1918, he became Professor of Political Economy in the Sydenham College of Commerce and Economics in Mumbai. Although he was successful with the students, other professors objected to his sharing a drinking-water jug with them.[13]

Dr. Ambedkar practiced as a legal professional and in 1926, he successfully defended three non-Brahmin leaders who had accused the Brahmin community of ruining India and were then subsequently litigated for defamation. Dhananjay Keer notes that "The victory was resounding, both socially and individually, for the clients and the doctor".

IMMENSE SUPPORTER OF EDUCATION TO UNTOUCHABLES AND WOMEN

Dr. Ambedkar was an immense advocate of education to untouchables and women. While practicing law in the Bombay High Court, he tried to promote education to untouchables and uplift them. His first organised attempt was his establishment of the central institution *Bahishkrit Hitakarini Sabha*, intended to promote education and socio-economic improvement, as well as the welfare of "outcastes", at the time referred to as depressed classes.[13A] For the defense of Dalit rights, he started many periodicals like *Mook Nayak*, *Bahishkrit Bharat*, and *Equality Janta*.[14] Through his periodicals and magezines, he highlighted the issues related with equality and social justice. He exposed the discriminatory and cruel face of casteism too. He was appointed to the Bombay Presidency Committee to work with the all-European Simon Commission in 1925.[15] This commission had sparked great protests across India, and while its report was ignored by most Indians, Ambedkar himself wrote a separate set of recommendations for the future Constitution of India.[16]

DR. AMBEDKAR'S FAMOUS MOVEMENTS AGAINST CASTE DISCRIMINATION

Mahad Satyagrah

Untouchables had no right to draw water from public tanks too and they had to struggle a lot for drinking water. Animals such as dogs, donkeys, buffalos etc could enter in public water tanks and drink water there but untouchables were not permitted either to enter or drink water there. By 1927, Ambedkar had decided to launch active movements against untouchability. He began with public movements and marches to open up public drinking water resources. He also began a struggle for the right to enter Hindu temples. He led *a satyagraha* in Mahad to fight for the right of the untouchable community to draw water from the main water tank of the town.[17] In a conference in late 1927, Ambedkar publicly condemned the classic Hindu text, the Manusmriti (Laws of Manu), for ideologically justifying caste discrimination and "untouchability", and he ceremonially burned copies of the ancient text.

Burning of Manusmriti

Dr. Ambedkar took Hindu religious books mainly Manusmriti as the sole cause of caste discrimination, inequality and brutality with the untouchable. Therefore, he decided to attack the Manusmriti by burning it publically. On 25 December 1927, he led thousands of followers to burn copies of Manusmriti.[18] Manuwadi people could not tolerate it and they attacked the satyagrahis. Really, it was a daring action of Babsaheb. He had not only ablazed the *Manusmriti* but also had set on fire the source of bondage of humiliation, discrimination and subjugation of untouchables and backwards.

Kalaram Temple Satygraha

In 1930, Dr. Ambedkar launched the Kalaram Temple movement. He made preparations for three months before starting the movement. About 15,000 volunteers assembled at Kalaram Temple satygraha making one of the greatest processions of Nashik. The procession was headed by a military band and a batch of scouts; women and men walked with discipline, order and determination to see the god for the first time. When they reached the gates, the gates were closed by Brahmin authorities.[19] There was a tussle between dalits and Brahmins. Dalits under Dr. Ambedkar wanted to enter the Kalaram temple but Brahmins forcefully stopped the. They attacked the dalists but croud didn't turn voilent. The movement was to have a right to enter temple, it was more towards having equal rights.

It was this period when Civil Disobedience Movement was initiated by Mahatma Gandhi and thus Satyagraha prevailed in the country. The Satyagrahis squatted before the temple, singing bhajans but a strong contingent of the Bombay police meted out the non violent Satyagrahis. The Bombay police was supported by the orthodox Hindus. These people considered it as an unholy act. Because of this attitude of theirs harsh treatment was given not only to the satyagrahis but also to the untouchables of near by villages. Their kids were expelled from the school, roads were closed for them, they were not allowed to buy articles of their daily needs from the local market. Despite this provocations, Dr. Babasaheb Ambedkar kept a check on his Satyagrahis and did not allow them to retaliate. Ambedkar in his speech on inauguration of Satyagraha said 'We don't want to go to temples though but we should have rights.'.. I didn't launch the temple entry movement because I wanted the Depressed Classes to become worshipers of idols which they were prevented from worshiping or because I believed temple entry would make them equal members in and an integral part of the Hindu Society.[19A] Dr. Ambedkar made serious efforts to mix with Hindu society but the caste Hindus failed his all efforts. Casteist Hindus are still not ready to accept that Dalits should mix with upper Hindus and get the respect that other Hindus get. Still dalits are struggling for entry in temples in many parts of the country. However, liberal Hindus including some Brahmins have changed their mind set towards the downtrodden and they have given some space to them. But it has happened in urban areas more rather than rural parts of the country.

POONA PACT (1932) AND RESEVATION POLICY

In 1932, the British colonial government announced the formation of a separate electorate for "Depressed Classes" in the Communal Award. Mahatma Gandhi fiercely opposed a separate electorate for untouchables, saying he feared that such an arrangement would divide the Hindu community.[20] Gandhi protested by fasting while imprisoned in the Yerwada Central Jail of Poona. Following the fast, congressional politicians and activists such as Madan Mohan Malaviya and Palwankar Baloo organised joint meetings with Ambedkar and his supporters at Yerwada.[21] On 25 September 1932, the agreement, known as the Poona Pact was signed between Ambedkar (on behalf of the depressed classes among Hindus) and Madan Mohan Malaviya (on behalf of the other Hindus). The agreement gave reserved seats for the depressed classes in the Provincial legislatures within the general electorate. Due to the pact the depressed class received 148 seats in the legislature instead of the 71, as allocated in the Communal Award proposed earlier by the colonial government under Prime Minister Ramsay MacDonald.[22]

The provision of the Communal Award proposed by the British Government, which was the result of the massive struggle of the champions of the Depressed Classes Particularly Dr. B.R. Ambedkar, can be considered as the beginning point of the reservation policy. Dr. Ambedkar, talking to Mahatma Gandhi, firmly demanded it stating,

"I want political power for my community. That is indispensable for our survival. The basis of the agreement should be: I should get what is due to me. I wish to tell the Hindus that I should be assured of my compensation"

(S.N. Busi, 1997)[23].

PROVISIONS OF POONA PACT

- Seats would be reserved for the 'Depressed classes' in the Provincial Councils.
- The number of seats reserved for the provinces depended on the strength of the provinces:
- Madras: 30; Punjab: 8; Bombay and Sindh: 15; Central Provinces: 20; Bihar and Orissa: 18; Bengal: 30; United Provinces: 20; and Assam: 7 (Total reserved: 148)
- In the Central Legislature, 19% of the seats would be reserved for the Depressed Classes.
- The members of the depressed classes who were eligible to vote would form an electoral college. This College would elect four candidates among the depressed classes on the basis of single vote. (That is, the candidates with the four highest numbers of votes would form the panel of four).
- Then, these four candidates would stand for election with the general candidates for election to the assembly. This time, the general electorate would vote. Thus, in effect, the depressed classes got a 'double vote' since they formed part of the general electorate also.
- This principle of **'Joint electorate and reserved seats'** was to be followed in the Central Assembly too.
- It was agreed that this system would continue for ten years unless it was ended by mutual consent sooner.
- It was also agreed upon to allocate a certain portion of money from the educational grant for the education of the depressed classes in all the provinces.
- Nobody would be discriminated against because they belonged to the depressed classes in the matter of election to the local bodies or appointment to government service.[23A]

But it was not so easy for Babasaheb to get political power for the Depressed Classes of which they were deprived for centuries. The caste Hindus did their best to force Babasaheb give up his demand. Mahatma Gandhi led the caste Hindus in this regard. To resist the Communal Award or the separate electorate policy for the Depressed Classes, Mahatma Gandhi took the shelter of the 'fast unto death', so-called peaceful mean. The physical condition of Mahatma Gandhi became critical because of the fast. All eyes set on Babasaheb for saving the life of Mahatma Gandhi. At that time, it seemed that it was within the hands of Babasaheb Ambedkar to grant lease of life to Bapuji or otherwise. On one side, he had the interests of his community and on the other, the life of Bapuji. In such an event, he was looking for an agreement that would not cost the interests of his community dearly but at the same time save the life of Gandhi ji. At long last, he quite generously and graciously agreed to an amicable solution. That solution is popularly known as the 'Poona Pact' of 1932. Babasaheb himself well explained the situation through which he had to pass, in these words:

"It was a baffling situation. I had to make a choice between two different alternatives. There was before me the duty, I owed as a part of common humanity to save Gandhi from sure death. There was before me the problem of securing for the untouchables the political right, which the Prime Minister had given them. I responded to the call of humanity and saved the life of Mr. Gandhi by agreeing to alter the Communal Award in a manner satisfactory to Mr. Gandhi". (S.N. Busi, 1997)[24]

DR. AMBEDKAR: A CRUSADER OF SOCIAL JUSTICE

The different concepts of justice, as discussed in ancient Western philosophy, were typically centered upon the community. Plato wrote in The Republic that it would be an ideal state that "every member of the community must be assigned to the class for which he finds himself best fitted. "Aristotle believed rights existed only between free people, and the law should take "account in the first instance of relations of inequality in which individuals are treated in proportion to their worth and only secondarily of relations of equality." Socrates is attributed with developing the idea of a social contract, whereby people ought to follow the rules of a society, and accept its burdens because they have accepted its benefits.

The issues of social justice have affected various developmental policy as well as whole development of social welfare programme for the down trodden and weaker sections of society. According to Dr. Ambedkar the root cause of social injustice to the Scheduled Castes and Scheduled Tribes is the Caste system in Hindu society. He observed,

Castes are enclosed units and it is their conspiracy with clear conscience that compels the ex-communicated to make them into a Caste. The logic of their obdurate circumstance in merciless and it is in obedience to its force that some unfortunate groups find themselves closed out with the result that now groups by a mechanical law are constantly being converted into Castes in a widening multiplicity. He further maintained that the root of untouchability is the Caste system and the root of the Caste system is religion, the root of religion attached to varnashram and the root of the varnashram is the Brahminism, the roof of Brahminism lies with the political power. [25]

THE ANNIHILATION OF CASTE AND HIS CONCEPT OF SOCIAL JUSTICE

Dr. Ambedkar outlined his thoughts in his speech that was published as a book, *The Annihilation of Caste*. He stood for a social system that is based on right relations between man and man in all spheres of his life. His concept of social justice stands for the liberty, equality and fraternity of all human beings. He had suffered of social inequality, discrimination and caste based brutality from his childhood. Therefore, he championed the cause of social equality and justice. He considered the caste system as the greatest evil of Hindu religion. The Varna system according to him is the root cause of all inequality and is also the originator of the caste system and untouchability. He wanted to dismantle the caste and caste system which was the source of discrimination, marginalization subjugation and humiliation. As a rationalist and humanist, he did not approve of any type of hypocrisy, injustice and exploitation of man by man in the name of caste or religion. He stood for a religion that is based on universal principles of morality and is applicable to all times, to all countries and to all races. It must be in accord with reason and must be based on the basic tenets of liberty, equality and fraternity.

DR AMBEDKAR'S IDEAL: A SOCIETY BASED ON LIBERTY, EQUALITY, AND FRATERNITY]

Dr. Ambedkar loved social justice and liberty, equality and fraternity as well. In his speech that was published as *Annihilation of Caste,* Dr. Ambedkar said, "I would not be surprized if some of you have grown weary listening to this tiresome tale of the sad effects which caste has produced. There is nothing new in it. I will therefore turn to the constructive side of the problem. What is your ideal society if you do not want caste, is a question that is bound to be asked of you. If you ask me, my ideal would be a society based on Liberty, Equality, and Fraternity. And why not? What objection can there be to Fraternity? I cannot imagine any...

In other words, there must be social endosmosis. This is fraternity, which is only another name for democracy. Democracy is not merely a form of government. It is primarily a mode of associated living, of conjoint communicated experience. It is essentially an attitude of respect and reverence towards one's fellow men.

2. Dr. Ambedkar asked a question, Any objection to Liberty? Few object to liberty in the sense of a right to free movement, in the sense of a right to life and limb. There is no objection to liberty in the sense of a right to property, tools, and materials, as being necessary for earning a living, to keep the body in a due state of health. Why not allow a person the liberty to benefit from an effective and competent use of a person's powers? The supporters of Caste who would allow liberty in the sense of a right to life, limb, and property, would not readily consent to liberty in this sense, inasmuch as it involves liberty to choose one's profession. But to object to this kind of liberty is to perpetuate slavery. For slavery does not merely mean a legalized form of subjection. It means a state of society in which some men are forced to accept from others the purposes which control their conduct. This condition obtains even where there is no slavery in the legal sense. It is found where, as in the Caste

System, some persons are compelled to carry on certain prescribed callings which are not of their choice.

3. Any objection to equality? This has obviously been the most contentious part of the slogan of the French Revolution. The objections to equality may be sound, and one may have to admit that all men are not equal. But what of that? Equality may be a fiction, but nonetheless one must accept it as the governing principle. A man's power is dependent upon (1) physical heredity; (2) social inheritance or endowment in the form of parental care, education, accumulation of scientific knowledge, everything which enables him to be more efficient than the savage; and finally, (3) on his own efforts. In all these three respects men are undoubtedly unequal. But the question is, shall we treat them as unequal because they are unequal? This is a question which the opponents of equality must answer

(https://ccnmtl.columbia.edu/projects/mmt/ambedkar/web/readings/aoc_print_2004.pdf)

DR. AMBEDKAR SACRIFICED HIS CHILDREN TO FIGHT FOR SOCIAL JUSTICE

Babasaheb had personal experiences as far as caste discrimination and hatred were concerned. He faced brutality, humiliation and torture on the basis of caste. He was made realise that he belonged to a low caste, therefore he deserved humiliation and brutality. He had to fight against caste based discrimination from his childhood. Therefore, he wanted to dismantle the brutal and heinous caste system. However, his struggle was very painful. He not only faced humiliation during the struggle but also had to loss his four children. It was an immense and unique scarification, which he faced personally in modern India.

DR. AMBEDKAR ATTACKED SOCIAL INJUSTICE UNVIOLENTLY THROUGH MAGZINES LIKE MOOK NAYAK

Dr. B.R. Ambedkar's thoughts on social justice were progressive. He did not believe in violence; he considered the press to be a powerful tool for social changes for justice and freedom. He published Mook Nayak, Janata and Samata magazines, but these magazines remained largely unsold, perhaps because of the progressive and unconventional thoughts expressed therein. If there are prohibitions on the social evil of untouchability in the Constitution, then this credit goes to Ambedkar to a great extent. Ambedkar's greatest achievement was that he made the downtrodden of India feel their separate powerful existence; the credit goes to him that he brought all the downtrodden - then, untouchable castes under the one name of SCs. If Ambedkar had not pursued special reservation facilities for the SCs/STs in the field of education and government services of the central and states governments, their conditions would have remained as before—laden with sorrow and sufferings. It is the result of Ambedkar's constant efforts that today there are members of parliament (MPs), members of the legislative assembly (MLAs), The Indian Administrative Service (IAS)/The Indian Police Service (IPS), professors and doctors from among these castes.

In the simplest sense, Dr. Ambedkar is also one of the proponents of social justice in modern India. His prime aim with the view of social justice is to remove all kinds of inequalities based upon caste, race, gender, religion, power, position, and wealth. The social justice brings equal distribution of the social, political and economic resources of the community. Dr. Ambedkar being the chief architect of the Indian Constitution was fully aware of the pattern and problems of the Indian society. He tried to achieve social justice and social democracy in terms of one man, one vote and one value. He treated social justice as a true basis for patriotism and nationalism. Dr. Ambedkar did not accept the theories of social justice as propounded by the Varna system, the Aristotelian order, Plato's Ideal State, Gandhian Sarvodaya order and not even the proletarian socialism of Marx. At the same time, we cannot deny the fact that in the field of social justice, much remains to complain about. Social differences and untouchability have not been removed due to the difficult caste system and the blind faiths that have been continuing for centuries. [26]

DR. AMBEDKAR'S STRUGGLE FOR SOCIAL JUSTICE

Dr. B.R. Ambedkar's name will be written in golden letters in the history of India as a champion of social justice. He was not only the main builder of the Constitution, but also the crusader of social justice for the betterment of the downtrodden. He spent his whole life for the betterment of the poor and exploited untouchables in the Indian society. In such a society, to bring about a great change, Dr. Ambedkar had only one power—his logic and thought. He relied on the power of his thoughts and ordinances.

French revolution highly influenced Dr. Ambedkar and he dreamt to achieve 'Liberty, Equality and Fraternity' in India too. Rousseau's saying 'Man is born free, but everywhere he is in chains' and his three words equality, liberty and fraternity had revolutionized France in 1789. Dr. Ambedkar also was very much influenced by Rousseau's words and he decided to fight for justice based on equality. Dr. B.R. Ambedkar wanted economic and social equalities before political equality; he tried his best to ensure that the downtrodden got a proper place in society. Hence, he gave more importance to social justice than political justice; on equal opportunity with individual liberty were laid much emphasis to root out the differences created by the caste system of the country.

DR. AMBEDKAR'S STRUGGLE FOR FREEDOM OF 'SLAVES OF SLAVES'

Dr. Ambedkar fought the battle of freedom at two fronts one, against Britishers and secondly against Brahmanical order that was discriminatory for downtroddens, backwards and women. No doubt, he was a national leader and wanted freedom for the country. Beside the concerns for nation, he had deep concerns for downtrodden, backwards and women too. He named his fight for freedom of downtrodden as a fight to liberate slaves (downtroddens) of slaves (Manuvadi forces who were the slaves of British). He was so committed for the liberation of the downtrodden, backwards and women that he wanted to get liberated them as soon as possible. He always gave preference to the upliftment of downtrodden, backwards and women.

DR. AMBEDKAR'S SUPPORT TO GENDER EQUALITY

Dr. Ambedkar wanted equality and social justice not only for men but also for women. That's why he was a great champion of gender equality. he was of the opinion that society cannot be developed if its women are lagging behind. He was in favour of women empowerment in all spheres of life and for the betterment of women he revolted against all oppressive features of Hindu society. His dream was to bring gender equality in the society that is yet to be realized and therefore his thoughts are important for the social reconstruction that favors women empowerment. Dr. Ambedkar expressed his concern on the miserable state of women. He emphatically stated that women must be treated equally and given equal respect. Being a Union Law Minister, he insisted on Hindu Code bill suggesting the basic improvements in the life of women. He also asserted and evoked all the parliamentary members to help to pass the bill in parliament. Eventually, he kicked off his minister ship and resigned for the cause of women, when government and other parliamentarian did not support him.

His deep concern and feelings for all round development of women is expressed from his thoughts. As a true feminist, Dr. Ambedkar's perception of women's question, emphasized their right to education, equal treatment with men, right to property and involvement in the political process. In his last speech in Indian Parliament, we can know his feelings and respect showed towards women. He quoted the famous thoughts of an Irish Patriot Daniel o Connal as, "No man can be grateful at the cost of his honor, no woman can be grateful at the cost of her chastity. And no nation can be grateful at the cost of his liberty.[27]

He had concerns of empowerment not only for Hindu women but also for Muslim and other women. In his famous book, "*Pakistan- Partition of India*" he expressed his views about Muslim women and their religious traditions, about wearing veil, their marriages and so on. Muslim women were suppressed under various religious traditions. Towards all the women, irrespective of their religion, casts and class, his views were humanitarian. He frequently raised his voice against all sorts of oppression and injustice towards women.[28]

Dr. AMBEDKAR'S FIGHT FOR WOMEN EMANCIPATION AND THEIR EMPOWERMENT

It will not be an exaggeration to state that Dr. Ambedkar was the greatest champion of women rights and women emancipation. He, right from his childhood, had massive concerns for women's miserable and disgraceful status in the society. He seriously believed in emancipation and empowerment of women. From his childhood, he was in favour of equality of education and opportunity to all including women.

Dr. Ambedkar believed in the strength of women and their role in the process of social reform. He had said, **"I measure the progress of community by the degree of progress which women had achieved"**. Let every girl who marries stand by her husband, claim to be her husband's friend and equal, and refuse to be his slave. I am sure if you follow this advice, you will bring honors and glory to yourselves. He strongly advocated for family planning measures for women in Bombay Legislative Assembly (Shambunath, 2018)[29].

He strongly advocated for family planning measures for women in Bombay Legislative Assembly. Dr. Ambedkar's work for women was not only limited to social reforms but he used the legal framework also to give women equal rights.

DR. AMBEDKAR'S LEGAL SAFEGUARDS TO WOMEN AS THE LABOUR MINISTER DURING BRITISH GOVERNMENT

How was Dr. Ambedkar careful of women rights, it seems in his efforts as a Labour Minister. In 1942, being a Labor Minister of Executive Council of Governor General, he introduced a **Maternity Benefit Bill**. He provided several provisions in the Constitution for protecting the welfare and civil rights of women. Besides, he highlighted the issues of Muslim women also. His secular perspective is known through his thoughts on "Purdah" (Veil) system, religious conversions and legal rights for Muslim women. Dr. Ambedkar's emphasis was on reconstruction of the Hindu society on the basis of equality rather than the social reforms initiated by Brahma Samaj or Arya Samaj because their attempts were limited only to the upper strata of the society. His in-depth study of Smritis and Shashtras and his experience from the response of upper castes during the temple entry movement crystallized his conclusions on Hindu philosophy and society (www.questjournal.org)[30]. no doubt to state that till today, no leader could rise to the heights of Dr. Ambedkar as far as the women rights and their empowerment were concerned. Only Dr. Ambedkar has resigned from the post of a cabinet minister in favour of women. He kicked off his post of Law Minister for the welfare of women. But it is a matter of immense sorrow that women do not find themselves grateful to Dr. Ambedkar, however he was great champion of women rights. He not echoed his voice for social justice from the point of view of Deprived people but also he fought for women betterment.

DR. AMBEDKAR'S RESIGNATION AS LAW MINISTER FOR WOMEN RIGHTS

Dr. Ambedkar was a great feminist thinker and leader as well. He always since his childhood raised vibrant voice in favour of women. No doubt to state that he was a huge champion of women rights and their upliftment. His dedication and seriousness can be seen for the women cause in his resignation from the post of Union Law Minister. In 1948, when the Hindu Code Bill was introduced in parliament and debated on the floor of the house, the opposition was strong against the Bill. Dr. Ambedkar as a Law Minister tried his level best to defend the Bill by pointing out the drawbacks of Indian society and arguing that the ideals in the Bill are based on the Constitutional principles of equality, liberty and fraternity and that in the Indian society characterized by the caste system and the oppression of women since women are deprived of equality, a legal frame work is necessary for a social change in which women have equal rights with men. He also pointed out that the aim of the Bill as "to codify the rules of Hindu Law which are scattered in innumerable decisions of High Courts and of the Privy Council which form a bewildering motley to the common man". (Arya, 2000:63) [31].

The opposition of the bill by Hindu orthodoxy and the dramatic move of the Prime Minister annoyed the then Law Minister Dr. Ambedkar and he protested the opposition democratically and decided to resign. Dr. Ambedkar resigned his post of Law Minister. It was a huge and historical step taken by Dr. Ambedkar in support of women interest and empowerment. His resignation shows his worthy and concrete fight for protecting women from deprivation and denial of rights.

SOCIAL JUSTICE THROUGH INDIAN CONSTITUTION

On 29th August, 1947, Drafting Committee was constituted under chairmanship of Dr. Ambedkar. Being the main architect of the Constitution of India, Dr. Ambedkar tried his best to institutionalize and practice social justice through the Constitution of India too. Dr. Ambedkar stood for a social system in which man's status is based on his merit and achievements and where no one is noble or untouchable because of his/her birth. He advocated the policy of preferential treatment for the socially oppressed and economically exploited people of the country. The Constitution of India, which was drafted under his chairmanship, contains a number of provisions that enjoins the state to secure to all its citizens, justice, social, economic and political, along with liberty, equality and fraternity. It also contains a number of provisions that guarantee a preferential treatment to the down-trodden people in various sectors. Article 17 of the Indian Constitution declares untouchability as abolished. Ambedkar, in his speech before the Constituent Assembly for the passage of the Constitution, said 'I have completed my work; I wish there should be a sunrise even tomorrow. The new Bharat has got political freedom, but it is yet to raise the sun of social and economic liberty." He highly emphasized the social and economic empowerment of the weaker sections of the society and preferred social and economic democracy over political one.

For ensuring social justice, he architected constitutional and legal order and safeguards that empower socially and educationally backwards. Several Articles in the Indian Constitution mainly, Articles 14 to 24 under the Fundamental Rights are framed to abolish the discrimination with the Dalits. The many provisions provide equal status to Dalit's with other segments of society. Abolition of untouchability and discrimination against them, provisions of fundamental rights to all, equal protection of laws, voting rights and reservation in education, jobs, promotion and political fields to all without discrimination of caste, race, sex and religion. There is a separate chapter on Indian Constitution and social justice in this book, in which detailed discussion has been made.

FAMOUS QUOTATIONS OF BABASAHEB DR. AMBEDKAR

In order to understand the greatness of Babsaheb Ambedkar and his ideological mindset, we will have to go through his ideas and famous quotes. Let us remember him for his own words. Here are 16 inspiring quotes by Babasaheb Ambedkar as under.

1. "They cannot make history who forget history".

2. "Be Educated, Be Organised and Be Agitated"

3. "I like the religion that teaches liberty, equality and fraternity"

4. "Life should be great rather than long".

5. "If I find the constitution being misused, I shall be the first to burn it."

6. "Cultivation of mind should be the ultimate aim of human existence".

7. "If you believe in living a respectable life, you believe in self-help which is the best help".

8. "We must stand on our own feet and fight as best as we can for our rights. So carry on your agitation and organize your forces. Power and prestige will come to you through struggle"

9. "The history of India is nothing but a history of a mortal conflict between Buddhism and Brahminism".

10. "I measure the progress of a community by the degree of progress which women have achieved."

11. "Men are mortal. So are ideas. An idea needs propagation as much as a plant needs watering. Otherwise both will wither and die."

12. "Every man who repeats the dogma of Mill that one country is no fit to rule another country must admit that one class is not fit to rule another class."

13. "The relationship between husband and wife should be one of closest friends."

14. "Political tyranny is nothing compared to the social tyranny and a reformer who defies society is a more courageous man than a politician who defies Government."

15. "A great man is different from an eminent one in that he is ready to be the servant of the society."

16. "Law and order are the medicine of the body politic and when the body politic gets sick, medicine must be administered."

(https://www.freepressjournal.in/india/16-famous-quotes-by-babasaheb-ambedkar-you-ought-to-know)

IN POPULAR CULTURE AND MEDIA

Several films, plays, and other works have been based on the life and thoughts of Ambedkar.

- Indian director Jabbar Patel made a documentary titled *Dr. Babasaheb Ambedkar* in 1991; he followed this with a full-length feature film *Dr. Babasaheb Ambedkar* in 2000 with Mammootty in the lead role.[32] This biopic was sponsored by the National Film Development Corporation of India and the government's Ministry of Social Justice and Empowerment. The film was released after a long and controversial gestation.[33]

- Other Indian films on Ambedkar include: *Balaka Ambedkar* (1991) by Basavaraj Kestur, *Dr. Ambedkar* (1992) by Bharath Parepalli, and *Yugpurush Dr. Babasaheb Ambedkar* (1993).

- David Blundell, professor of anthropology at UCLA and historical ethnographer, has established *Arising Light* – a series of films and events that are intended to stimulate interest and knowledge about the social conditions in India and the life of Ambedkar. [34] In *Samvidhaan*, a TV mini-series on the making of the Constitution of India directed by Shyam Benegal, the pivotal role of B. R. Ambedkar was played by Sachin Khedekar.[35] The play *Ambedkar Aur Gandhi*, directed by Arvind Gaur and written by Rajesh Kumar, tracks the two prominent personalities of its title.[36]

- *Bhimayana: Experiences of Untouchability* is a graphic biography of Ambedkar created by Pardhan-Gond artists Durgabai Vyam and Subhash Vyam, and writers Srividya Natarajan and S. Anand. The book depicts the experiences of untouchability faced by Ambedkar from childhood to adulthood. CNN named it one of the top 5 political comic books.[37]

- The Ambedkar Memorial at Lucknow is dedicated in his memory. The chaitya consists of monuments showing his biography.[38]

- Jai Bhim slogan was given by the Dalit community in Delhi in his honour in 1946.[39]

- Google commemorated Ambedkar's 124th birthday through a homepage doodle on 14 April 2015.[40] The doodle was featured in India, Argentina, Chile, Ireland, Peru, Poland, Sweden and the United Kingdom.[41]

- An Indian television show named *Ek Mahanayak: Dr. B. R. Ambedkar* portraying his life aired on &TV in 2019.[42]

- Another show, *Dr. Babasaheb Ambedkar - Mahamanvachi Gauravgatha*, has aired in Marathi on Star Pravah from 2019.[43]

LEGENDARY WORKS OF DR. AMBEDKAR

The Education Department, <u>Government of Maharashtra</u> (Mumbai) published the collection of Ambedkar's writings and speeches in different volumes.[44]

i. <u>*Castes in India: Their Mechanism, Genesis and Development*</u> *and 11 Other Essays*

v. *Ambedkar in the Bombay Legislature, with the Simon Commission and at the Round Table Conferences*, 1927–1939

v. *Philosophy of Hinduism; India and the Pre-requisites of Communism; Revolution and Counter-revolution; Buddha or Karl Marx*

v. *Riddles in Hinduism* <u>ISBN978-81-89059-77-4</u>

v. *Essays on Untouchables and Untouchability*

v. *The Evolution of Provincial Finance in British India*

v. *The Untouchables Who Were They And Why They Became Untouchables?*

v. <u>*The Annihilation of Caste*</u> *(1936)*

v. *Pakistan or the Partition of India*

v. *What Congress and Gandhi have done to the Untouchables; Mr. Gandhi and the Emancipation of the Untouchables*

v. Ambedkar as member of the Governor General's Executive Council, 1942–46

v. <u>*The Buddha and his Dhamma*</u>

v. *Unpublished Writings; Ancient Indian Commerce; Notes on laws;* <u>*Waiting for a Visa*</u> *; Miscellaneous notes, etc.*

v. Ambedkar as the principal architect of the Constitution of India

v. (2 parts) Dr. Ambedkar and The Hindu Code Bill

v. *Ambedkar as Free India's First Law Minister and Member of Opposition in Indian Parliament (1947–1956)*

v. *The Pali Grammar*

v. Ambedkar and his Egalitarian Revolution – Struggle for Human Rights. Events starting from March 1927 to 17 November 1956 in the chronological order; Ambedkar and his Egalitarian Revolution – Socio-political and religious activities. Events starting from November 1929 to 8 May 1956 in the chronological order; Ambedkar and his Egalitarian Revolution – Speeches. (Events starting from 1 January to 20 November 1956 in the chronological order.)

<u>**REFERENCE**</u>

*https://www.google.com/searchq=dr+ambedkar+hd+image&rlz=1C1ONGR_enIN982IN982&oq=&aqs=chrome.3.69i59i450l8.413109943j0j15&sourceid=chrome&ie=UTF-8#imgrc=zDbWe-rm3LYtHM

1. Jaffrelot, Christophe (2005). Ambedkar and Untouchability: Fighting the Indian Caste System. New York: <u>Columbia University Press</u>. p. 2. <u>ISBN0-231-13602-1</u>.

2. Pritchett, Frances. <u>"In the 1890s"</u> (PHP). <u>Archived</u> from the original on 7 September 2006.

3. <u>"Mahar"</u>. <u>Encyclopædia Britannica</u>. britannica.com. <u>Archived</u> from the original on 30 November 2011.

4. Ahuja, M. L. (2007). <u>"Babasaheb Ambedkar"</u>. Eminent Indians : administrators and political thinkers. New Delhi: Rupa. pp. 1922–1923. <u>ISBN978-8129111074</u>. <u>Archived</u> from the original on 23 December 2016.

5. Jaffrelot, Christophe (2005). Ambedkar and Untouchability: Fighting the Indian Caste System. New York: <u>Columbia University Press</u>. p. 2. <u>ISBN0-231-13602-1</u>.

6. ambedkaritetoday.com

7. <u>https://en.wikipedia.org/wiki/B._R._Ambedkar</u>)

7A. <u>"Bhimrao Ambedkar"</u>. columbia.edu. <u>Archived</u> from the original on 10 February 2014.

8. <u>"Rescuing Ambedkar from pure Dalitism: He would've been India's best Prime Minister"</u>. <u>Archived</u> from the original on 6 November 2015

9. Mahanayak Serial &TV, 30 December, 2021

10. Mahanayak Serial &TV, 30 December, 2021

11. Pritchett, Frances. "In the 1890s" (PHP). Archived from the original on 7 September 2006.

12. Pritchett, Frances. "In the 1910s" (PHP). Archived from the original on 23 November 2011.

13. "Ambedkar teacher". 31 March 2016.

14. 13A. Kshīrasāgara, Rāmacandra (1994). Dalit Movement in India and Its Leaders,

15. 1857-1956, M.D. Publications Pvt. Ltd. ISBN978-8185880433.

16. Ambedkar, Dr. B.R. "Waiting for a Visa". columbia.edu. Columbia University. Archived from the original on 24 June 2010.

17. Keer, Dhananjay (1971) [1954]. Dr. Ambedkar: Life and Mission. Mumbai: Popular Prakashan. pp. 37–38. ISBN8171542379. OCLC123913369.

18. Harris, Ian, ed. (2001). Buddhism and politics in twentieth-century Asia. Continuum International Group. ISBN978-0826451781.

19. Tejani, Shabnum (2008). "From Untouchable to Hindu Gandhi, Ambedkar and Depressed class question 1932". Indian secularism : a social and intellectual history, 1890–1950. Bloomington, Ind.: Indiana University Press. pp. 205–210. ISBN978-0253220448. 19A. https://www.ambedkaritetoday.com/2020/03/kalaram-temple-entry-movement-by-ambedkar.html

20. Jaffrelot, Christophe (2005). Dr Ambedkar and Untouchability: Analysing and Fighting Caste. London: C. Hurst & Co. Publishers. p. 4. ISBN1850654492.

21. Ambedkar, B. R. (1979). Writings and Speeches. **1**. Education Dept., Govt. of Maharashtra.

22. "Annihilating caste". frontline.in. Archived from the original on 28 May 2014.

23. Menon, Nivedita (25 December 2014). "Meanwhile, for Dalits and Ambedkarites in India, December 25th is Manusmriti Dahan Din, the day on which B R Ambedkar publicly and ceremoniously in 1927". Kafila.

24. https://en.wikipedia.org/wiki/B._R._Ambedkar)

25. S.N. Busi, (1997). Mahatma Ganghi and Babasaheb Ambedkar: Crusaders Against Caste And Untouchability, Saroj Publications, Andhra Pradesh, p. 199.

26. S.N. Busi, 1997

27. www.ijcrt.org © 2020 IJCRT | Volume 8, Issue 12 December 2020 | ISSN: 2320-2882 IJCRT2012278 International Journal of Creative Research Thoughts (IJCRT) www.ijcrt.org 2619

28. www.ijcrt.org © 2020 IJCRT | Volume 8, Issue 12 December 2020 | ISSN: 2320-2882 IJCRT2012278 International Journal of Creative Research Thoughts (IJCRT) www.ijcrt.org 2620

29. https://www.dailyexcelsior.com/ambedkar-on-women/

30. https://www.dailyexcelsior.com/ambedkar-on-women/

31. Shambunath, 2018

32. www.questjournal.org

33. Arya, Sudha., (2000). Women Gender Equality and the State, Deep and Deep Publications, New Delhi..

34. Dhananjay Keer (1971). Dr. Ambedkar: Life and Mission, Popular Prakashan. pp. 280–. ISBN978-81-7154-237-6.

35. Geoffrey A. Oddie (1991). Religion in South Asia: Religious Conversion and Revival Movements in South Asia in Medieval and Modern Times. Manohar. p. 198. ISBN978-81-85425-46-7.

36. Gauri Viswanathan (11 May 2021). Outside the Fold: Conversion, Modernity, and Belief. Princeton University Press. pp. 224–. ISBN978-1-4008-4348-0.

37. Bryant, Edwin (2001). The Quest for the Origins of Vedic Culture, Oxford: Oxford University Press. pp. 50–51. ISBN9780195169478

38. Bryant, Edwin. The Quest for the Origins of Vedic Culture, Oxford: Oxford University Press, 2001. pp. 50.

39. Sharma, Arvind (2005), "Dr. B. R. Ambedkar on the Aryan Invasion and the Emergence of the Caste System in India", J Am Acad Relig (September 2005) 73 (3): 849.

40. Sharma, Arvind (2005). "Dr. B. R. Ambedkar on the Aryan Invasion and the Emergence of the Caste System in India". Journal of the American Academy of Religion. **73** (3):843–870. doi:10.1093/jaarel/lfi081. ISSN0002-7189. JSTOR4139922.

41. Kumar, Vivek (20 January 2018). "Resurgence of an icon". Business Line. Kasturi & Sons.

42. Viswanathan, S (24 May 2010). "Ambedkar film: better late than never". The Hindu. Archived from the original on 10 September 2011.

43. Anima, P. (17 July 2009). "A spirited adventure". The Hindu. Chennai, India.

44. "Ambedkar Memorial, Lucknow/India" (PDF). Remmers India Pvt. Ltd. Archived (PDF) from the original on 2 November 2013.

45. Tripathi, Ashish; Apr 18, Arunav Sinha / TNN / Updated; 2016; Ist, 14:55. "Chronologically 'Jai Bhim' is older than 'Jai Hind': Experts | Lucknow News - Times of India". The Times of India. Retrieved 13 March 2021.

46. "Archived copy". Archived from the original on 14 April 2015.

CHAPTER ELEVEN

DR. RAM MANOHAR LOHIYA

Source*

EARLY LIFE AND EDUCATION

Dr. Ram Manohar Lohia has been a great name in Indian politics who echoed his voice for not only socialism but also for social justice and social change. Indian citizens should recall how Ram Manohar Lohia wove social justice with socialism. He was born on 23rd March 1910 at Akbarpur village of Uttar Pradesh in a Marnari family. His father, Hiralal, was a devoted freedom fighter and a follower of Gandhi. Lohia was greatly influenced by his father Hiralal and Gandhi. It was from his father that Lohia derived his interest in his early years in the nationalist politics led by Gandhi. The political interest of Ram Manohar Lohia took a radical character during His student life in India. After his primary education in the village he was admitted to a school in Bombay (Marhari Vidyalaya) and passed

High School examination from Bombay in 1925. He had his college education in Benaras (1925-1927) and Calcutta (1927-1929), and in August 1929 he went to Europe for Higher studies.

RECALLING THE FAMOUS QUOTES OF LOHIA

Ram Manohar Lohia's quest for social justice can be understood by his thoughts and famous quotes, which are being recalled as under-

- BHARAT ME ASAMANTA SIRF AARTHIK NAHI HAI; YEH SAMAJIK BHI HAI
- (Inequality in India is not just economic; It's social too.)
- JATI PRATHA KE VIRUDDH VIDROH SE HI DESH ME JAGRITI AAYEGI
- (It is only through the revolt against the caste system that there will be awakening in the country.)
- JATI TODNE KA SABSE ACHCHHA UPAY HAI, KATHIT UCHCH AUR NIMN JATIYON KE BEECH ROTI BETI KA SA SAMBANDH
- (The best way to break the caste is the relationship of bread and daughter between the alleged upper and lower castes).
- BHARAT ME RAJ KAUN KAREGA YE TEEN CHEEJON SE TAY HOTA HAI-OONCHI JATI, DHAN AUR GYAN. JINKE PASS INME SE KOI DO CHEEJEN HOTI HAIN VAH SHASAN KAR SAKTA HAI.
- (Who will rule in India is decided by three things. High caste, wealth and knowledge. Those who have any two of these things can rule).

- "Satyagraha without constructive work is like a sentence without a verb"
- JINDA KOMEN SARKAAR BADALNE KE LIYE PANCH SAAL TAK INTIZAR NAHI KARTI
- ("Live communities don't wait for five years (the term of the Parliament)"
- "The use of English is a hindrance to original thinking, progenitor of inferiority feelings and a gap between the educated and uneducated public. Come, let us unite to restore Hindi to its original Glory."
- JATI AVASAR KO SIMIT KARTI HAI. SIMIT AVASAR KSHAMTA KO SANKUCHIT KARTA HAI. SANKUCHIT KSHAMTA AVASAR KO AUR BHI SIMIT KAR DETI HAI. JAHAN JATI KA PRACHALAN HAI, VAHAN AVASAR OR KSHAMTA HAMESHA SE SIKUD RAHE KUCHH LOGON KE DAYARE TAK SIMIT HAI.
- "Caste restricts opportunity. Restricted opportunity constricts ability. Constricted ability further restricts opportunity. Where caste prevails, opportunity and ability are restricted to ever-narrowing circles of the people." (Ram Manohar Lohia Quotes in Hindi (achhikhabar.com)1

Quotes and slogans expressed by Ram Manohar Lohia show that he was against caste and caste based discrimination and hegemony and wanted to dismantle it through intercaste relations of bread and daughter. It meant that Lohiaji wanted to establish an egalitarian society for which he supported and promoted inter-caste dining and wedding.

LOHIA'S DREAM OF SOCIAL CHANGE BY INVOLVING LAGGING BEHIND SECTIONS OF THE SOCIETY IN THE INDEPENDENCE MOVEMENT

Lohia unfortunately died very soon on 12th October 1967. But his short life acts as a thread that links the stories of Gandhi, Ambedkar and post-1960s politics. Influenced by Gandhian ideas of civil disobedience, Lohia took an active part in the freedom struggle. Lohia dreamt of social change and began to independently anticipate the idea of making social change by involving socially backward communities, women, the poor, the peasants, and the working classes in the Independence movement.

Lohia's efforts, along with leaders like Jayaprakash Narayan, Acharya Narendra Dev and others, led to the formation of Congress Socialists, within the Indian National Congress. This group sought to promote socialist ideas in the freedom struggle. After Gandhi's assassination in 1948, Ram Manohar Lohia chose to part ways with Jawaharlal Nehru and Sardar Patel, and launched his own party, and focused on the challenge of bringing about social change. Lohia's politics in independent India was different. Besides leading the socialist movement, according to scholar Anand Kumar, Lohia's unique contribution to the political discourse lies in his formulation of an "intersectionalist approach for understanding the inequalities, exclusions and exploitations in the power system of contemporary India".2

LOHIA'S ADVOCACY FOR WAR AGAINST TWO SEGREGATIONS OF CASTE AND SEX

Unlike other socialist leaders and Communists Lohia did not focus the factor of class. He showed interest towards social differences rather than economic one. Lohia attacked caste and gender discrimination. He said that it is the two segregations of caste and gender that have caused unjust social, economic and cultural order in India. In his work *The Two Segregations of Caste and Sex,* Lohia stated, "All war on poverty is a sham, unless it is, at the same time, a conscious and sustained war on these two segregations". Lohia said that destruction of the caste-based hierarchical system was central for democracy to sustain itself. He was thoroughly against such practices that promoted caste and castiesm. He was angered by then President Rajendra Prasad's act of publicly bathing the feet of 200 Brahmins in Varanasi and openly criticised him, stating, "To bathe another's feet publicly is vulgar... To bathe another's feet on the ground that he is a Brahmin is to guarantee the continuance of the caste system, of poverty and sadness". In other words, Lohia held caste and sex or gender core responsible factor of injustice against downtrodden, backwards and women. Therefore, he wanted to start a war against these two segregations of caste and sex. He wanted to create an egalitarian society free from the inequality and discrimination on the basis of two segregations of caste and gender. At a time when Nehru was India's undisputed leader, Lohia contested elections against him in the 1952 general elections to symbolise that no one is infallible and questioned his commitment for social justice by observing, "Aside from general and airy fulminations against the caste system, it would be interesting to know what the Prime Minister has done to smash caste and to encourage fellowship among all". Lohia's remarks can be used as a benchmark to measure the commitment of ruling political regimes even today.3

LOHIA'S ATTEMPT TO WORK WITH DR. AMBEDKAR

Lohia had immense belief in the greatness of Dr. Ambedkar and wanted to meet him, the greatest warrior of social justice. Probably, his attempt to join hands with Ambedkar in the 1950s was a part of his strategy to develop a broad radical agenda for social justice. Unfortunately, Ambedkar died before they could meet with each other. It was too late when Lohia ji decided to meet Babasaheb. Later, in his election speeches, Lohia asked people to reject the "old caste policy" that created a "vertical solidarity of the castes", and move towards the "new caste policy" of the socialists that sought to bring a "horizontal solidarity" of the Dalits, Adivasis, backwards, religious minorities, women, the working class and the poor people. Years later, BSP founder Kanshiram appeared to have borrowed Lohia's idea to conceptualise the idea of the Bahujan identity of horizontal solidarity

FAVOUR TO EQUALITY FOR JUSTICE

Both Equality and justice are two great values without which the democratic countries can not run properly. Indeed, equality and justice both are supplementary to each other because without equality justice is unexpected and without justice equality is meaningless. Justice can not be achieved without the establishment of equality of man in the society. Lohia ji writes that all those who desire for world peace through the world government must aspire to achieve a world view of equality against class or caste or regional inequalities. Lohia conceives equality not only within a nation but also among nations and that such equality must not be limited to the field of law. Lojia advocated for equality in all fields of life such as economic, political, social and other areas also. Material equality among nations appears more difficult to achieve than material equality within the nations. No nation can for long remain equal within its frontiers-if it is unequal against other nations. As water finds its level, human society tends to approximate to its lowest levels, provided these levels are otherwise not raised.

Lohia's attitude towards equality was very broad and he views equality in four aspects, viz., inward and outward as well as spiritual and material, he pleads for an integrated approach. He advocated, "Equality must therefore, be grasped in all its four meanings. Material equality must mean the outward approximation among nations as well as the inward approximation within the nation. Spiritual equality must mean outward kinship as much as it means inward equanimity, kinship, material equality within the nation and among nations is worthy to become a supreme aim of life and its purpose.

LOHIA'S SOCIALIST MOVEMENT FAVOURED BACKWARDS-DALITS UNITY

He was Dr. Ambedkar who alone was fighting the battle of social justice for deprived and backward people. It was pleasant to see the fight for equality and social justice begin to strengthen when Dr. Lohia later on joined the fight for social justice. No doubt, he proved a helping hand to Dr. Ambedkar as far as battle of social justice was concerned. However, both could not meet and fight together. But Dr. Lohia echoed a vibrant voice for equality and social justice that Dr. Ambedkar was doing. He wanted to make a blend of backward-dalit unity in which he could not succeed. The Mandal-OBC politics is the direct impact of Lohia's socialist movement, which questioned upper-caste dominance and advocated intersectional caste-based affirmative action, including his demand for 60 per cent reservation for the backwards. However, Lohia's name as a political leader has remained alive because of the efforts of his political followers like Mulayam Singh Yadav, Lalu Yadav and Sharad Yadav but today his followers have forgotten Lohia's ideas, his dialogues with Ambedkar and his concern for Dalits. Backward leaders did not show serious interest towards thoughts and ideology of Dr. Ambedkar. They hardly paid respect to Babasaheb, whereas Babasaheb had much contributed to the empowerment of not only Dalits but also of backwards. Most of backward leaders did not show enthusiasm towards issues of Dalits. For instance, the SP opposed the bill for reservation in promotion for SC/ST in Parliament in 2012, whereas that bill was of much significance for the Dalits. It is a matter of concern for Bahujan politics. This attitude of backward leaders could not bring Dalits and backwards on a common front. However, Kanshi Ram made sincere efforts to unit the force of Dalits and backwards through his organisations such as BAMSEF and DS4.

On the occasion of Lohia's birth centenary in 2010, political commentator Yogendra Yadav had observed that Lohia's legacy has been ignored in the same way that Ambedkar's was before it was revived after his birth centenary.4 In the views of Yogendra Yadav, Dalit leaders who accepts Dr. Ambedkar as a great icon, have failed to acknowledge Lohia's rich legacy and his efforts to launch a common struggle for social justice. It is true to state that Dalit leaders except Kanshi Ram ignored Lohia and other icons from backward community. But we also can not deny that backward leaders too simultaneously ignored Babasaheb and his legacy. This attitude of Dalit and backward leaders damaged both. Thus, to achieve social equality and social justice as per the dreams of Dr. Ambedkar and Ram Manohar Lohia, there is a strong need of not only to link Ambedkarite and Lohian ideology but also to cristlise unity between backwards and Dalits. By doing so, Dalit-backward unity will be established that will lead Indian democracy towards becoming a social and economic democracy, which is the real form of democracy in the vision of Dr. Ambedkar. Bahujanvadi Politicians, Intellectuals and activists should come forward and join hands of each other to ensure equality and social justice in the country. At present, there is a momentous need to safeguard the Constitution of India that is a document of equality and social justice and it is possible only with the alliance of Dalits, backwards and other supporters of social justice.

LOHIA'S CONTRIBUTIONS TO SOCIALIST THOUGHT AND ACTION

Lohia's contributions to socialist thought and action are manifold. He wanted to free the individual from ignorance, backwardness and all kinds of superstitions and prejudices. He put maximum emphasis about restoring the dignity and individuality of human being. Lohia highlighted the ideological problems of the socialist movement in India. He wanted to assimilate the fundamental tenets of Marxism with Gandhian ideas. Though he was inspired by Marxism yet he did not blindly accept some of the postulates of Marxism. Lohia was of the opinion that Gandhian ideas and principles should be re-examined and reconsidered in the light of the changes in the socialist and communist movements all over the world. He made it a point to look into the economic problems country is facing. It should be "pointed out that Lohia's ideas and thinking on socialist thought and movement came to be influenced by Gandhian teachings and techniques. One scholar says: "Among those who tried to give a new orientation· of Marxist and Gandhian principles. Lohia who led to work out the doctrinal foundation of socialism occupies the pride of place." A democrat by conviction socialism appealed to Lohia as a way of life. He strongly advocated the plea that socialist movement in India should have a distinct Indian character. Lohia championed "the principle of equal irrelevance of capitalism and communism in respect of the creation of a new human civilization." This 'new civilization' is called by Lohia 'socialism'.

SUPPORT FOR POLITICAL AND ADMINISTRATIVE DECENTRALISATION

Being a socialist thinker, Lohia noted that the primary task of Indian socialism is to create prosperity. He pleads that the four-pillar state which provides the political structure of the future socialist state is supposed to activate every section of the society to a new life. Lohia is in favour of administrative decentralization so that each group of the society may share the power even at grassroots level. He suggests that economic decentralization, corresponding to political and administrative decentralisation, may be brought about through maximum utilization of small machines. Lohia hoped that "a state organised like this ... will surely be able to rouse popular enthusiasm and encourage initiative in the social world; it will dispel popular apathy and democratise and purify the administration." N.C. Mehrotra opines: "Through the means of democratic institutions and decentralization Lohia wanted to safeguard the society from the domination of bureaucracy." V.R. Mehta rightly points out: "The most important contribution of Lohia is his development of the concept of political decentralization." Lohia was a staunch critic of centrelisation as he felt that centralization leads to dictatorship and whimsical exercise of power. Lohia was of the firm belief that a truly non-violent society can be achieved only on the basis of decentralization.

To sum up, Dr. Ram Manohar Lohia has been a great socialist leader who echoed his voice for not only socialism but also for social justice and social change. Indian citizens should recall how Ram Manohar Lohia wove social justice with socialism. Lohia was greatly influenced by his father Hiralal and Gandhi. From his father, Lohia derived his interest in his early years in the nationalist politics led by Gandhi. The political interest of Ram Manohar Lohia took a radical character during His student life in India. Later Dr. Lohia wanted to meet Dr. Ambedkar and also wanted to work with him to echo the voice for social justice. But it could not happen. Lohia ji gave new meanings of socialism that was a blend of the thoughts of Karl Marx and Mahatma Gandhi. He wanted to free the individual from the shackles of ignorance, backwardness and all kinds of superstitions and prejudices. He put maximum emphasis about restoring the dignity and individuality of human being. Really, he was a great warrior of social justice.

<u>**REFERENCE**</u>

Wikipedia

*https://www.google.com/searchq=ram+manohar+lohia&rlz=1C1ONGR_enIN982IN982&sxsrf=ALiCzsYsgkF1JkW433xG3btyt6qk5epZEg:1665832685835&source=lnms&tbm=isch&sa=X&ved=2ahUKEwiV9vmrjuL6AhWzDgGHfgJBZ8Q_AUoAXoECAEQAw&biw=1920&bih=860&dpr=1#imgrc=QpROeE72tJH3iMhttps://madhyapradesh.pscnotes.com/paper-iv-ethics/ethical-values-of-ram-manohar-lohiya/

1. राम मनोहर लोहिया के 31 अनमोल विचार Ram Manohar Lohia Quotes in Hindi (achhikhabar.com)

2.   https://theprint.in/opinion/dalit-leaders-have-failed-to-acknowledge-ram-manohar-lohia-work-on-social-justice/133180//

3.   https://theprint.in/opinion/dalit-leaders-have-failed-to-acknowledge-ram-manohar-lohia-work-on-social-justice/133180//

4.   https://theprint.in/opinion/dalit-leaders-have-failed-to-acknowledge-ram-manohar-lohia-work-on-social-justice/133180//

CHAPTER TWELVE

MANYAWAR KANSHI RAM

Source*

ITRODUCTION

Kanshi Ram was born on 15 March 1934 and lived as a champion of social equality, social justice and political consciousness among Bahujans till 9 October 2006, when he passed away. He has been also known as **Bahujan Nayak** or **Manyavar** or **Saheb**. He was not only an Indian politician but also political mobiliser and social reformer who worked for the upliftment and political mobilisation of the Bahujans, the backward or lower caste people including untouchable groups at the bottom of the caste system in India.[1] Towards this end, Kanshi Ram founded two non-political organisations namely Dalit Shoshit Samaj Sangharsh Samiti (DS-4) and the All India Backward and Minority Communities Employees' Federation (BAMCEF) in 1971. He was a staunch supporter and follower of the ideology of Babasaheb Dr. B.R. Ambedkar who stressed upon grabbing political power that is the key to open all locks or solve the all problems social, educational, economic and political. Therefore, Kanshi Ram founded the Bahujan Samaj Party (BSP) on 14th April 1984. He conceded leadership of the BSP to Mayawati who has served four terms as Chief Minister of Uttar Pradesh and presently she is continuing the mission Ambedkar to achieve social equality and justice after Manyavar Kanshi Ram.

EARLY LIFE AND EDUCATION

Kanshi Ram was born to a Ramdasia Sikh family of Chamar caste on 15 March 1934 in Ropar district, Punjab, British India.[2] Shri Hari Singh was his father and Shrimati Bishan Kour was his mother. He had five siblings-Dalbara Singh, Gurcharan Kaur, Swaran Kaur, Kulwant Kaur, Harbans Singh. According to Some sources, his birthplace was the village of Pirthipur Bunga[3] and others that it was Khawaspur village.[4] After studies at various local schools, Kanshi Ram got higher education and graduated in 1956 with a B.Sc. degree from Government College Ropar.[5]

KANSHI RAM'S EXPERIENCES WITH CASTE SYSTEM IN PUNJAB

It is very interesting to see that Kanshi Ram had made a different observation about the Brahmins. As his biographer writes: In Punjab, Brahmins were not much prominent economically or culturally. It was the Jat Sikhs who constituted the dominant community. Sikhism never encouraged Brahminism. The social, economic and political status of Bramans was not as good as in other states of the country. Kanshi Ram once recalled in a lecture that as a small boy when he saw how some Brahman boys he knew lived, he thought that Brahmans were a very poor, backward community. Only much later did he come to realise that socially they were way above the dalits. The only memory of "exploitation of the downtrodden" he seemed to have recalled from his personal life was the story of his father having been asked to do begaar (unpaid labour) by a bureaucrat, an official at the "canal guest house" close to his village (Narayan 2014: 17)[6]. The nature of his childhood experience of caste perhaps had an influence on his later life. Kanshi Ram was out of the grip of inferior complex and he carried himself with a sense of dignity and confidence all his life. While he was working in Pune, rarely did anyone think of him as being a Dalit because "he was tall" and "fair skinned." Some rumors were aired about him being a non-Dalit fellow. Later on, the BSP even had to officially release a pamphlet denying rumours that he was not a Dalit himself because he did not look like one.

INCIDENCE THAT MADE KANSHIRAM COMMITED TO SOCIAL JUSTICE

Kanshi Ram joined the offices of the Explosive Research and Development Laboratory in Pune[7] under the government's scheme of affirmative action. It was at this time that he first experienced caste discrimination[8] and in 1964 he became an activist. Those who admire him point out that he was spurred to this after reading B. R. Ambedkar's book *Annihilation of Caste* and witnessing the discrimination against Dinabhana a Dalit employee who wished to observe a holiday celebrating Ambedkar's birth. The Dinabhan episode proved a turning point in the life of Manyawar Kanshi Ram. He took a solid step in favour of Dinabhana. Later on, he went through the literature on Babasaheb Dr. Ambedkar. Kanshi Ram strongly inspired by B. R. Ambedkar and his philosophy.[9]

Kanshi Ram initially supported the Republican Party of India (RPI) but became disillusioned with its co-operation with the Indian National Congress. Kanshi Ram found RPI incapable to fulfil the goal of social equality and justice and decided to form independent organistions to fight for social justice. In 1971, he founded the All India SC, ST, OBC and Minority Employees Association and in 1978 this became BAMCEF, an organisation that aimed to persuade educated members of the Scheduled Castes, Scheduled Tribes, Other Backwards Classes and Minorities to support Ambedkarite principles. BAMCEF was neither a political nor a religious body and it also had no aims to agitate for its purpose. Suryakant Waghmore says it appealed to "the class among the Dalits that was comparatively well-off, mostly based in urban areas and small towns working as government servants and partially alienated from their untouchable identities".[10]

Later, in 1981, Kanshi Ram formed another social organisation known as Dalit Shoshit Samaj Sangharsh Samiti (DSSSS, or DS4). He started his attempt consolidate the Dalit vote and in 1984 he founded the Bahujan Samaj Party (BSP). He fought his first election in 1984 from Janjgir-Champa seat in Chhattisgarh.[11] The BSP found success in Uttar Pradesh. However, BSP initially struggled to bridge the divide between Dalits and Other Backward Classes[12] but later under leadership of Mayawati bridged this gap.[13] Under leadership of Mauawati, BSP achieved huge victory in 2007 and it succeeded in winning majority on its own. It was due to unity of Dalits and backwards. But this unity could not continue for long. Death of Manyawar Kanshi Ram really proved a setback to the unity of Dalits and other backwards classes.

DALIT PANTHERS AND DALIT MOVEMENT

No doubt to say that Babasaheb was the biggest face of Dalit movement who single handedly led it to the peaks till he lived alive. The movements initiated and led by Dr. Ambedkar were of great worth. Dalit movement under Babasaheb not only exposed caste based hatred and torture but also attacked inequality and social injustice. Chavdar Pond and Kala Ram temple entry movements remarkable that paved the path of Dalit movement in the country. Dalit is not a caste category, a synonymous of ex-untouchables. It is a political construct. It represents an articulation of a specific view on the subject of caste that rejects its popular anthropological theorisations that approach it as a uniquely Indian cultural reality, a consensual framework of living a Hindu life. The idea of Dalit rejects the ideology of caste and karma and foregrounds the experience of violence that it implied for those classified as "untouchables."

The invocation of Dalit-ness is to foreground the political and oppressive nature of the relational framework of caste. It, thus, frames the caste question in the language of modern citizenship. The category, however, began to acquire prominence only in the post-1970s India when the Dalit Panthers movement emerged in Maharashtra (Murugkar 1991)[14].

As the name indicates, its leaders were influenced by the Black Panthers of the United States. Its popular support base was "the educated Dalit youth wishing to give a political expression to their anger against caste and class injustices" (Jaoul 2007: 199)[15]. The Panthers expressed their disappointment with the existing leaders of the SCs, those in the Republican Party of India (RPI) and those working with the national political parties, particularly the Indian National Congress, who were all able to get elected because of the quotas and the reservation system but did not have an independent voice. However, their influence did not last for very long.

KANSHI RAM AND DALIT MOVEMENT

Dalit movement started by Dr. Ambedkar addressed the question of Dalit empowerment and it paved the path for social justice to be achieved in the country. Dr. Ambedkar energetically echoed his voice for equality and social justice as a Dalit leader and made possible efforts to ensure it in independent India as a constitution architect. After Dr. Ambedkar, Kanshi Ram led the movement more relevantly as compared to other Dalit leaders and shaped the next wave of the Dalit movement in the post-Ambedkar period. Though his movement found its realisation in northern India, he too was "educated" about the dynamics of caste in Maharashtra. After completing his education in science from Punjab, he joined as a junior scientist in a public-sector unit, Explosives Research and Development Laboratory (ERDL), located in Pune. It was here that he closely encountered caste as it was being experienced in the modern organisations during those times.

Incidence related with Dinabhana proved a turning point in Kanshi Ram's life. As the story goes, Ambedkar's birthday used to be a holiday in his organisation. However, the management suddenly decided to withdraw the holiday. Some of the Dalit employees protested against the move but the administration did not concede. A Class IV employee, Dinabhana, who had led the protest was charged with insubordination and was fired. Even though Kanshi Ram was in a senior cadre, he openly came out in support of Dinabhana and helped him during his legal struggle. As his biographer writes, when his upper-caste colleagues asked him to stay away from trade union activities of the Class IV staff, as he had nothing in common with them, Kanshiram retorted that the similarity indeed existed as Dinabhana was a Bhangi and he himself was a Chamar; they both had the same problems that this struggle was not for the Class IV workers alone. (Narayan 2014: 20–21)[16] Thus, his most critical encounter with caste was not in the village where he was born or in the school where he went to study but in the office of a modern organisation, as a member of the officially designated SCs.[17]

BAMCEF AND FIGHT FOR SOCIAL JUSTICE

Maharashtra's Dinabhana's incidence proved a turning point in the life of Kanshi Ram. Kanshi Ram decided to fight against the injustices of caste and he also did not go back to his village. He became very active to the cause of social justice and began to mobilise Dalits, backwards and minorities to fulfil the goal of social equality and justice. He decided to build a platform for the protection of upwardly mobile Dalits like himself and set up the BAMCEF (Backward and Minority Communities Employees Federation) in 1978. This step also shaped his perspective on caste and politics. To pursue his objectives, he left his job and decided to focus completely on his political work. He stayed on in Maharashtra for some time, engaging and working with Dalit activists in the cities of Pune and Bombay. He was fascinated by Dr. Ambedkar's writings and his vision but he grew dissatisfied with the local activists and role of RPI. He found the RPI "divided into many factions," which made it incapable of any serious political action. The Panthers too "were wasting their time on endlessly debating the relevance of Marxism and Buddhism to the Dalit cause." The real need was "organizing a social movement" (Pai 2006: 2)[18].

Though Kanshi Ram's motive was to make a blend of Dalits, backwards and minorities for political action but initially he focused upon the Dalit masses of the country. He saw the Dalit employees as his primary constituency. He not only organised them through the BAMCEF but also criticised them for not being sufficiently sensitive towards the communities of their origin, thereby invoking a moral claim that he had over them. "They were educated and monetarily secure." Their training in bureaucratic set up enabled them to work "in a disciplined manner" (Kumar 2013: 73)[19].

DALIT SHOSHIT SAMAJ SANGHARSH SAMITI (DS-4)

However, the task of acquiring political power required popular mobilisations, from across the length and breadth of the country. It was with this objective in mind that he set up a new organisation with the name Dalit Shoshit Samaj Sangharsh Samiti (DS-4) in 1981, followed by the formation of BSP in 1984. Along with a group of his comrades, he initiated a rally on bicycles, which took him across the country, cycling around 3,000 kilometers over a period of 40 days. It was during this march that he coined the famous slogans that reflected his notion of bahujan, the majority, which was to be visualised in caste terms and included a broad section of Indians. As he put it through a slogan, except for the three upper-caste Hindu groups, the Thakurs, the Brahmins and the Baniyas, everyone else was included in the DS-4 (**Thakur, Brahmin, Baniya chhod; baki sab hai DS-4**). This "ruling minority" was only around 15% of the total Indian population. Even though India became a democracy in 1947, they, the minority, have been ruling over the majority (Kumar 2013: 81–86)[20]. They were able to do so because the majority was willing to be fooled and manipulated.

This is what needed to be questioned and stopped: **Vote hamara, raj tumhara; nahin chalegaa, nahin chalegaa!** (Our votes, and your rule; no longer, no longer!) Moving beyond Dalit-ness Kanshi Ram stayed firmly committed to Ambedkar's persona and his ideals of building a society grounded on the culture of equality and human dignity, free from the oppressions of caste hierarchy. He also stayed fi rmly committed to the idea of electoral democracy as the only mode for bringing about change, through acquisition of political power. However, he did not deify Ambedkar and occasionally expressed his disagreement with him on the strategic modes of moving on the path he had shown. For example, he disagreed with the idea of foregrounding the agenda of annihilation of caste, which, for Ambedkar, was to be the broader moral imperative of the Dalit movement. Kanshi Ram approached it as a resource, to be mobilised and consolidated to fight against its oppression.

FOUNDATION OF BSP AND HIS POLITICAL JOURNEY

In 1982, he wrote his famous book *The Chamcha Age*, in which he used the term *chamcha* (stooge) to describe Dalit leaders such as Jagjivan Ram and Ram Vilas Paswan.[21] He stressed upon independent politics of Bahujan Samaj without joining Congress and BJP. He argued that Dalits should work politically for their own ends rather than compromise by working with other parties.[22] After forming BSP Kanshi Ram said the party would fight first election to lose, next to get noticed and the third election to win.[23] In 1988 he contested Allahabad seat up against a future Prime Minister V. P. Singh and performed impressively but lost polling close to 70,000 votes.[24]

He contested from East Delhi Lok Sabha constituency against HKL Bhagat and Amethi Lok Sabha constituency against Rajiv Gandhi in 1989 and obtained third position on both the seats. Then he represented the 11th Lok Sabha (1996-1998) from Hoshiarpur. Kanshiram got also elected as member of Lok Sabha from Etawah in Uttar Pradesh. After Demolition of the Babri Masjid in 1992, Mulayam Singh Yadav and Kanshi Ram joined hands to keep communal forces out of power by creating unity among the backward and Dalit castes. The BSP-SP alliance gave the popular slogan "**Mile Mulayam-Kanshi Ram, Hawa Ho Gaye Jai Shri Ram**". BJP got drubbing in the election and a coalition government of SP and BSP was formed in UP under the leadership of Mulayam Singh Yadav, although due to some differences and Mayawati's ambition, this alliance broke up in June 1995. BSP made alliance with BJP and Mayawati became first time Dalit Chief Minister of Uttar Pradesh with support of BJP. In the late 1990s, Kanshi Ram described the BJP as the most corrupt (*mahabrasht*) party in India and the Indian National Congress INC, Samajwadi Party and

Janata Dal as equally corrupt.

IDEOLOGY AND OBJECTIVES OFBAHUJAN SAMAJ PARTY

The BSP claims its ideology and strategies of mobilization are based upon the writings and speeches of Dr. Ambedkar, but draws heavily from those of Kanshi Ram, and to a lesser extent Mayawati. (Sudha, 2000)[25] To teach the Ambedkarism to the Dalits, Kanshi Ram traveled a long journey on foot and bicycle. Its ideology and objectives have been changing from time to time as part of strategy. He started as a social reformer. By contrast, in the 1970s, his activities were focused on welfare and reform. (Mendelssohn, 1998)[26]

But by late 1970s, his strategy had changed and he no longer believed in the primacy of social reform and emphasized on sharing of political and administrative power to bring about desired social change. (Mendelssohn, 1998) He declared to his supporters: 'we have a one point programme - take power'. (Omvedt, 1996)[27] On the whole, Kanshi Ram did not have clear-cut ideological basis, but still he rose as a prominent leader and floated his party, the BSP. (Massey, 1995)[28] The main objective of this party was to fight for the Dalit cause and interest of the OBCs.

1. To execute the mission Ambedkar, securing self-respect and a life full of dignity for the Dalits, and annihilation of caste system, was the first and basic objective of the BSP. Its aim was to replace Brahmnical political rule by that of the Dait-Bahujans, as it would provide the latter better status and faster economic betterment (Massey, 1995)[29].For it, BSP drove strong anti-Manuvadi movement to mobilize Dalits, Backwards, and Muslims. To mobilize Dalits and bring them under his own flag, Kanshi Ram did not hesitate in using even the hard language against caste Hindus.

2. BSP is of opinion that the population of forward and self-declared upper castes is just 15 per cent of the total population of the country. Therefore, the remaining 85 per cent population is of Dalits, OBCs and minorities and these sections have been under deprivation, neglect and marginalization. On the other hand, 15 per cent forward castes have been using all facilities and privileges. The majority has always dominated the minority and still it is going on. Therefore, it gave slogans like *vote hamara raj tumhara nahi chalega, nahi chalega*" meaning that we (deprived) will not allow you (15 per cent forward) to rule us because majority of votes are in our hands. *Vote se lenge PM/ CM, arakshan se SP/DM. "jitani jiski sankhya bhari, utni uski hissedari*" meaning that representation and share should be given according to the population ratio in the fields of education, employment and political leadership. Actually, these slogans played tremendous role in mobilizing Dalits with BSP.

KANSHI RAM'S ATTITUDE TOWARDS DOMINANT POLITICAL PARTIES

Kanshi Ram was of the opinion that Congress, BJP and other parities including Communist Parties were uncommitted towards the welfare of dalits and backwards. He called Congress Sanpnath and BJP the Nagnath both harmful for dalits and backwards. He nouned CPI and CPM as Hair Ghas ke Hare Sanp (green snackes of green grass). Kanshi Ram rejected the mainstream parties as welwishers of dalits and backwards and appealed them to support and vote BSP. In the late 1990s, he described the BJP as the most corrupt (*mahabrasht*) party in India and the Indian National Congress (INC), Samajwadi Party and Janata Dal as equally corrupt.[30]

KANSHI RAM AND DALIT ASSERTION AND POLITICAL CONSCIOUNESS

By the late 1980s, Kanshi Ram emerged as the face of Dalit political assertion mainly in North India and BSP registered significant electoral successes in the state of Uttar Pradesh (UP) and elsewhere. As leader of BSP, He himself was elected as a member of the Indian Parliament. He played a critical role in articulating Dalit political agenda and in making Dalits a political force. He mobilized Bahujans and prepared them to have dreams of solving their issues by achieving political power. Kanshi Ram saw himself as taking forward B R Ambedkar's political work and he scored success in it. Dalits under his leadership emerged as a huge strength as far as political spectrum is concerned. BSP with its political force succeeded in winning some Lok Sabha and legislative assembly in states like UP, MP, Punjab, Haryana, Rajasthan etc. BSP succeeded in forming government for four times in UP. Even those who think that "a comparison between these seemingly incomparable personalities could be misleading," agree that he has been "the biggest and most creative leader in the post-Ambedkar Dalit movement" (Teltumbde 2006: 4531)[31].

Due to his pioneering struggles and educational achievements, Dr. Ambedkar has also come to be very widely recognised as an important thinker of modern India, far beyond the Dalit universe, who provided a powerful and critical perspective on Indian society. As compared to Dr. Ambedkar, Kanshi Ram's life course was quite different from that of Dr. Ambedkar's. They were not only born in different regions of India, but also in different time periods.

He neither went abroad to study nor wrote books like Ambedkar did. However, both had many similarities. Dr. Ambedkar planted a seed of social equality, justice and political consciousness but Kanshi Ram nurtured that plant into a huge tree. Kanshi Ram committed to the principles and ideology of Dr. Ambedkar and travelled on the path that had already been defined by Ambedkar. He emphasized upon grabbing political power as he quite like Dr. Ambedkar, saw electoral politics as an instrument of social change. To serve this purpose (grabbing political power) he founded Dalit organisations and a political party. While Ambedkar's party could not win electoral battles or form a government headed by a Dalit, Kanshi Ram's party succeeded in achieving political successes and BSP made governments for terms, one on its own strength in 2007, when it scored majority. In this way, the rise of the BSP in UP, politically the most important state of India, marked a phenomenal shift in the politics of North India. Its rise changed the electoral sequences in several states of northern India and beyond. Rise of BSP proved an immense dent to the political position of the Congress as the members of SC community were among the hardcore voters of the Congress party before Kanshi Ram's entry in the political arena.

KANSHI RAM IN THE MAINSTREAM MEDIA

No doubt, Dr. Ambedkar was not only an undisputed stalwart leader of Dalits but also a unique national icon of the country. He has not only recognition as a world famous leader, scholar, thinker and economist but also a true champion of social justice. Despite of Mahatma Gandhi's efforts to dilute his popularity as a Dalit champion, he succeeded to attract the attention of national and international media. He himself too began many newspapers and news magazines. However, unlike Dr. Ambedkar, the persona of Kanshi Ram "did not receive the kind of attention and recognition he deserved" (Kumar 2014: 73)[32]. Even when he is remembered and written about, it is mostly in relation to the Dalit politics of UP, where the political party he founded managed to form a government with his confidante, Mayawati, as the chief minister (Bose 2008)[33]. He is rarely talked about as someone who contributed to the making of the Indian democracy, or even in shaping Dalit identities. Mainstream political analysts began to forget him soon after he exited the scene. When he died in 2006, "the electronic and print media reported it but did not spend much time or space on it" (Pai 2006: 1)[34].

KANSHI RAM'S CRUCIAL ROLE IN SHAPING INDIAN ELECTORAL POLITICS

However, despite such cold-shouldering by the mainstream media, Kanshi Ram remains an important symbol of Dalit assertion and political activism and an important member of India's political elite who have not only changed but also shaped the nature of democratic and electoral politics of independent India. Still, his passion to make Bahujans the ruling class of the country continues to inspire the newer generation of leaders coming from different Dalit communities in different state and regions of India. He is also remembered for the language and the idioms of politics that he added into national political and electoral gamut and Dalit activism. The coming generations hardly will forget his contribution and will remember him for enhancing representations of dalits and backwards in the electoral politics. However, Dalits were becoming MLAs and MPs but their representation in the councils of ministers was insufficient. Backward castes were lagging behind as far as the electoral and political representation was concerned. Rise of Kanshi Ram gave strength to not only Dalit representation but also to backwards. He contributed much to political empowerment of backwards.

KANSHIRAM STRONGLY FAVOURED OBC RESERVATION

The question of caste began to be discussed in relation to India's political spectrum since independence. Renowned political scholar Rajni Kothari evaluated the influence of caste on Indian politics in his famous book *Caste in Indian Politics*. however, so called upper castes remained dominant for a long time as far as electoral politics was concerned. Rise of backward castes as a serious issue on the electoral scene could be seen during the 1970s when Janata Party government led by Morarji Desai set up second Backward Commission in 1978 to study the causes of backwardness of the backward communities or OBCs. However, backwards began to be visible in the regional and national politics during the 1990s.

Kanshi Ram had mobilized and awakened backwards through his non-political organisation BAMCEF, which was a federation of Backward and Minorities Communities Employees. As a leader of BAMCEF and BSP, he was mounting pressure on the central government to implement the report of Mandal Commission since 1980 when the report was submitted. Even before the implementation of Mandal Commission Report, when the debate on the Mandal

Commission Report was gaining momentum in the parliament and outside, Kanshi Ram emphasised the claims of the OBCs. This is evident from one of his speeches during the election campaign for the Vidhan Sabha of Haryana in 1987, when he emphasisedly demanded for implementation of the report.

He had admitted that in some respects the conditions of the Scheduled Castes were better than those of the OBCs. He also observed that the Scheduled Castes and the Scheduled Tribes had a larger presence in the bureaucracy because of reservations than the OBCs. Kanshi Ram concluded that the number of OBCs is 50 to 52% but we don't see any of them as District Magistrate. He seriously insisted upon reservation to OBCs and opined that the issue which is special for us, is that reservation is not a question of our daily bread; reservation is not a question of our jobs, reservation is a matter of participation in the government and administration. He put a question mark on Indian democracy. He argued that there is democracy in this country but 52 percent of the people cannot participate, then what is the system in which they can participate?

Kanshi Ram devotedly favoured reservations for this OBCs, which he regarded as underprivileged. One of the BSP's slogans has been '**Mandal ayog lagu karo, varna kursi khali karo**' (Implement the Mandal Commission [Report] or vacate the seat [of power]). This was part of his strategy of constituting the Bahujan Samaj into a political force and ruling class of the country. Therefore, in post Mandal era the BSP undoubtedly benefited from the atmosphere created by the 'Mandal affair'. Many OBC castes came closer to BSP and casted vote to it at the time of elections. BSP promoted many OBC leaders and fielded them as BSP candidates in elections. In 1999 Lok Sabha elections Kanshi Ram made a systematic policy to nominate candidates in proportion to caste and community composition of society. Out of 85 candidates, he fielded 17 Muslims (20%), 20 Scheduled Castes (23.5%) 38 OBCs (45%) and 10 upper castes (12%) – 5 Brahmins and 5 Rajputs.[35]

KANSHI RAM'S LECTURE IN FIRST WORLD DALIT CONVENTION

Speaking at the first World Dalit Convention at Kuala Lumpur in Malaysia in 1998, he said: When I read the Annihilation of Caste in 1962–63, I too felt that it was possible to annihilate caste. However, when I closely looked at the caste system and how deeply it is ingrained in the lives of common people, I changed my opinion. It is hard to forget caste. Even when poor Indians migrate from their villages to urban slums, the one thing that they all carry with them is caste. If it matters so much to common people, how could we destroy it? While I continue to work for a society free of caste, I have no illusions that it cannot be destroyed simply because we wish to do so. If that is the case, how do we move forward? We must recognize that caste has been put in place for a purpose, by those who gain from it. They are also the rulers of India. How will they let us destroy it?

Caste is a double-edged sword. We need to learn to handle it. The savarnas have so far used it against us, even though they are only 15 percent of the population and we are 85 percent ... If we have such large numbers, why can't we use it for ourselves. However, the challenge is to learn to use caste, politically. What appears to us as a source of all our problem could also be a source of opportunity for us. If we use it intelligently, we can be in power ... And power is the key to all solutions. We need to be the rulers of this country. (Nath and Kureel 1999: 1–8)[36] Political power was the key. He underlined the need for a new imagination and a political organisation that would bring together 1,000 caste communities and organise them as a united political force, the Bahujans. Dalits were to provide leadership to this process. He was critical of the Dalits of Maharashtra who had been opportunistically aligning with parties of the upper caste and gaining some personal benefits. He stated that we have people from Maharashtra in this Convention. I have learnt a lot from them. I learnt half of my political lessons on how to run an Ambedkarite movement from Babasaheb Ambedkar. I have also learnt a lot from the Mahars of Maharashtra. While Ambedkar taught me how to run a movement; from the Mahars of Maharashtra I have learnt how not to run a movement. (Nath and Kureel 1999: 10–11)[37] Towards the end of the lecture, he went on to pronounce his views on Dalit-ness (dalitpan) and how that had become a problem. While caste was a useful tool and a resource for moving towards acquiring power, he was very critical of dalitpan which he saw as a reflection of a defeated mindset. He appealed to his audience to come out of it, if they wished to become rulers of India. "Dalitpan has become the biggest weakness of Dalits. It makes them dependent like beggars. Beggars can never become rulers" (Nath and Kureel 1999: 16)[38].

KANSHI RAM'S VIEWS ON POONA PACT

The arguments presented in the Kuala Lumpur lecture were an extension of the ideas that he had developed very early on during his political life, some of which were put together in the only book he wrote, *The Chamcha Age.* (SPECIAL ARTICLE-EPW, January 16, 2021 vol lVI no 3)[39] The book was published in 1982, on the 50th anniversary of the Poona Pact. The book was dedicated to the "pioneers of anti-caste movement, thinkers and reformers, such as Jyotirao Phule, B R Ambedkar, Periyar E V Ramasamy" and "many others," who had worked hard to prepare the ground for Dalit struggles to achieve social equality and justice in the society.

The Poona Pact signed in 1932 between Gandhi and Ambedkar was the result of Mahatma Gandhi's fast unto death against the British decision to grant separate electorates to the "untouchable" communities of India on the demand of Dr. Ambedkar. As per the conditions of the "Pact," Dr. Ambedkar was to withdraw his demand for separate electorates and in return the "untouchable" were to be given a quota of seats, from those allocated to the Hindus. While other minorities could keep their separate, community specific, electorates, the Dalits were to be elected by the common electorates. As Kanshi Ram argues, Dr. Ambedkar had worked hard for separate electorates, which could give an autonomous or sovereign voice to the Dalits. But he had to surrender to the pressure of Gandhi's fast and the fear of the possible consequences if Gandhi would have died due to the fast.

Kanshi Ram, in a sense, extended and articulated the anxieties that Ambedkar himself had about the pact. The separate electorates would have undermined the power of the upper caste, who constituted only a small proportion of India's total population. Had the separate electorates been allowed to prevail, they would have considerably shrunk the influence of upper castes, perhaps equal to the size of their population and thereby reducing them to a small minority. Ambedkar's success in winning the separate electorates for the Dalits was an indication of the things to come for the upper castes. They were quick to grasp their imminent marginalisation in a democratic India. This was the reason for Gandhi's hunger fast. While Gandhi managed to blackmail Ambedkar into signing the Poona Pact, it implied a defeat for the Dalits. Their hope and vision of a "Bright Age" was thus lost. The Chamcha Age, he argued, was a consequence of the Poona Pact. It made Dalit leaders stooges of the upper castes. Even when a good number of seats were reserved for them, Dalit electorates had very little say in getting their representative elected. Given their demographic distribution across the country, no SC candidate could win without the support of upper caste voters. This is how the "upper-caste" national parties gained control over the Dalit representatives. The elected members of the national parties did not represent their fellow Dalits. For the sake of getting elected and holding on to positions of power, they became chamchas of their masters and worked for them, not for the welfare of their communities. (Surinder,January 2021)[40]

SUPPORTER OF POLITICAL REPRESENTATION TO EACH COMMUNITY

Kanshi Ram's political ideology can be understood by viewing his slogans that he gave from time to time. He gave a slogan, **"jiski jitnee sankhya bhari, us ki utnee hissedari "**, which meant that he was strong supporter of political representation to each community in proportion to their numbers. He wanted representation to all communities in education, administration and political power. Such a framing enabled him to visualise an autonomous politics of the Dalits and their coming to power through an alliance with the OBCs and religious minorities, mainly Muslims. To realise his plan, he needed the Dalit political elite to come out of the patronage of upper-caste elite and the mainstream political parties. Such an imagination would have required a shift in focus that was the postponement of the agenda of caste annihilation and working towards consolidation of caste communities. It was only through numbers, and the consciousness of communities seeking their legitimate share in the power structure, that the Dalits could move forward, taking them closer to the representational politics of the rural "dominant caste." He emphasised on the assertion of eighty five percent people being dominated by fifteen percent people. He awared the OBCs, SCs, STs and Minorities including women and called them to grab political power tha is the Guru Killi (Master Key) in opinion. He gave a call to the 85 percent people come out from the clutches of 15 percent. He used to show a pen in his meetings to explain the hegemony of 15 percent over 85 percent people.

His language of politics also gave a new lease of life to Dalit activism, a new confidence and a new hope, of being rulers and sharers of power. His success was quite evident. The decade of the 1990s saw a sudden decline of the Indian National Congress in UP and the rise of the BSP. Renewal of Kanshi Ram's vision of democratisation through community based power sharing soon confronted a major block and a new challenge in Indian politics. It was not so easy to make a coalition of Dalits, backwards and minorities. They were not ready to help each other and the prime factor was differntiality of caste. caste system was a huge obstacle to the path of unification of these communities. Even the Dalits belonging to different sub castes do not see themselves as a singular ethnic formation. The growing self-awareness of deprivation and marginalisation too were not sufficient factors that could necessarily bring them together as a political community. Undoubtedly, it was Identity politics based purely on the principle of hissedari or representational power-sharing, worked towards consolidation of Dalits and backwards. However, this consolidation could not enhance the unity of Dalits and backwards in an expected manner.

Though it might appear contradictory, the rise or success of the BSP and its constant reminder of caste identity would have likely produced an aspirational elite, "Dalit movement entrepreneurs," as Amit Ahuja (2019) describes them, within the individual jatis, aware of their numbers and accounting for their possible hissa (share). The post-Mandal moment of politics that expanded space for caste-based political mobilisations would have only enabled such a process of sharpening of jati-specific community identities. The idea of bahujan alliance in the absence of a new political language that could go beyond the additive process of jatis/castes coming together could at best be short-lived. The rhetoric of "power-sharing" could also encourage a jati-level fragmentation within the officialised clusters of SCs and OBCs. The process of caste-based mobilisation and jati-based fragmentation has also had implications for the relationship of caste with electoral politics at a broader level. It made everyone available for political maneuvering, for viable electoral alliances. Its translation is quite evident in post-2014 electoral politics, when leaders of the Bharatiya Janata Party (BJP) with superior resources at their command were able to successfully carry out such a maneuvering. At the local level, every jati has its own leaders and they negotiate for their share in the power that can be acquired through electoral politics. Growing mobilisations for sub-classification of SCs and OBCs across regions of India further sharpened the internal divisions within the officially classified categories. (SPECIAL ARTICLE –EPW, January 16, 2021 vol lVI no 3) [41]

A mere symbolic representation may not necessarily empower the backward communities at the local level and could bring them back to interest-based political alliance building. In other words, the BJP's ability to secure Dalit votes does not necessarily imply the triumph of Hindutva over caste. If the realities of caste persist-exclusionary, discriminatory and humiliating-it would be very hard for any political formation to take their support for granted. However, to move forward, the new generation of Dalit leadership will need to invent a different language of politics, beyond the tokenism of hissedari, and towards an imagination of substantive citizenship or "absolute equality," in the words of Kanshi Ram. (Surinder,January 2021) [42]

SUPPORTER OF INDEPENDENT DALIT LEADERSHIP

Providing a broader context, he took the help of historical reference. Kanshi Ram remarkably argued that Dalits had no possibility of gaining a voice of their own during the precolonial period. The British rule gave them access to education and a space for gaining a new consciousness and confidence. Reform movements initiated by Phule was the beginning of this process. Following Phule, Ambedkar worked hard to win freedom for his people. The separate electorates would have enabled the Dalits to produce their own leaders, elected by them and accountable to them. They would have taken the Dalits out of the "Dark Age" and into a "Bright Age." In the absence of genuine political leadership, even Dalit bureaucrats suffered. Kanshi Ram was an immense supporter of independent leadership of Dalits that would be their real caretaker. Therefore, he founded a political party, BSP to provide independent leadership free from clutches of Congress, BJP, Communist Parties etc.

The SC employees were rarely given substantive positions of authority in the system. They too were, therefore, turned into chamchas. Besides the persistent marginalisation of large sections of the Dalit masses in the social and political life of the country, the opportunist motilies of a section of Dalits in the chamcha age thus produces, what he calls, an "alienation of the elite." Kanshi Ram's objective was not simply to criticise everything and everyone, but also to argue for or propose a new kind of sovereign politics of the Dalit, which, according to him, was the real vision of Ambedkar. The BAMCEF was to protect the interests of employees belonging to the marginalised groups and to instill a sense of empathy among its members for the larger masses of the socially excluded communities that they came from.

Kanshi Ram openly opined that the politics of the Congress party for Dalits was primarily framed in the narrative of deprivation. He shifted his narrative to the question of dignity, which could be achieved only if Dalits extended their aspiration from economic mobility to political power. This is well illustrated in Kanchan Chandra's paper on the BSP in Hoshiarpur (Punjab). Writing about those who were attracted to Kanshi Ram's politics, she observes: they were predominantly Scheduled Castes ... all born after independence; educated ... in the lower echelons of government service ... better off than their parents and the rest of the Scheduled Caste population. They were ... upwardly mobile ... having hit the glass ceiling that separated them from the rest of society, turned back to themselves and their own community for respect. (Chandra 2000: 36)[43]

UNDERSTANDING KANSHIRAM'S VISION THROUGH HIS SLOGANS

If we want to understand Kanshi Ram's social, economic and political ideology and his vision, then we will have to have look on his prime slogans he used in his meetings and rallies to mobilise the lagging behind people. However, the main moto of his slogans and political quotes was to awaken the dalits and backwards from their long slumber of unconsciousness. Undoubtedly, his slogans worked a lot to bring political awakening among them. His fundamental slogans were as under-

A) Thakur, Brahmin, Baniya Chhod; Baki Sab Hai DS-4,

B) Mandal Ayog Lagu Karo, Varna Kursi Khali Karo

C) Jiski Jitnee Sankhya Bhari, Uski Utnee Hissedari,

D) Vote Humara Raj Tumhara Nahi Chalega, Nahi Chalega,

E) Vote Se Lenge PM/CM, Arakshan Se SP/DM

F) Ab Bahujan ki Bari hai, Ikkeeshvi Sadi Hamari hai

Above slogans show that he wanted to unite dalits, backwards and minorities against the political hegemony of forward castes. By grabbing political power that he called the master key, he wanted achieve the goal of social justice. He focused on power sharing and encouraged people of backward and Dalit communities to achieve power as they are majority as far as number of votes are concerned. He suggested a formula of representation of all communities as according to their number. His slogan 'Madal Commission Report Lagu karo, varna kursi khali karo' shows that he was an immense supporter of the empowerment of OBCs.

His supporters and party workers gave some other slogans for Kanshi Ram as under:

A) Kanshi Ram Teri Nek Kamai, Tune Soti Kom Jagai

B) Babasahab Tera Mission Adhura, Kanshi Ram Karenge Poora

C) BSP aur Kanshi Ram, Jindabad

D) BSP ki kya Pehchan, Neela Jhanda Hathi Nishan

A remarkable slogan was echoed during Uttar Pradesh assembly election which BSP fought in alliance with Samajwadi Party of Mulayam Singh Yadav in 1993. It was **'Mile Mulayam Kanshiram, Hawa ho gaye Jai Shri Ram'**. This slogan highly influenced the voters and the BSP-SP alliance succeeded in forming government.

IMPACT OF KANSHI RAM ON DALITS, BACKWARDS AND INDIAN POLITICS

The BSP under the leadership of Kanshi Ram had placed noticeable impact on the Indian politics. Kanshi Ram as a social activist and leader of BSP brought consciousness among the Dalits and other backward classes of the society. His labour, struggle and charisma laid the foundation for crucial changes in Indian politics too. The considerable and significant impact of the BSP can be viewed as under:

1. Mobilization and polarization of the deprived people, on a large scale, have been the big contribution of Kanshi Ram and BSP. The political consciousness among Dalits and OBCs has increased. Now, it is not easy to exploit them. They have become a political force in Indian politics. Before this, they were just a vote-bank for the Congress Party, which they supported and voted blindly. Kanshi Ram's arrival worked as a big boost in making the oppressed and marginalized, politically conscious and empowered. Kanshi Ram awakened the deprived from their long slumber. Under Kanshi Ram's leadership, the BSP won 14 parliamentary seats in the 1999 Lok Sabha elections.

2. Another significant impact of Kanshi Ram and his party, BSP can be seen in that the marginalized and neglected people have shifted to BSP and other parties from the Congress Party. This has proved threatening to the Congress because its dominance in political and electoral fields has eroded. In other words, the emergence of BSP has been

a big blow to the Congress Party. The BSP has spoiled the political equations of the Congress Party. Its impact can be seen in north Indian states particularly in Uttar Pradesh where the Congress Party is fighting to maintain its existence.

3. Kanshi Ram believed in the ideology and principles of Babasaheb Dr. Ambedkar and he propagated his ideology and principles at the national level. This made Ambedkarite movement more popular all over the country. Kanshi Ram was demanding Bharar Ratna award to Babasaheb for a long time. Pressure of Knashi Ram worked positively and V.P. Singh government had to award the Bharat Ratna, the highest national award to Babasaheb in 1990. Statues of Babsaheb were installed not only all over the country but also in the premises of Indian Parliament.

4. The emergence of BSP under the leadership of Kanshi Ram caused Dalits' social and political assertion. Possibly, the pressure of increasing popularity of BSP among the deprived castes forced other political parties to provide some share for these people in the key posts in their organisations and governing bodies in order to win their support. That is why, Dr. K.R. Narayanan, a Dalit, was elected as the President of India. It brought self-respect and proud for the Dalits. G. M. Balyogi was elected as the first Dalit Speaker of the Lok Sabha. Justice Balakrishanan had been appointed first Chief Justice of India (CJI) from the Dalit community. It was a huge impact of emergence of the Dalit consciousness aroused by BSP under Manyawar Kanshiram.

5. Dalits and backwards were given representation in political parties and cabinets. Lakshman Bangaru and Suraj Bhan, the Dalit faces in the BJP were given important berths in the party. Congress also appointed Sushil Kumar Shinde as the Chief minister in Maharashtra. It was the first time, when Congress had to appoint a Dalit as C. M. of any state. The Communist Parties are also giving importance to the dalit leaders by offering them representation in their parties. The BJP recognizing the need to broaden its base, organized "samoohik bhojans" (inter-caste dining) and a Dalit laid the foundation stone of the Ram Mandir in Ayodhya. The process of Ambedkarisation took place in India. Dalit assertion started with separate identity, self-respect, a celebration of Ambedkar birth anniversary, wide spread dissemination of the ideas and writings of Dr. Ambedkar. Dalit began to greet each other using 'Jai Bhim' in place of 'Ram'. (Pai, 2000) [44]

6. Kanshiram was in favour of implementation of Mandal Commission Report. Hence he demanded for implementation of this report. He organized a rally in Delhi and gave slogan 'Mandal Commission Report lagu karo, varna kursi khali karo'. Under the mounting pressure of Saheb Kanshiram and BSP, V.P. Singh government decided to implement the report in 1990. It was a huge impact of the rise of Kanshiram and BSP. This was the turning point of Indian politics and Mandal issue gave a new life to backward politics. However, BJP could not digest the decision of V.P. Singh government and began Kamandal politics raising Ram Mandir issue. But it is unfortunate that many OBCs are either unaware about this fact or they neglect the role of Kanshiram in implementation of Mandal Commission Report, which opened the door for progress to OBCs through reservation in education and government jobs.

7. Kanshi Ram and BSP have stressed upon the idea of "proportional representation for all castes" as according to their populous number. On the basis of this idea, it has boosted the political awareness among the different castes mainly OBCs, which were on the bottom line as far as political participation and representation is concerned. This idea has opened the door for them too to share political power.

8. The erosion of the votes by the Congress party, due to emergence of BSP, provided fillip to the BJP. The data are witness to the fact that the BJP was very weak before the emergence of the BSP. Increase in the BSP's strength brought decrease in the strength of Congress. As the votes of Congress shifted to the BSP, therefore the anti BJP votes divided and it proved beneficial for the BJP.

9. The last two decades are witness to coalition politics and coalition governments in India. The rise of the BSP has strengthened the concept of coalition politics. BSP's entry into politics highly damaged the Congress's support base. The traditional social groups supporting the Congress shifted to the BSP. Consequently, Congress became politically weak and BJP got opportunity to emerge as a significant political force. Therefore, the division of votes among several political parties made it difficult to get absolute majority by any single party and paved the way for the emergence of coalition politics.

CHAMPION OF THE BAHUJANS AND MENTOR OF BACKWARD LEADERS OF UTTAR PRADESH

Saheb Kanshi Ram was known as the champion of the poor, deprived, backwards and minorities. He emphasized on political empowerment of lagging behind people who called them Bahujan and favoured power sharing as per the populous numbers. He not only made a blend of Dalits, Backwards and Minorities but also trained them to fight for social justice and grab political power through the process of election. No doubt to say that Manyawar Kanshi Ram not only collected and united the backwards but also mentored them to grab political power. He cultivated them with Ambedkarite ideology. Hence, he could be called a mentor to the prominent leaders of backward community such as Swami Prasad Maurya, Omprakash Rajbhar, Dr. Sanjay Nishad, Sonelal Patel etc. The major contest within the Uttar Pradesh meeting elections is believed to be between the Bharatiya Janata Party and the Samajwadi Party. But even these large events must depend upon smaller events, whose function is taken into account to be crucial within the electoral battle. These embrace Omprakash Rajbhar, Sanjay Nishad, Sonelal Patel and Keshav Dev Maurya of Mahan Dal. The political mentor of all these leaders has been Kanshi Ram, who's right now seen solely because the icon of the Bahujan Samaj Party. But right now all these political disciples of Kanshi Ram are enjoying an essential function within the politics of UP based mostly on caste equation. Omprakash Rajbhar, who did politics in Purvanchal by forming Suheldev Bharatiya Samaj Party, mentioned in a dialog with our affiliate newspaper Economic Times, 'Manyavar Kanshi Ram at all times used to say that to deliver consciousness in your caste, you need to type a caste based mostly social gathering. This is the proper technique to declare your share. Rajbhar attended a gathering of Kanshi Ram throughout his faculty days and was tremendously impressed by his concepts. After this he turned part of the Dalit Shoshit Samaj Sangharsh Samiti group fashioned by Kanshi Ram in 1981.

Rajbhar mentioned that he used to prepare conferences and clarify Kanshi Ram's ideas and issues to the folks. constituted. He mentioned, "Kanshi Ram used to say {that a} day will come when large political events will run after small caste based mostly events. In right now's time, we're seeing this occurring ourselves.' At the identical time, the preliminary political affiliation of Nishad Party President and BJP ally Sanjay Nishad has additionally been with Kanshi Ram. Nishad was a part of the BAMCEF (Backward and Minority Community Employment) group which was run by Kanshi Ram. Sanjay Nishad informed ET that his job was to prepare conferences and create new cadres for BAMCEF in Gorakhpur and surrounding areas. Dr Sanjay Nishad informed that after the formation of BSP, Kanshi Ram had requested him to stay energetic in BAMCEF. When Kanshi Ram was not energetic in politics, Sanjay fashioned his personal group twice in Nishad. But finally he fashioned the Nishad Party. His supporters blocked a railway line close to Sahjanwan station in Gorakhpur district in June 2015. Sanjay Nishad (File picture) A person in police firing throughout an agitation demanding Scheduled Caste standing for the Nishad neighborhood died. Dr. Sanjay Nishad went to jail and continued to demand SC standing for Nishad. He mentioned that BJP has promised to present reservation to Nishads after the elections, so we're supporting them. At the identical time, Apna Dal founder Sonelal Patel has additionally been in contact with Kanshi Ram since his college days and has been influenced by his ideology. Sonelal Patel was amongst those that performed an essential function within the formation of the Bahujan Samaj Party. But when Kanshi Ram gave extra significance to Mayawati, Patel fashioned a brand new social gathering named Apna Dal. Idols of Mayawati, Ambedkar, Kanshi Ram He by no means obtained success within the election however his daughter Anupriya Patel obtained success, who took the Apna Dal (Sonelal) faction ahead and went on to grow to be a Union Minister. Today Apna Dal is split into two components. The second faction is within the palms of Sonelal Patel's spouse Krishna Patel and daughter Pallavi Patel, who've fashioned an alliance with the Samajwadi Party by forming Apna Dal (Communist). Keshav Dev Maurya, president of the Mahan Dal, is the same story. In a dialog with Economic Times, Keshav Dev mentioned, 'I used to be a small employee of BSP and later additionally went to Samajwadi Party. I by no means obtained an opportunity to work intently with Kanshi Ram. But I used to be impressed by those that gave political energy and voice to Dalit and backward castes.[44A] Today, they are playing relevant role in Uttar Pradesh politics. leading politics of social justice involving backwards and giving them representation.

PROPOSED CONVERSION TO BUDDHISM

In 2002, Kanshi Ram announced his intention to convert to Buddhism on 14 October 2006, the 50th anniversary of Dr. Ambedkar's conversion. He intended for 50,000,000 of his supporters to convert at the same time. Part of the significance of this plan was that Kanshi Ram's followers include not only untouchables, but persons from a variety of castes, who could significantly broaden Buddhism's support. However, he died on 9 October 2006. [45]

Mayawati his successor said "Saheb Kanshi Ram and I had decided that we will convert and adopt Buddhism when we will get "absolute majority" at the Centre. We wanted to do this because we can make a difference to the religion by taking along with us millions of people. If we convert without power, then only we two will be converting. But when you have power you can really create a stir".[46]

DEATH OF MANAYWAR KANSHI RAM, A SET BACK TO MISSION AMEDKAR

Kanshi Ram was a diabetic. He suffered a heart attack in 1994, an arterial clot in his brain in 1995, and a paralytic stroke in 2003. He died in New Delhi on 9 October 2006 of a severe heart attack at the age of 72. He had been virtually bed-ridden for more than two years. According to his wishes, his funeral rites were performed according to Buddhist tradition, with Mayawati lighting the pyre. His ashes have been placed in an urn and kept at Prerna Sthal, where many people paid their respects.[47] In his condolence message, Indian Prime Minister Manmohan Singh described Kanshi Ram as "one of the greatest social reformers of our time ... his political ideas and movements had a significant impact on our political evolution ... He had a larger understanding of social change and was able to unite various underprivileged sections of our society and provide a political platform where their voices would be heard." [48] His death was a huge damage to Bahujan politics. Indeed, death of Manyawar Kanshi Ram was a severe set back to Mission Ambedkar. After him, his many supporters left BSP and they either founded their own parties or joined other political parties.

MAYAWATI AS SUCCESSOR OF KANSHI RAM

Kanshi Ram not only mentored Mayawati as a strong Dalit leader and presented her in Indian politics but also he declared Mayawati as his successor and supreme leader of BSP. He groomed Mayawati as not only as a strong Dalit leader but also as his inheritor and in 2001, he publicly announced Mayawati as his successor. She was on born 15 January 1956 is an Indian politician, social reformer and a pioneering leader of Bahujan and Ambedkarite Movement. She is the national president of the Bahujan Samaj Party (BSP), which focuses on a platform of social change for *Bahujans*, more commonly known as Other Backward Castes, Scheduled Castes and Scheduled Tribes as well as converted minorities from these castes. She has served four separate terms as Chief Minister of Uttar Pradesh briefly in 1995 and again in 1997, then from 2002 to 2003 and from 2007 to 2012. After Coming to power, she launched many programs and schemes for the betterment of people manly the marginalized. Keeping the social justice and social change, Mayawati has seen through to completion of several memorials dedicated to icons of Bahujan Samaj build first time in India, including the Manyawar Shri Kanshiram Ji Green Eco Garden (inaugurated March 2011), the Rashtriya Dalit Prerna Sthal and Green Garden (inaugurated October 2011), and the Dr Bhimrao Ambedkar Samajik Parivartan Prateek Sthal (opened November 2012).[49] She renamed Amethi district as Chattrapati Sahuji Maharaj Nagar,[50] Kanpur Dehat as Rambai Nagar, Sambhal as Bheem Nagar, Shamli as Prabuddha Nagar, Hapur as Psanchseel Nagar, Kasganj as Kanshiram Nagar, Hathras as Mahamaya Nagar and Amroha as JP Nagar.[51]

Mayawati during her tenure directed all the Commissioners and the District Magistrates to distribute 3 acre land pieces or pattas to weaker sections of society by launching special drive for illegal possesses of pattas be dispossessed of them and the eligible poor be identified by regular monitoring of pattas and strict action against the mafias and musclemen through spot verification of different development and public welfare programmes.[52] In 2010, 5596 people belonging to the SC and ST communities were allotted 1054.879 hectares of agriculture land.

It is true to say that BSP, under Kanshi Ram, began its struggle with the support of Dalits and OBCs. Its dedication to the interest of these people portrayed it as a party of Dalits only. Its leaders Kanshi Ram and Mayawati did their best to get the master key of political power, which was the solution of all social, political and economic problems in the views of Dr. Ambedkar.

The BSP concentrated on its basic idea that is "every social group should get participation and representation in the political power according to their populous ratio". To realize it, Mayawati changed her stretagy and made a combination of 'sarvajanas', which the political thinkers and intellectuals have called the "social engineering", a strategic move of Mayawati. The BSP attained success in making an alliance of Dalits, Muslims and Brahmins. Mayawati adopted the policy of "sarvajana hitaya, sarvajana sukhaya" in place of "bahujan hitya, bahujan sukhaya". As a result, BSP got success in gaining 77 per cent of Dalit votes, 27 per cent of Other Backward Class, 17 per cent of Muslims and 16 per cent of votes of forward castes, which led it to win 206 seats out of 403. Its winning candidates were 58 from Other Backward Class, 62 from Dalits, 29 from Muslims and about 50 from forward castes.

Mayawati as a successor of Manyawar Kanshi Ram is on the way to realize the dream of Dr. Ambedkar, which was to break down the rigid caste system and to enable Dalits to live a life of respect and dignity. Voters' verdict in 2007 in favour of BSP under Mayawati had given an opportunity to Mayawati to implement ideology Babasheb and Manyawar and she tried her best in this regard. With emergence of a political coalition of Dalits and Brahmans, centuries old casteism seemed to dissolve. The rigid Hindutva ideology seemed to lose its magic because through social engineering, Mayawati had written a history. Following the policy of inclusive democracy, Mayawati gave representation to 19 Dalits, 11 OBCs, 8 Brahmins, 5 Muslims and others in her council of ministers also that was a good move towards creating a social and political system based on equality and social justice. However, Mayawati and Dalit movement-a fight for social justice has been in a weak position since 2012 and she could not echo her voice strongly for social justice for which she was known. Political force of BSP has got a severe setback since 2014. Now BSP has totally shrank to an unrelevent party even in Uttar Pradesh as it has managed to win only one seat in the recent Assembly election, 2022. But no doubt, she has echoed her strong voice in favour of equality and social justice since she joined politics under the leadership of Kanshi Ram and still remains relevant as far as Dalit movement and fight for social justice is concerned. Still she is regarded and considered as a most influential Dalit leader in the country. Now, she has to rethink and prepare new strategy so that Dalit movement and voice for social justice could be revived. She will have to go back to the basics of Dalit politics and should take concrete steps to make a new blend of Dalit, Backwards and Minorities as Manaywar Kanshiram had done during 1990s.

KANSHI RAM'S BOOKS AND LEGACY

The Chamcha Age (The Era of the Stooges) is a famous book written by Kanshi Ram in 1982. In this book, he used the term *chamcha* (stooge) for Dalit leaders who he alleged had selfish reasons to work for parties such as the Indian National Congress (INC) and Bharatiya Janata Party (BJP). His book *Birth of BAMCEF* has been also published. Badri Narayan Tiwari has written his biography, *Kanshiram: Leader Of The Dalits*. His speeches are compiled in books like *Bahujan Nayak Kanshiram Ke Avismarniya Bhashan* by Anuj Kumar, *Writings & Speeches of Kanshiram* compiled by S. S. Gautam and *The Editorials of Kanshi Ram* by Bahujan Samaj Publications in 1997.

As per his ideas and dreams, Mayawati government launched many government programmes and schemes and public institutions have been named after Kanshi Ram in Uttar Pradesh. A memorial with his statue has been constructed at his birthplace, Pirthipur Bunga Sahib. Manyawar Shri Kanshiram Ji Green Eco Garden in Lucknow has been named in his memory. His statues have been erected in Dalit Prerna sthal in Lucknow and Noida, Uttar Pradesh. In 2017, a Hindi-language Biopic film *The Great Leader Kanshiram* was released in India, directed and produced by Arjun Singh, based on the story of DS4, BAMCEF and Bahujan Samaj Party founder Kanshi Ram from his childhood to 1984.

<u>**REFRENCES**</u>
*https://www.google.com/searchq=KANSHIRAM&rlz=1C1ONGR_enIN982IN982&sxsrf=ALiCzsYuIP4_32-EBXFVOyXktjNP7KmJeQ:1665833155174&source=lnms&tbm=isch&sa=X&ved=2ahUKEwiWkuCLkOL6AhVcv2MGHQFWCIIQ_AUoAXoECAEQAw&biw=1920&bih=860&dpr=1#imgrc=OBrZ3lxNdsjKQM
1. Narayan, Badri (11 May 2012). "Ambedkar and Kanshi Ram – so alike, yet so different". The Hindu.

2. "I will be the best PM and Mayawati is my chosen heir". archive.indianexpress.com. Retrieved 21 September 2020.

3. "Kejriwal to visit BSP founder Kanshi Ram's family". hindustantimes.com. 7 March 2016.

4. "Kanshi Ram Death Anniversary: Know contributions made by Bahujan Nayak for upliftment of Dalits". Newsd.in. 15 March 2019. Retrieved 21 September 2020.

5. Bose, Ajoy (2009). Behenji: A Political Biography of Mayawati. Penguin UK. p. 35. ISBN9788184756500.

6. Narayan, Badri (2014). Kanshiram: Leader of the Dalits. Penguin UK. p. 25. ISBN9789351186700.

7. "The man who saw tomorrow". The Indian Express. 24 May 2014. Retrieved 16 October 2016.

8. Bose, Ajoy (2009). Behenji: A Political Biography of Mayawati. Penguin UK. p. 35. ISBN9788184756500

9. Waghmore, Suryakant (30 September 2013). Civility against Caste: Dalit Politics and Citizenship in Western India. Sage. p. 39. ISBN9788132118862.

10. Waghmore, Suryakant (30 September 2013). Civility against Caste: Dalit Politics and Citizenship in Western India. Sage. p. 40. ISBN9788132118862.

11. Bagchi, Suvojit (17 November 2013). "Chhattisgarh polls: Towards a photo finish". The Hindu. ISSN0971-751X. Retrieved 9 August 2018.

12. Rawat, Ramnarayan (23 October 2006). "The Dalit Chanakya". Outlook. Retrieved 16 October 2016.

13. Lal, Ratan Mani. "17 castes included Shakyas, Rajbhar, Saini, Maurya and others members of this community are more inclined towards Mayawati and her BSP".

14. Murugkar, Lata (1991): Dalit Panther Movement in Maharashtra: A Sociological Appraisal, Bombay: Popular Prakashan

15. Nicolas Jaoul · 2007. "Dalit Processions: Street Politics and Democratization in India" in Staging Politics Power and Performance in Asia and Africa edited by Julia C Strauss and Donal B Cruise O'Brien, I.B.Tauris 2007

(https://www.semanticscholar.org › paper › Dalit-Processio)

16. Narayan, Badri (2014). Kanshiram: Leader of the Dalits. Penguin UK. p. 25. ISBN9789351186700.

17. SPECIAL ARTICLE Economic & Political Weekly EPW january 16, 2021 vol lVI no 3 41

18. Pai, Sudha, State Politics: New Dimensions, "The BSP in Uttar Pradesh", Shipra Publications, Delhi, 2000, p.120.

19. Kumar, Vivek (2013): Dalit Assertion and Bahujan Samaj Party: A Perspective from Below, New Delhi: Samyak Prakashan.

20. Kumar, Vivek (2013): Dalit Assertion and Bahujan Samaj Party: A Perspective from Below, New Delhi: Samyak Prakashan.

21. "The man who saw tomorrow". The Indian Express. 24 May 2014. Retrieved 16 October 2016.

22. "Return of the chamcha age". The Indian Express. 3 November 2014. Retrieved 27 February 2016.

23. "a new party loses the first election, gets noticed in the next and wins the third, these are Kanshiram ji's words – Yogendra Yadav".

24 SUBRAHMANIAM, VIDYA. "A quarter century of Kanshi Ram & Mayawati".

25. Pai, Sudha, State Politics: New Dimensions, "The BSP in Uttar Pradesh", Shipra Publications, Delhi, 2000, p.120.

26. Mendelssohn, Oliver and Vivziani, Marica, The Untouchable: Subordination, Poverty and the State, Cambridge University Press, Cambridge, 1998, p. 223.

27. Omvedt, Gail, 'The Anti-Caste Movement and the Discourse of Power', in T.V. Sathyamurthy (ed.), Region, Religion, Caste, Gender and Culture in Contemporary India, Oxford University Press, New Delhi, 1996, pp. 344-46.

28. Massey, James, Dalits in India: Religion as a source of bondage or liberation with special Reference to Christians, Manohar Publication, New Delhi, 1995, p. 157

29. Massey, James, Dalits in India: Religion as a source of bondage or liberation with special Reference to Christians, Manohar Publication, New Delhi, 1995, p. 157

30. "The man who saw tomorrow". The Indian Express. 24 May 2014. Retrieved 16 October 2016.

31. Teltumbde, Anand An Enigma Called Kanshi Ram | Request PDF - ResearchGate

January 2006; Economic and Political Weekly 41(43):4531-4532. DOI:10.2307/4418854. https://www.researchgate.net › publication › 262126826_...

32. Kumar, Vivek (2013): Dalit Assertion and Bahujan Samaj Party: A Perspective from Below, New Delhi: Samyak Prakashan.

33. Bose, Ajoy (2009). Behenji: A Political Biography of Mayawati. Penguin UK. p. 35. ISBN9788184756500.

34. Pai, Sudha, State Politics: New Dimensions, "The BSP in Uttar Pradesh", Shipra Publications, Delhi, 2000

35.(https://www.forwardpress.in/2013/03/building-a-bahujan-front-kanshi-ram-and-the-obcs/)

36. Nath, M Gopi and K Kureel (1999): Jati Vihin Samaj Ki Sthapna Ke Liye Aapko Desh Ka Hanuman Banana Hoga (in Hindi), New Delhi: Baba Sahib Dr Ambedkar Press.

37. Nath, M Gopi and K Kureel (1999): Jati Vihin Samaj Ki Sthapna Ke Liye Aapko Desh Ka Hanuman Banana Hoga (in Hindi), New Delhi: Baba Sahib Dr Ambedkar Press.

38. Nath, M Gopi and K Kureel (1999): Jati Vihin Samaj Ki Sthapna Ke Liye Aapko Desh Ka Hanuman Banana Hoga (in Hindi), New Delhi: Baba Sahib Dr Ambedkar Press.

39. SPECIAL ARTICLE Economic & Political Weekly EPW january 16, 2021 vol lVI no 3 41

40. Surinder S. Jodhka. (January 2021) "Kanshi Ram and the Making of Dalit Political Agency Leadership Legacies and the Politics of Hissedari", Economic and Political Weekly 56(3):35-

41. SPECIAL ARTICLE Economic & Political Weekly EPW january 16, 2021 vol lVI no 3 41

42. Surinder S. Jodhka. (January 2021) "Kanshi Ram and the Making of Dalit Political Agency Leadership Legacies and the Politics of Hissedari", Economic and Political Weekly 56(3):35-41

43. Chandra, K (2000): "The Transformation of Ethnic Politics in India: The Decline of Congress and the Rise of the Bahujan Samaj Party in Hoshiarpur," Journal of Asian Studies, Vol 59, No 1, pp 26–61.

44. Pai, Sudha, State Politics: New Dimensions, "The BSP in Uttar Pradesh", Shipra Publications, Delhi, 2000, p.124.

44A.   https://www.reportwire.in/rajbhar-nishad-patel-kanshi-ram-had-sown-the-crop-now-the-political-disciple-has-proved-to-be-a-game-changer-in-up/

45. The Hindu, . 10 October 2006.

46. https://redif.com/news/2006/oct/16look.htm?zcc=r

47. (https://en.wikipedia.org/wiki/Kanshi_Ram)

48. (https://en.wikipedia.org/wiki/Kanshi_Ram)

49. Srivastava, Rajiv (9 November 2012). "Mayawati's dream project ready for 1090 helpline cell". The Times of India. Archived from the original on 2 August 2013. Retrieved 2 August 2013.

50. "Amethi to form part of new Uttar Pradesh district". DNA India. 1 July 2010. Retrieved 4 November 2019.

51. "UP government changes names of eight districts, Mayawati fumes". The Economic Times. 23 July 2012. Retrieved 4 November 2019.

52. "Uttar Pradesh CM Mayawati directs officials to distribute pattas by launching special drive". Orissa Diary. 16 June 2010. Archived from the original on 17 June 2016. Retrieved 16 May 2016.

Note-Some words indicating the names of some castes belonging to Scheduled Castes have been used which can be objectionable in the text somewhere. But, there is no intention to disrespect any community here.

KARPOORI THAKUR

source*

LIFE, EDUCATION AND CAREER

Karpoori Thakur (24 January 1924 – 17 February 1988) was an Indian politician from the Bihar state. He was popularly known as **Jan Nayak** (people's hero). He served as the Chief Minister of Nihar from December 1970 to June 1971 as leader of Socialist Party/Bhartiya Kranti Dal, and from December 1977 to April 1979 as a leader of Janata Party. Today's youth know relatively lesser about life and contribution of Karpoori Thakur and his popularity during the 1960s and the 1970s. No doubt to say that he was not only a very influential politician but also a popular leader of backward community and warrior of social justice. In 1965, he led a powerful mass movement against the

Congress's repressive anti-student regime so much so that the Congress had to take recourse to violent suppression of the popular agitations.

Karpoori Thakur was born in the Nai (Barber) caste at Pitaunjhia (now Karpuri Gram) village in Samastipur District of Bihar. His father and mother were Gokul Thakur and Ramdulari Devi respectively. He was influenced by nationalistic ideas as a student, and joined the All India Students Federation.[1] As a student activist, he left his graduate college to actively participate in the Quit India Movement. For his participation in the Indian independence movement, he spent 26 months in prison. After India gained independence, Thakur worked as a teacher in his village's school. But later on, he joined politics and became a member of the Bihar Vidhan Sabha in 1952 from Tajpur constituency as a Socialist Party candidate. He was arrested for leading P & T employees during the general strike of the Central Government employees in 1960. In 1970, he undertook a fast unto death for 28 days to promote the cause of Telco labourers.[2]

Thakur was a supporter of Hindi language and not in favour of making English as a compulsory subject. When he became the education minister of Bihar, he removed English as the compulsory subject for the matriculation curriculum. It is alleged that the Bihari students suffered due to the resulting low standards of English-medium education in the state.[3] Thakur had served as a minister and Deputy Chief Minister of Bihar, before becoming the first non-Congress socialist Chief Minister of Bihar in 1970. He was not only a politician but also a social reformer and a champion of social equality. He was against consumption of alcohol and also enforced total prohibition of alcohol in Bihar. During his reign, many schools and colleges were established in his name in the backward areas of Bihar. He was a bifg supporter of resevation to the backward castes. Karpoori Thakur launched an agitation in favour of reservation policy in the 1970s.

FOLLOWER OF JAYA PRAKASH NARAYAN

Jaya Prakash Narayan had been a prominent socialist leader of the country who influenced Indian politics significantly. Jaya Prakash Narayan is well known for his national movement during 1970s, which he called *Sampoorna Kranti,* 'Total Revolution'. It was JP movement that feared then PM Indira Gandhi. She felt unsecure and declared national emergency using the constitutional provisions under article 352. As a socialist leader, Karpoori Thakur was close to Jaya Prakash Narayan who gave the call of "Total Revolution" a mass movement that aimed at non-violent all round transformation of the Indian society.[3] The impact of the movement led by Narayan was so massive that Indira Gandhi government imposed emergency (1975–77) in the country. In the post emergency period, in the Bihar Legislative Assembly election held in 1977, the ruling Indian National Congress suffered a heavy defeat at the hands of Janata Party. Janata Party was a recent amalgam of disparate groups including Indian National Congress (Organisation), Charan Singh's Bharatiya Lok Dal (BLD), Socialists and Hindu Nationalists of Jana Sangh. The sole purpose of these groups joining together was to defeat Prime Minister Indira Gandhi, who had imposed a nationwide emergency and curtailed many freedoms. There were also social cleavages with Socialists and BLD representing backward castes and Congress(O) and Jana Sangh the upper castes.[4]

AS A LEADER OF BACKWARDS

According to Jagpal Singh (*Economic and Political Weekly*, 2015), Karpoori, in the final phase of political career (1980 to 1988), was in search of a popular base among the lower OBCs, Dalits and the poor, struggling after being marginalised by the dominant OBCs. So much so that he once aired his anguish, saying, 'I would not have faced such humiliation if I were born a Yadav'. During this period, he attempted to mobilise the Hindu community of fishermen (Mallah/Kaivatas/Nishads/Sahnis), listed as *Ati Pichhrha* (Most Backward). He addressed their rallies on June 19, 1983 and also on February 14, 1988, just three days before his death.

MASSIVE ADVOCATE OF RESERVATION FOR BACKWARD CASTES

Karpoori Thakur was an immense advocate of reservation for backward castes. After the Janata Party came to power, Karpoori Thakur became Chief Minister of Bihar for the second time by winning the legislative party election against Bihar Janata Party President Satyendra Narayan Sinha, formerly of Congress [O], by a vote of 144 to 84.[5] Infighting in the party broke over the question of Thakur's decision to implement the Mungeri Lal Commission report, that recommended the institution of reservations for Backward Castes in government jobs. Upper caste members of the Janata Party tried to water down the reservation policy by unseating Thakur as Chief Minister. To wean away Dalit MLAs, Ram Sundar Das, a Dalit himself, was nominated as the candidate. Though both Das and Thakur were socialists, Das was considered more moderate and accommodating than the Chief Minister. Thakur resigned and Das became the Chief Minister of Bihar on 21 April 1979. The reservation law was weakened by allowing upper castes to obtain a greater percentage of government jobs. The internal tensions in the Janata Party caused it to split into multiple factions which led to Congress to return to power in 1980.[6] However, he could not last his full term because he lost the leadership battle in 1979 from Ram Sundar Das whom his adversaries placed against him and was replaced as chief minister.[7] When Janata Party split in July 1979, Karpoori Thakur sided with the outgoing Charan Singh faction. He was elected from Samastipur (Vidhan Sabha constituency) to Bihar Vidhan Sabha as Janata Party (Secular) candidate in 1980 elections. His party changed its name to Bharatiya Lok Dal later, and Thakur was elected to Bihar Vidhan Sabha as its candidate in 1985 election from Sonbarsa constituency.[8]

CHAMPION OF THE POOR AND MENTOR OF BACKWARD LEADERS OF BIHAR

Being a backward leader, Thakur was known as the champion of the poor.[9] He reluctantly wanted empowerment of backwards and took concrete steps for their upliftment when he came into power. He introduced reservation for the backward classes in the Government jobs, in 1978. In 1977; Devendra Prasad Yadav resigned from the Bihar Vidhan Sabha and paved the way for Thakur to contest the Phulparas Vidhan Sabha constituency by-election. Thakur won by the margin of 65000 votes, defeating Ram Jaipal Singh Yadav of INC.[10] Thakur served as the President of Samyukta Socialist Party. He is called a mentor to the prominent Bihari leaders such as Lalu Prasad Yadav, Ram Vilas Paswan, Devendra Prasad Yadav and Nitish Kumar.[11] Karpoori Thakur inspired many leaders of bihar mentioned above and paved the path of political consciousness among backward leaders. Being inspired by Thakur, Lalu Yadav, Nitish Kumar and Ram Vilas Paswan emerged as influential leaders of bihar and they earned significant identity and popularity. Today, Bihar politics is moving around the Lalu Prasad Yadav, Nitish Kumar and late Paswan and they are leading politics of social justice involving backwards and giving them representation.

KARPOORI THAKUR AS A WARRIER OF EQUALITY AND SOCIAL JUSTICE

Not very far off from Tajpur-Samastipur highway lies the Karpoori Gram, the ancestral place of late Karpoori Thakur, the towering backward leader who served as Bihar chief minister thrice much before the Mandal Commission was implemented. No doubt, Karpoori Thakur was the stalwart of backward politics and he showed the path for backward politics to emerge. Known for his simplicity and probity, Karpoori was the embodiment of social justice. This small hamlet, which was originally called Pitraunjia, was renamed Karpoorigram after the demise of veteran Socialist in the late 1980s. The locals in Karpoorigram feel proud in recalling how Karpoori led a simple life even after becoming the chief minister in the 70s. "Once when his wife Phuleshwari Devi fell sick in Patna, she was required to be taken to a doctor. But Karpooriji, a stickler of norms, said that instead of CM's official car (then an Ambassador), she should go in a rickshaw. He was man of integrity in real sense," recalls an octogenarian. A quick glimpse inside the Karpoori's ancestral house, now renamed Karpoori.[12] Trully speaking, Karpoori Thakur was a vibrant voice for the equality and social justice. He tried to uplift the backward people and promoted social cause. He contrinuted lot to promot the equality and social justice. Indeed he was a warrior of equality and social justice.

AS A POPULAR LEADER

Karpoori Thakur led many agitation in favour of poor, backwards and employees. He also protested to ensure job security for Tatas employees in Jamshedpur. He went on a fast unto death for 28 days. The Tata management had to yield and eventually conceded the workers' demands. Similar dramatic mobilisations of workers, teachers, engineers, journalists, etc. were undertaken in 1974 during Bihar movement. Thakur appealed to the Opposition, intelligentsia, students and youth to declare a *jihad* against Congress misrule. His pro-people performance as deputy chief minister in 1967 and as chief minister in 1970-1971, helped him connect with the people.

He was a worried politician for the poor and backwards. He echoed strong voice for the betterment of the poor people. He mobilized poor and backward people and made them conscious towards social justice. His slogan, '*Poora rashan, poora kaam, nahin to hoga chakka jam*' caught the popular imagination. He went to the extent of proposing to arm poor peasants against violent subjugation by the landed elites of upper and intermediate castes. They have hardly been able to launch such popular mass agitational movements against the incumbent regime. For instance, despite Muslims being their tremendous unflinching support-base, they did not hit the streets on the issue of lynching. In this way, he emerged as a true popular leader and a champion of social justice.

<u>**REFERENCES**</u>

Source- https://en.wikipedia.org/wiki/Karpoori_Thakur

*https://www.google.com/searchq=karpoori+thakur+hd+image&rlz=1C1ONGR_enIN982IN982
&oq=&aqs=chrome.3.69i59i450l8.413639405j0j15&sourceid=chrome&ie=UTF-8#imgrc=VnpYz3YEsxbKpM

1. "Karpoori Thakur: A Socialist Leader in the Hindi Belt". 15 August 2016.

2. <u>"Karpoori Thakur"</u>. FreeIndia.Org. Retrieved 14 January 2008.

3. "Bihar wants Bharat Ratna for Karpoori Thakur". <u>CNN-IBN</u>. 14 January 2008. Retrieved 14 January 2008.

4. Sanjay Kumar (2018). Post-Mandal Politics in Bihar: Changing Electoral Patterns. SAGE Publications. <u>ISBN9789352805860</u>.

5. G.G. Mirchandani (2003). Bihar chief ministership battle 1977. 320 Million Judges. Abhinav Publications. p. 211. <u>ISBN9788170170617</u>. Retrieved 4 June 2007.

6. "State mourns death of ex-CM on festival day". Daily Telegraph. 7 March 2015.

7.<u>30 years ago in India Today</u> (slide 3). India Today.

8. "Bihar Assembly Election Results in 1985".

9. Santosh Jha (2 June 2002). "The depth of Opulence". Spectrum. The Tribune. Retrieved 14 January 2008.

10. "Bihar CM Karpoori Thakur wins crucial by-election from Phulpuras". India Today. Retrieved 27 April 2021.

11. Akshayakumar; Ramanlal Desai, eds. (1986). Agrarian Struggles in India After Independence. Oxford University Press, 1986. p. 87. <u>ISBN0195616812</u>. Retrieved 2 April 2021.

12. https://www.deccanherald.com/content/504731/karpoori-thakur-epitome-justice.html)

CHAPTER FOURTEEN

BABU JAGDEO PRASAD KUSHWAHA

Source*

LIFE AND EDUCATION

Like other heroes of social justice, Babu Jagdeo Prasad has been one of the pioneers of the struggle against inequality, social exclusion, caste based discrimination, deprivation, marginalistion and subjugation. He made sincere efforts to mobilise the poor and backwards against social inequality and injustice. He echoed his voice in favour of exploited who comprise 90 percent part of Indian masses as according to Babu Jagged himself. He always remained an advocate of social justice. Babu Jagdeo Prasad was born into a poor Kushwaha family on 2 February 1922 in Kurhari, Kurtha block, Bihar – close to Bodh Gaya, where Mahatma Buddha attained enlightenment. His father Prayag Narayan Kushwaha was a teacher in a primary school in the neighbourhood while his mother Raskali was unlettered. After passing his middle-school exam, he went to Jehanabad for high school. Jagdeo Prasad's son, Nagmani is a veteran politician who started his career from his father's party itself. He later joined Rashtriya Janata

Dal and remained minister in RJD government.[1]

He lived a short life as he was killed in police firing on 5 September 1974. He announced a statewide satyagraha from 5 September 1974. On that day, he was marching on the streets in Kurtha, holding the black flag of his party in his hands, followed by thousands of supporters, when the DSP on duty asked him to stop. Jagdeo Babu refused and fell into a trap so meticulously laid by his rivals. The police opened fire and a bullet hit him on his neck. He fell down but instead of taking him to hospital, the policemen took him to the police station. The police even tried to secretly dispose of his body but failed due to public pressure. His body was brought to Patna on 6 December. People from all parts of the country reached Patna to join his funeral procession. Lakhs bid their last farewell to him. Vinayak Prasad Yadav, then a member of the Samyukta Socialist Party, resigned from the Legislative Assembly of Bihar in protest of this killing at Kurtha.[2]

STRUGGLER BUT RADICAL AGAINST CASTE DISCRIMINATION FROM CHLDHOOD

Having been born into a lower-middle class family, he became a struggler from his early days. Like Jyotiba Phule and Babasaheb Ambedkar, he too faced caste discrimination during his school days. When the adolescent Jagdeo Prasad went to school wearing clean clothes, the upper-caste students made fun of him. One day, he lost his temper, thrashed his tormentors black and blue and threw dust into their eyes. His father had to pay a fine and tender an apology for his son's outburst. He was also given a severe dressing-down in the school. Another day, a teacher slapped Jagdeo Prasad for no fault of his. A couple of days later, that teacher fell asleep in the class and began snoring. Jagdeo Prasad slapped him hard across the face. The teacher complained to the headmaster. When confronted, he told the headmaster, "Everyone should get the same punishment for committing a mistake – whether he is a teacher or a student." (https://en.wikipedia.org/wiki/jagdeo_prasad)

BABU JAGDEV - LENIN OF BIHAR

From childhood, Babu Jagdev was of radical thoughts and a strong critic of inequality and social injustice. He strongly opposed the oppression and exploitation of the poor and backward castes. He led the Shoshit Samaj Dal and during the early 1970s, at the height of the caste tensions known as the Bihar Movement, he was able to attract much support from both members of the Other Backward Classes and the Dalits in their opposition to upper-caste landlords.[3] Jagdeo is said to have revolutionary mindset since his early childhood as in his adolescence. He fought to end prevailing practices like "Panchkathia System", in which farmers had to leave *5 katta* of their land for the elephant of landlord to graze.[4] He was referred to as the "Lenin of Bihar" due to his charisma[5] and revolutionary nature.

Due to his strong voice in favour of equality and social justice, the people of Bihar began describing him as the "Lenin of Bihar'. A massive students' movement was launched under the leadership of Jay Prakash (JP) against the authoritarian Congress government of Bihar but the leadership of the movement was in the hands of the Anglicized dominant sections of society. Jagdeo Babu did not agree with this kind of a students' movement. He tried to give a wider sweep to the movement. In May 1974, he addressed a series of public meetings all over the state in support of his six-point charter of demands but the corrupt administration and the Brahmanical government were unmoved.

STRONG OPPOSER AND CRITIC OF THE CASTE BASED DISCRIMINATION

Babu Jagdeo Prasad was a not only a politician in Bihar but also a voiceful champion of social justice. Being a revolutionary and progressive since his early childhood, he openly opposed social injustice. Due to his revolutionary mindset against exploitation and marginalisation, he is also known to have been a strong opposer and critic of the caste based discrimination happening in the society. He was highly influenced with the ideology of western political thinker, T.H. Green. Every time he spoke, Jagdeo Babu broadened the horizons of the exploited sections. He exemplified political thinker T.H. Green's belief that "Human consciousness postulates liberty; liberty involves rights; rights demand the state".[6]

SUPPORT TO SOCIALISM AND RAM MANOHAR LOHIA

Later, he came into contact with Chandradeo Prasad Verma, who persuaded him to study the political philosophers to know the prevalent societal condition in depth. Jagdeo agreed and soon he became sympathetic to idea of socialism. Later, he joined Samyukta Socialist Party and in the days of ideological wars between Ram Manohar Lohia and Jayprakash Narayan, he chose to go with Lohia. Jagdeo also became editor of the magazine of SSP called *Janata*. Later he moved to Hyderabad and started editing two more magazines *Uday* and *Citizen*. His ideas brought great fame to the magazines but he had to face intimidation from orthodox section of society. This led him to leave the magazine and move to Patna once again.[7]

FORMATION OF SHOSHIT SAMAJ PARTY

Though, initially he remained an active member of SSP (Samyukta Socialist Party) but he could not remain its member for a long time. He later realised that the fruits of labour of many are reaped by few in the party and given his ideological difference with Lohia, he resigned and formed a new party called Shoshit Samaj Party (SSP). He also remained active member of Arjak Sangh, a platform led by Ramswaroop Verma.[8] The Shoshit Samaj Party was more a revolutionary organisation than a political party as it urged the landless labourers to grab the lands of landlords, a practice which gave rise to a number of caste armies and private senas in Bihar.[9]

MAIN SLOGANS COINED BY BABU JAGDEO PRASAD

Babu Jagdeo gave many slogans to mobilige and awaken backwards and dalits. Following ones are very remarkable and appealing slogans which really proved fruitful.

"DAS KA SHASHAN NABBE PAR,

NAHIN CHALEGA, NAHIN CHALEGA

(the rule of ten over ninety cannot continue)

SAU MEIN NABBE SHOSHIT HAIN,

SHOSHITON NE LALKARA HAI,

DHAN, DHARTI AUR RAJPAAT MEIN,

NABBE BHAAG HAMARA HAI"

(Ninety of hundred are exploited,

We are owners of ninety parts

We should have ninety per cent share in wealth, land and power)

MANAVVAD KEE KYA PEHCHAN,

BRAHMIN, BHANGI EK SAMAAN,

(The identity of humanism is that Brahmins and Bhangis (sweeper) are equal)

PUNARJANM AUR BHAGYAVAAD,

INSE JANMA BRAHMANVAD

(Belief in rebirth and Fatalism has given birth to Brahmanism)

Babu Jagdev Prasad[10]

Due to his critic of upper caste dominance, Prasad many a times is branded as Anti-forward caste. He remained Deputy Chief Minister of Bihar for a brief period of time when SSP was at peak. People used to call Jagdev Prasad as Bihar's Lenin in his lifetime due to his radical views, he also coined the politically radical slogan:

"ABKI SAAL KE BHADON MEIN, GORI UNGLI KADO MEIN

(Next paddy sowing season will see the slim white fingers of upper caste women in mud, transplanting paddy)"[11]

Itmeans he was not happy to see the poor and backward communities women labouring hard in the fields. He wanted upliftment of women belonging to backward castes. Due to poverty, women from backward and Dalit communities worked hard going into the mud. On the other hand, women of upper strata of the society enjoyed luxury life. Therefore, he did not like backward and Dalit women to labour in the fields. He stressfully stated that women from upper castes too should work in fields as backward women do. This was revolutionary move of Babu Jagdev. This attitude of Babu Jagdev showed his concern for betterment of backward women.

HARBINGER OF THE "REVOLUTION OF THE EXPLOITED"

Babu Jagdeo Prasad, was the harbinger of the "revolution of the exploited" in north India, a great protagonist of Arjak culture and literature, an inspiration for the setting-up of the Mandal Commission and the founder of Shoshit Samaj Dal and later the Bahujan Samaj Party. A great hero of the proletariat, Jagdeo Babu laid the path on which the non-savarnas of the country today are marching towards social, economic, political and cultural progress.

He strengthened the organizational structure of the Socialist Party and indigenised the socialist ideology so as to make its reach wider. JP quit active politics and joined the Bhoodan Movement of Vinoba Bhave. JP was a sham revolutionary who served the interests of the socialists of the forward castes. The land that the landlords donated after a "change of heart" was largely barren. It was distributed among the poor and the landless, who, through their industry and toil, turned it fertile. But once that happened, the landlords started staking a claim on the land and assaulting and forcibly evicting Dalits and OBCs from their fields. At that time, Karpoori Thakur openly flayed Vinoba Bhave and described him as a "Havai Mahatma" (an airy Mahatma).**

No doubt to state that Babu Jagdev Prasad Kushwaha was a great warrior of equality and social justice. He believed in upliftment of the backwards and dalits and for this cause he remained active always till his death. Due to his pro poor, labourer and backward attitude, he was called Lenin of Bihar.

REFERENCES

*https://www.google.com/searchq=jagdev+prasad&rlz=1C1ONGR_enIN982IN982&sxsrf=ALiCzs Yj5xGCc1W2skuisiwZtRZPOw:1665883164551&source=lnms&tbm=isch&sa=X&ved=2ahUKEw i6ooqyyuP6AhVSZWwGHTaBiYQ_AUoAXoECAIQAw&biw=1920&bih=860&dpr=1#imgrc=iOce Ujrr4ABNXM

1. Tiwari, Lalan (1987). Democracy and Dissent: A Case Study of the Bihar Movement, 1974-75. Mittal Publications. pp. 86–87. ISBN978-8-17099-008-6.
2. Sinha, A. (2011). Nitish Kumar and the Rise of Bihar. Viking. p. 95. ISBN978-0-670-08459-3.
3. "'Lenin' waits wrapped in plastic". www.telegraphindia.com. Retrieved 9 September 2021.
4. PATEL, ANOOP (5 May 2016). "babu-jagdev-prasad-bahujans-real-hero". forward press.
5. Kumar, Sanjay (2018). Post-Mandal Politics in Bihar: Changing Electoral Patterns. SAGE Publishing India. p. 39. ISBN978-9-35280-587-7.
6. https://en.wikipedia.org/wiki/jagdeo_prasad)
7. PATEL, ANOOP (5 May 2016). "babu-jagdev-prasad-bahujans-real-hero". forward press. Archived from the original on 23 October 2016.
8. PATEL, ANOOP (5 May 2016). "babu-jagdev-prasad-bahujans-real-hero". forward press. Archived from the original on 23 October 2016.
9. Law Kumar Mishra. "'Three-days-chief minister' Satish Prasad Singh dies of COVID-19". The Free Press Journal. Archived from the original on 14 November 2020.
10. https://en.wikipedia.org/wiki/jagdeo_prasad)
11. "Translation: Three day-jagdev-fair-started-with-the-rally". Jagran.com.

**Pathak, Narendra (2008) Karpoori Thakur Aur Samajvad, Medha Books, Delhi

CHAPTER FIFTEEN

RAM SWAROOP VERMA

Source*

LIFE, EDUCATION AND POLITICAL CAREER

Ramswaroop Verma (22 August 1923 – 19 August 1998), was an Indian humanist and a great warrior of equality and social justice. He was not only a massive voice for social justice but also was staunch critic of Brahaminism and Brahminical hegemony over society, economy and politics. He was a firm critic of Ram Rajya. He gave call for revolution in all spheres of life, social, economic, political and religious. He did not hesitate to criticize the President of India and the Prime Minister when they did some acts that were considered as promotion of Brahmanism.

He was the founder of Arjak Sangh, a humanist organisation.[1] The Arjak Sangh emphasises social equality and is strongly opposed to Brahmanism and caste based discrimination. Verma denied the existence of god and soul. He was strongly opposed to the doctrine of *Karma* and *Fatalism*. Verma campaigned tirelessly against Brahmanism and Untouchability. According to him, Brahmanism is rooted in the doctrine of rebirth and it is not possible to eradicate it without attacking the doctrine of rebirth. Verma strongly asserts that Brahmanism cannot be reformed, and it has to be negated totally.[2] Ramswaroop Verma was born on 22 August 1923 in Gaurikaran village of Kanpur district in the state of Uttar Pradesh, in a Kurmi peasant family. Verma was married to Siyadulari as a student, but his wife died soon.[3]

Ramswaroop Verma did his M.A. in Hindi from Allahabad University in 1949. He was Law Graduate from Agra University, Uttar Pradesh. He had been a brilliant student and he secured first position in the first class in in both the examinations. He qualified in the written examination of the Indian Administrative Services, but did not appear for the interview. Verma was of the view that an administrator has to work within limitations. He wanted to work for social change as a free citizen. He came in contact of prominent Indian democratic socialist leaders of his time such as Acharya Narendra Dev and Dr. Ram Manohar Lohia. Consequently, he became a member of the Socialist Party. Several times he was elected to the Uttar Pradesh Legislative Assembly. In 1967, he was for some time the finance minister of Uttar Pradesh in the government headed by Charan Singh, who later became the prime minister of India.[4]

COMMITTED AMBEDKRITE AND CRITIC OF BRAHMANICAL LITERATURE

Ramswaroop Verma was totally inclined towards the ideology of Dr. Ambedkar and he has been described as a committed Ambedkarite. Like all other Bahujan intellectual, he also nurtured a different perspective on the Brahmanical litterateurs and characters like *Ramcharitmanas* of Tulsidas and its lead character, Lord Rama. There necessarily exists two streams of thoughts on the characters like Rama and Krishna in the political circle. While one group of intellectual, the traditional elite, belonging to *Dvija* castes classify them as the ideal human beings, the Bahujan intellectuals consider them as purely mythical characters, crafted in order to keep the lower castes subjugated under the banner of religion. Several ideologues have composed their own version of texts on the litterateurs like *Ramcharitmanas* which identifies lord Rama as a negative character and the protector of hated *Varna System*. In his book *Brahmin Mahima Kyo aur Kaise?*

Verma has described the *Ramcharitmanas* as a pro-upper caste text written by Brahmins in order to justify their superiority over the other caste groups. Verma had compiled this book from his letters written on various occasions to some of the notable politicians like then Prime Minister, Indira Gandhi and the contemporary Chief Minister of Uttar Pradesh, who according to him were acting against the secular feature of Indian constitution by organizing commemoration ceremony of the day of compilation of various Hindu texts. Verma in his book, has described various verses of the text *Ramcharitmanas*, which justifies the superiority of the Brahmins over the other caste groups. The book also contains verses in which the castes like Kewat, Ahir and Kalwar are classified as "impure".[5]

FORMATION OF ARJAK SAMAJ (EARNERS ASSOCIATION) AND ITS PROPOSALS

Ramswaroop Verma was a huge supporter of equality in all spheres of life, social, economic and political. He strongly condemned inequality and social injustice based on caste system. After being active in party politics for a long time, Verma concluded that political and economic equality could not be achieved without a social and cultural revolution. Consequently, he founded Arjak Sangh on 1 June 1968 for achieving this aim. This was an organisation of working people who belong to Dalit and backward communities and work hard to earn their bread. To echo the voice of deprived and backward people, he also had started *Arjak Saptahik*, a Hindi weekly. He was the chief editor of the weekly.

Vermaji felt that it is meaningless to uplift the backward people till they remain chained in the bondage of religion and culture. Therefore, he attacked religion and culture and decided to hold conferences to educate people. There were three general conferences of the Uttar Pradesh branch of Arjak Sangh. The first conference was held in Lucknow in 1971, the second at Kanpur in 1972 and the third at Allahabad in 1979. Altogether eight resolutions were passed in these conferences.

All these proposals were religious and cultural. Four of these proposals were very revolutionary, which are discussed as under.

Attack on Reincarnation and Fatalism

Thefirst is that the Earning Association accepts the principle of human-human equality. He believes that the root cause of inequality in the country is reincarnation and fatalism, the foundation bricks of Brahmanism. In his view the feelings of caste, untouchability, high-low and poor-rich are the product of this Brahmanism. According to the proposal, 'Today the truth has come to the fore in front of the whole world that caste-caste, high-low, untouchable and rich and poor are not due to luck, but due to manipulative society-enemies. The conference came to the conclusion that reincarnation is not possible in this world made of matter, just as all rivers end their existence by joining the ocean, similarly all living beings merge into matter after death, thereby raising the question of their rebirth. Doesn't even get up Therefore, when there is no rebirth, then where did luck come from? Gone.

Emphasis on 'Sit Equal and Sit Equally'

In the second resolution, a resolution was taken to 'Sit Equal and Sit Equally'. Under this it was said that in Brahmanism, a cow that eats a cauldron is pure and a Bhangi is impure. There was no such humiliation of human beings as seen in India. Similarly, the lower castes are also insulted by calling them in bad name. This uncivilized unfair treatment needs to end.

Interpretation of *Dharma* and Advocacy for Freedom of Religion

The third resolution said, 'Dharma is the one by which human society is sustained and progressed.' Admit it, that too cannot be a religion. It was accepted in the resolution that every person attaining the age of 18 years should have the freedom to leave his religion and adopt another religion. The conference also demanded that the Central Government should immediately bring the Adoption Bill and give it the form of a law.

Criticism of Teaching of Brahmanism in Schools

Vermaji was highly against the teaching of Bramanism abd religious texts in schools. In the fourth resolution, there was a demand to remove from the curriculum 'Our Ancestors' and other text books taught in the schools of the Uttar Pradesh government, in which education of reincarnation, fatalism, caste-caste and high and low was being taught. In the opinion of the conference, this teaching of Brahmanism was against the Constitution of India. In this there was a demand to keep education as a central subject and to implement a uniform education system.

In the words of Maharaj Singh Bharti, the objectives of 'Arjak Sangh' was to secure freedom of thought and expression to all. Everyone has complete freedom to express, say, write and change their views, it follows. Therefore, despite being contrary to the scientific point of view, Arjak Sangh does not want to debate on the soul like God. But it denies reincarnation at the sting, because the Hindu culture, which was robbed of the previous birth itself, has made the basis of exploitation through the Brahmanical system. When every oppressed is suffering the punishment of the sin of his past lives, how can he blame any system or person for his sufferings? The Arjak Sangh, an organisation founded by Verma was also active in the obliteration of <u>Brahmanism</u> and the emancipation of downtrodden in the several belts of <u>Uttar Pradesh</u>. It was supported by other organisations working in this field and Verma himself visited several places where the discrimination against the Dalits were recorded.

DIFFERENCES WITH DR. RAM MANOHAR LOHIA ON CULTURAL ISSUES

According to Bahujan thinker Mudrarakshas, Ramswaroop Verma had deep differences with Dr. Ram Manohar Lohia, due to which he himself left the party. The issues on which these differences took place have been described by Mudrarakshasa in one of his articles as follows-I met Vermaji one afternoon at Dr. Ram Manohar Lohia's bungalow on Gurdwara Road in Delhi, when he was having a very stimulating debate with Dr. Lohia about Ramcharitmanas. Dr. Lohia's favorite book was Ramcharitmanas, he loved Manusmriti equally. I had also clashed with him on Manusmriti and Ramcharitmanas. He also looked at Hindutva almost from Gandhi's point of view. He certainly saw something in the Hindus, in which reforms should be done, but he did not like to reject Hindutva, and Ramswaroop Verma considered freedom from Hindutva as necessary for revolutionary and fundamental change in Indian society. Dr. Lohia did not like Hindutva to be rejected at all. Dr. Lohia had a huge dispute with Vermaji on these issues and this dispute became the reason for Vermaji's separation from Dr. Lohia's party. How right Vermaji was on this issue, the second big proof is that Lohia's relationship with the then Jana Sangh had become very deep. It was the result of his

Hindutva love that he had campaigned in favor of Upadhyay in the election for the parliamentary seat of Jana Sangh chief Deendayal Upadhyay and people like his important colleague George Fernandez directly joined the Bharatiya Janata Party.

In fact, it was the establishment of Arjak Sangh that separated Ramswaroop Verma from the ideology of Dr. Lohia and his Socialist Party. The cultural uprising for which Vermaji wanted to work could not be done by staying in the Socialist Party. In fact, the objectives of the Arjak Sangh were cultural, not political, and were so revolutionary that socialists like Lohia could not agree with it. The socialist movement in India was not opposed to Brahmanism. Just as the Indian communist movement was inspired by Marx and Lenin, in the same way the socialist movement was not influenced by them. His sources of inspiration were others, including Vivekananda and Gandhi, as well as Vedas and Tulsidas. So the socialist leaders of India were against the class struggle. Perhaps this was the reason why he was also very early towards Gandhism, including Acharya Narendra Dev, Jayaprakash Narayan and Dr. Ram Manohar Lohia. The sources of inspiration for the Arjak Sangh were anti-Brahmanical heroes like Karl Marx and Lenin as well as Jyotiba Phule, Dr. Ambedkar and Periyar Ramasami Naikar.

INFLUENCE OF DR. AMBEDKAR ON RAMSWAROOP VERMA

Vermaji was highly influenced and inspired by Dr. Ambedkar. He remained active in party politics for a long time. However, he is best known and remembered as a humanist thinker, writer and founder of the Earners Association. He wrote articles and books and gave many lectures to promote humanism. Ramswaroop Verma wrote and spoke in Hindi only. He died on 19 August 1998 in Lucknow.[6]

Dr. Ambedkar wrote in the preface to 'The Mook Nayak' of 1927: Find out what the original controversy is? In this article he emphasized on finding the root of the problem. After this Ramswaroop Verma wrote a long and important article titled 'Initiation to get to the bottom of the problems'. Although it is his political writings that highlight the brahmanical culture of the Congress, the impeccably explored root of the problem reminds us of Ambedkar's socialist thought. He has blamed Gandhi and the Congress party for the establishment of Brahminism in the politics of India at the very beginning of the article.

VERMAJI OPPOSED HEGEMONY OF BRAHMINS OVER CONGRESS

Vermaji was not only a critic but also a solid opponent of hegemony of Brahmins over Congress. He was of the opinion that the prayer meetings of Mohandas Karamchand Gandhi began with songs praising Vaishnavism and Ram Rajya. Ever since Gandhiji started propagating Vaishnavism in the Congress, minority leaders like Muhammad Ali Jinnah etc. and social reformers like Ramaswami Naykar and revolutionary leaders like Bhagat Singh, who believed in materialistic philosophy, kept away from the Congress. The major problem of Brahminists has been the number of minorities, Dalit and adivasis, whom they consider as mlechchha and untouchables. 30 percent Muslims and 24 percent Dalit-Adivasis together form the majority. For Brahmanism to flourish, it is necessary to maintain authority over governance.

Varmaji, while explaining Hindu communalism, further said, the leadership of Hindu communalism has always been governed by Brahmins. Be it the Brahmin side, or the opposition, they play this game together. The Brahmins of the opposition propagate Hindu communalism with respect to non-Brahmin Hindus and the majority of Brahmins stay in the Congress and talk about secularism. That's why the minority class stays with the Congress fearing Hindu communalism. Vermaji was in favour of inclusive governance representing all communities and he opposed the Brahmanical nature of Congress and hegemony of Brahmans over Congress. Varmaji had understood the game of Brahmin very well. So he made a precise analysis that the leadership of both secularism and communalism is in the hands of Brahmins. He said that any party spreading communalism cannot succeed without Brahmins. According to him Hindu communalism benefits the Brahmins, and the non-Brahmin Hindus suffer. (Ramswaroop Varma's Arjak sangh movement against Brahmanism and superstition (mediavigil.com)[7]

VERMAJI'S VIEWS ON CONGRESS'S *RAM RAJYA*

Gandhi wanted to bring *Ram Rajya* in India that is in simpler sense a Brahmin dominated state. Congress started to work on *Ram Rajya* as soon as India became independent, making Nehru the first Prime Minister of India and appointing Brahmins first to the Chief Minister posts of the states. What is Ram Rajya and why do Brahmins like it? Ramswaroop Verma's thinking on this subject is wonderful. See his statement-

The story of Ramayana is not a history, but a fictional literature. If Ramayana was history, then the economic aspects of Ramayana should also have been written in it. Rama and the people of his caste, all Brahmins and sages did not do any production and construction with their own labor, yet Rama used to spend a lot of money in the service of all Brahmins and sages. No minerals were mined in Ramrajya, yet all the family members are laden with gold ornaments and crowns. No paved roads, no bridges over rivers, no factories, no dams, canals or tube wells. Whatever little the farmer had produced from irrigated farming, the servants of Raja Ram first took away the share. Then the local Thakur was given to the Brahmin. What was left, carpenters, potters, weavers etc. subjects, landless laborers and the farmer himself had to spend his life. The monarchy system based on terrible exploitation is the wish of Ramrajya, but no one, from Pandit Valmiki to Pandit Tulsidas, considered it appropriate to discuss it.

According to Verma ji, Ram Rajya was called an ideal state because the saints, Brahmins and Kshatriyas were happy and respected in it. Regarding Vaishyas, Varmaji was of the opinion that Brahmanism has placed Vaishyas in a very pathetic condition. He is a milch cow for the Brahmins, and his wealth runs the kingdom of the Brahmins. 'Thus a Vaishya earns many times more for Brahmins and Kshatriyas than he has to earn for himself.' Therefore, he has to adopt every means of exploitation. According to Varmaji, the mentality of Vaishya is also very Brahmanical, that is why he exploits the farmers and artisans horribly. He uses his illegal money to build temples and perform yagyas. He is of the opinion that this Brahmanical mentality of Vaishya is hurting the economy of India. We can see this in the writings of Vermaji. (Ramswaroop Varma's Arjak sangh movement against Brahmanism and superstition (mediavigil.com)

VERMAJI RIDICULED *RAMCHARITMANAS* AS PROPAGATOR OF BRAHMANISM

In 1974, on the occasion of the completion of four hundred years of *Ramcharitmanas*, the then Congress government organized 'Manas-Chatushati' with pomp. Preparations for this event took place in 1970. The then Prime Minister Smt. Indira Gandhi allocated a budget of one crore rupees for this event and announced to distribute four crore copies of *Ramcharitmanas* free of cost to the public with a view to promote maximum. Ramswaroop Verma strongly opposed it on behalf of Arjak Sangh. He not only wrote letters against it to the then Prime Minister Indira Gandhi and President V.V. Giri, but also wrote a book titled 'Brahmin Mahima: Why and How'. In the preface of this book, Vermaji wrote that there is no program with the Prime Minister to remove the poverty of crores of earners, but one crore rupees is being spent from the hard earned money of the earners to maintain the Brahmanshahi. He said that only after seeing the destruction of Brahmanism due to the development of scientific knowledge, the Brahmin class is undertaking to celebrate the fourteenth anniversary of the nutritious text of Brahmanism. He said in sharp words that giving power to the preachers of Brahmanism is no less dangerous than giving a torch to a monkey.(mediavigil.com)

HE HELD PROPAGATION OF *RAMCHARITMANAS* AS UNCONSTITUIONAL

Vermaji was very unhappy due to propagation of Ramcharitmanas and he strongly opposed celebrations of Tulsi Chatushti. He wrote four letters to the then Prime Minister Mrs. Gandhi and President V.V. Giri in protest against Manas Chatushati. The first letter was sent to Shri VV Giri on 18 June 1970. Some special parts of its text were as follows-

greetings,

Celebration of Tulsi Chatushati is being organized in the country. I have heard that you are the patron of the said event and the Hon'ble Prime Minister of India, Indira Gandhi is going to become the chairperson of the said function committee. It seems that you are considering Pandit Tulsidas as the ultimate benefactor of the nation of India, only then you became the patron of Tulsi Chatushti celebrations. It cannot be said that you have not studied the Ramcharitmanas of Pandit Tulsidas. You have taken an oath to implement the Constitution of India. Not only this, when you came to Lucknow during the presidential election and being the convener of the Uttar Pradesh 'Giri Jitao' committee, you addressed the meeting of MLAs called under my chairmanship in the common room of Darul Shafa-e-Block. Even then you had said that if you win, you will uphold the dignity of the Constitution of India.

The Constitution of India is secular. In it, every citizen of India has been given many fundamental rights. In short, the Constitution of India accepts the principle of human-human equality, and does not even imagine inhuman differences like man-woman, Shudra-Brahmin, Mlechha Hindu. Then how did you patronize the celebration of the fourth century of Pandit Tulsidas, the antithesis of the above inhuman difference? Isn't this act a violation of the Constitution? Doesn't this hurt the vast majority of the country?

In the texts of Pandit Tulsidas, only the rendition of reincarnation and fatalism is found. Due to reincarnation and fatalism, the feeling of high and low and untouchability inevitably flourishes in human beings. The Constitution of India declares the spirit of untouchability as unfair and the law of the country declares untouchability a crime. But in the book *Ramcharitmanas* of Pandit Tulsidas, Kewat or Mallah has been called untouchable. 'Lok Veda Sabhi Vid Neecha, Jasu Chhah Chui Leia Sincha.'

Today the Constitution of India considers it to be a crime to call a caste inferior or sinful. Pandit Tulsidas in his Ramcharitmanas has called many castes as inferior and sinful 'Je Varnadham Teli Kumhara, Vapach, Kirat, Kol, Kalwara. Aabhir, Yavan, Kirat, Khal Vapchadi Ati Ardhrup J.' Give protection to those who call crores of people of the country inferior, lowly, sinners, untouchables, then this contradiction will be said to be impossible to quell.

"Pandit Tulsidas considers teaching a Shudra to be like giving milk to a snake. That is, Shudra is snake and education is milk. According to popular belief, feeding a snake with milk makes it more venomous. Similarly, according to Pandit Tulsidas, a Shudra becomes more dangerous by acquiring knowledge. In the Kakbhusundi-Garuda dialogue of Ramcharitmanas, Kakbhusandi says, saying that he was a Shudra in his previous birth, he should get education in the lower caste, let him drink milk as ahi (snake).

The Constitution of India takes a pledge to introduce compulsory education and Pandit Tulsidas calls it dangerous to teach education to Shudras. From the above examples, although it may not be possible to give a good introduction to the anti-constitutional tendencies of Pandit Tulsidas, but keeping in mind your busy time, it did not seem right to increase the cover of the letter. Therefore, considering these examples as sufficient to test like Batloi's rice, I would request you to graciously and graciously separate yourself from the guardianship of the Tulsi-Chatushati ceremony and announce it immediately and your Prime Minister should also be prohibited from participating. Do it You may have been made the custodian of the Chatushati ceremony of Pandit Tulsidas, who made Bhagiratha efforts to bring glory to the Brahmins. But this will be completely opposite to your glorious position, and those who voted to make you the President, considering you to be an attempt to build a classless society, will have great anguish and anguish.

Yours,

Ramswaroop Verma

(mediavigil.com)

VERMAJI'S LETTER TO MRS. INDIRA GANDHI AGAINST PROPAGATION OF BRAMANISM

Similarly, Vermaji wrote another letter to the same effect on 27 June 1970 to the then Prime Minister Indira Gandhi. The main content of this letter are as follows-

Honorable Indira Gandhi

Madam,

It has come to know from newspapers and other types of news that you have accepted the presidency of Tulsi Chatushati ceremony. It pains me to learn that despite taking an oath of allegiance to the Constitution of India, you have accepted the presidency of the quadrennial ceremony of a communal person like Tulsidas.

You are not involved in celebrating the Chatushti of Pandit Tulsidas because you too have taken birth in a Brahmin family and Pandit Tulsidas was also a Brahmin. It will not be benevolent for you, because you are the Prime Minister of secular Indian Republic and Pandit Tulsidas was a strong proponent of Brahmanism and propagator of so called Sanatan Dharma. Therefore, being the Prime Minister of India, you cannot participate in the Chatushti of Pandit Tulsidas, because in his Ramcharitmanas, Pandit Tulsidas has severely insulted the majority of the people of India by calling the Shudras, Antyajas, Yavanas very sinful and despicable. Such a poet can neither be national nor beneficent of the nation.

'You are a woman. Naturally, your heart has more capacity to understand their sorrow and happiness. Pandit Tulsidas has put a flurry of blasphemy in his texts. According to him, even Brahma could not know the speed of a woman's heart, because she is the mine of all deceit, sin and demerits'.

In this letter also, Vermaji had requested the president to break his association with the Tulsi Chatushati ceremony by giving many quotes from the scriptures.

However, both the President and the Prime Minister did not respond to his letter for two months. Then Varmaji again wrote letters to him on 6 August 1970 and 14 August 1970 respectively, and reminded again that Pandit Tulsidas was neither a national poet nor his Ramcharitmanas is a national book, but an anti-constitutional book, whose function to participate in would be a violation of the constitution. But this effort of Vermaji also failed, and Manas-Chatushadi was celebrated with pomp by the government.

Both these letters are given in the beginning of Ramswaroop Varma's book 'Brahman-Mahima'. After that there are three chapters on Tulsidas and his brahmin-glory, whose titles are: 'Maryada Purushottam or Brahmin-slave Rama', 'Is Ramcharitmanas a religious text?' and 'Rama and Ravana are fictional characters.' Done for the crores of Bahujan earners who are suffering from Brahmanism and are sleeping on the bullet of ignorance. (mediavigil.com)

STAUNCH CRITIC OF *RAMCHARITMANAS*

Ramswaroop Verma was a staunch critic of Hindu religious texts and he had no belief in *Ramcharitmanas* as a religious text. His opposition to religious texts mainly *Ramcharitmans* begins with an incident happened in 1974. Then, an MLA in the Uttar Pradesh Legislative Assembly expressed his resistance by tearing a page of Ramcharitmanas in protest against Manas-Chatushati. This incident created fury among the Brahmins. On this, Vermaji wrote that even in 1957, a legislator named Bhup Kishore had torn Ramcharitmanas in the house, but there was no noise at that time. On this, Vermaji wrote: 'The Uttar Pradesh of 1957, due to its attainment of independence on the basis of human-equality, was somewhat convinced of humanism. That is why the Brahminists were left stunned after tearing down the Ramcharitmanas. But now the country is rapidly moving towards Brahmanism. it is this It is evident from the evidence that Brahminical newspapers and people are making outrage after tearing the page of Ramcharitmanas in 1974, that is, now Brahmanism is at its climax. And now what's the point of anyone tearing the biggest book of Brahmanism? This is an insult to Brahmanism, and how can he tolerate this insult as a ruler?'

Vermaji has written second chapter in his own book 'Brahman-Mahima' keeping this incident in the center. A Supreme Court judgment was cited on behalf of the Brahmins that tearing a religious book is a punishable offence. In this context, Vermaji refuted the fact that Ramcharitmanas is a religious text. He said that a religious text is that which is written by the originator of the religion, or which contains a collection of teachings of the originator, such as the Tripitaka, which contains the words of Buddha, or such as the Qur'an, in which the Prophet of Allah was revealed to Muhammad. There are verses, or such as the Bible, in which the thoughts of Jesus Christ are stored. He questioned that on this basis, how can Ramcharitmanas be called a religious text? Was its founder Pandit Tulsidas the founder of any religion, or did he claim so? Then why Brahmins are considering Ramcharitmanas as a religious text?

Vermaji further made another thought provoking revelation, which is very relevant from the point of view of the Bahujans. They said - One thing makes this dispute clear that it is usually Brahmins who prove Ramcharitmanas as religious texts, literary texts, ideal texts etc., because Ramcharitmanas is a book of Brahminists. By reading this book, the superiority of the Brahmin settles on the thoughtless mind and the inferior people of undeveloped intellect become easily victims of Brahminical exploitation by taking it as such. Therefore, the Brahmin group of the country is ready to protect it because of using it like the upper castes to trap the non-varna fish.

In the third chapter, Varmaji has propounded the view that Rama and Ravana are imaginary characters. He told with reference to the letter written by the Dravida Kazhagam to the then Prime Minister Indira Gandhi in 1974 that the Dravida Kazhagam had requested the Prime Minister to stop the Ramlila which hurt the Dravidians in North India, because according to him Ravana was a Dravidian, whose burning was humiliating for them. He had also threatened in the letter that if Ramlila was not stopped, he would be forced to burn the effigies of Rama, Sita and Lakshmana in response. Indira ji took no notice of his letter, and as a result she 'burned huge 18 feet high effigies of Rama, Lakshmana and Sita by performing Ravana-lila on 25 December 1975.'

Varmaji has clarified with many pushkal evidences that Rama and Ravana are imaginary characters. He propounded his opinion, 'It seems, Valmiki Ramayana was created in opposition to Ashvaghosha's 'Buddhacharitam' written in relation to Mahamana Buddha. It is not found in the royal lineage tradition.' According to him, 'Rama being born in Treta and killing the humanist Ravana to establish Brahmanism is a mere fantasy.' Punishable only. Therefore, doing Ramlila is totally inappropriate. To harm the national unity for the fictional characters like Ram-Ravana would be called completely unreasonable. (mediavigil.com)

VERMAJI AS A FOLLOWER OF CONSTITUTION AND SECULARISM

Vermaji being a great supporter of the Indian Constitution and its secular nature, loved equality and secularism which are important parts of the basic structure of the Indian Constitution. He considered the Constitution of India and its values supreme. According to him, the Constitution of India is secular and it provides many fundamental rights to every citizen of the country. He was against the propagation of religious beliefs and traditions by the office bearers holding constitutional posts. According to him, the Constitution of India accepts the principle of human-human equality, and does not even conceive of inhuman differences like man-woman, Shudra-Brahmin, Mlechcha Hindu. He not only opposed the steps of the government for the promotion and propagation of religion but also raised some serious questions. How then did you patronize Pandit Tulsidas's celebration of the fourth century, which contrasts with the above inhuman distinction? Isn't this act a violation of the constitution? Doesn't this hurt the vast majority of the country?

VERMAJI'S THOUGHTS ON REVOLUTION: WHY AND HOW?

Vermaji was a great supporter of social change in India. He wanted to establish equality and social justice by destroying social inequality. He was a strong supporter of restoration of predetermined values of social life in the interest of human beings. Therefore, he believed in revolution to destroy the existing social, economic and political conditions and wanted to bring changes in favor of downtrodden and backward people. In other words, he believed in social change and social justice, which was possible only through revolution. But what is revolution? And how will she come? This is described by Varmaji in his most famous book 'Kranti Kyun and Kaise'. He has explained it very well in this book. He advocated revolution in every sphere of life. According to him, social, economic, cultural and political revolutions were simultaneously needed in India, without which complete social change was not possible and talking of social justice without social change was a waste of our energy. According to him, people use revolution indiscriminately, but they do not know the meaning of revolution. According to him, the parties which believe in Brahminical culture and caste system also raise slogans of 'Inquilab Zindabad' or 'Kranti Amar Rahe'. They ask, after all, what is the meaning of revolution? He himself answers: 'Revolution is the name of the restoration of the predetermined values of life in the interest of man. Then they have to be reevaluated in the background of Bahujan Hitaya and Bahujan Sukhay. This evaluation has been named revolution. He further explains in the language of the historian Tinvi: 'Hemant's suffering is related to the passivity of autumn and then the enthusiasm of spring'. His interpretation of revolution closely resembles that of the German philosopher Georg Wilhelm Friedrich Hegel's dialectic, thesis-antithesis-synthesis.

Hegel's dialectic applied to the true self versus the false self (or self) is an interesting example. The thesis-antithesis-synthesis cycle doesn't just take away the stress but takes us a little closer to heaven. Right and wrong do not mean good or bad. Rather, it is to support the right to improve human life.

Emphasizing on the need for **social revolution**, Vermaji told that what are the predetermined values of life? Varmaji explains: 'A person born in Brahminical values is born in a high or low caste and a person born of Muslims and Christians is born as a human being. So in this case social values have to be re-determined. Does a person rise or fall as soon as he is born? It is clear that Brahminical social values are unequal, in this the question of human judgment does not arise. So this social value of life is worth re-determining. Social values can be reestablished in such a way that human beings are equal. Similarly, social revolution lies in the rediscovery of all social values.

What are economic revolutions? It has been established that both poverty and rich are the gift of God, says Verma. Will have to think again on this. Are the poor and the rich really created by God? Vermaji says no, the reason for this is mismanagement and economic exploitation. According to him, 'The gap between poverty and wealth widens only when an individual has authority over the fields of production. In maintaining this occupation in the name of fate, the progress of the country is going towards sluggishness. This is the economic revolution.

For **cultural revolution,** Varmaji's emphasises on the destruction of Brahmanical culture that is root cause of discrimination on the basis of caste and varna. According to him, the development of humanistic culture is essential. He says that unless there is the rise of egalitarian earning culture and the destruction of unequal Brahminical culture based on rebirth and fatalism, cultural revolution is not possible. That is why he said that the Arjak culture is establishing the age of logic through the efforts of his Arjak Sangh. The earning youths have become aware of their exploitation, and have waged jihad to get rid of it. Scientific knowledge and democracy are opening their eyes and they are beginning to experience their immense power. He says that the speed with which scientific knowledge will increase, so will the Brahmanical culture be destroyed.

What is political revolution? Vermaji says that even in politics, predetermined values of life dominate. That's why 'Democracy has arrived, but in the absence of redistribution of predetermined monarchical values, democracy has withered, and an extensive oligarchic system of monarchy has permeated the administrative tradition of the whole country. Now all are dominated by governance and administration, and the development of democratic values is in jeopardy. In Vermaji's view both revolution and change are different. According to him, the revolution moves with the whole life, and it is mental, whereas the change is material and it does not take the whole life. He was of the opinion that revolution without change is futile and vain. This is the reason that even after changing the governments in the country, there is no revolution. He said that if the people adopted the path of revolution, it would change the whole map of the country and 'man too would become like a human being'. (mediavigil.com)

HE FAVOURED HUMANISM AND CRITICISED INDIRA GANDHI FOR PROMOTING BRAHMANISM

Ramswaroop Varma was a great humanist as well as a critic of Brahmanical nationalism. He has given serious discussion on nationalism and mainly on Hindu nationalism in his book titled 'Humanism Vs Brahmanism'. He has drawn attention to the fact that in India, the oppressed people, that is, the exploiting class, talk a lot about emotional unity and also raise slogans of being a nation, but do not tell how this unity has to be maintained. He asked: 'In a country where eight crore untouchables, four crore tribals, six crore Muslims and one crore Christians are forbidden to drink even water touched by their hands, if such brahminical system is not an obstacle in the way of unity in the country. , So what? People like Shankaracharya, a strong pillar of Brahmanism, are not ready to accept Shudras and Mlechchas as human beings. Then the question of eating food prepared by them does not arise. This is the policy of anti-national discrimination of Brahmanism, which will make unity impossible in India.

Vermaji had hit out hard on the attempts by the government and constitutional functionaries to promote Brahmanism. He favoured humanism and criticised the government for promoting Brahamanism. He was against the superstition and Brahmanical order. He had said that the rulers of India take the oath of the Indian Constitution in a democracy, but they uphold and nurture Brahmanism. According to Vermaji, the then Prime Minister Indira Gandhi completed the Veda-sthapana ceremony on 11 April 1974, the last day of the 11-day event organized by 'Guru Gangeshwar Chaturveda Sansthan' for the propagation of Vedas. Speaking on the occasion, he said that Vedas are the storehouse of knowledge and they teach tolerance and equality. Varmaji said in his rebuttal that mantras must have come in the Vedas to bring unity among brahmins, but in them such mantras are sufficient, in which the Aryans were given to the Dasyus; Prayers have been made for the destruction of Shudras. He said that Indira Gandhi's saying that Vedas are a storehouse of knowledge is beyond truth. The Vedas were composed by the Aryans as a prayer to please their gods, who are full of trivial things and those prayers are also performed.

He raised some serious questions on caste discrimination which he found an obstacle in the path of unity. He also criticised the attempts by some to make India a Hindu Rashtra. According to him those who walk by imagining a Hindu Rashtra, they deceive themselves. How can a Hindu be a community divided into about four thousand castes? He insisted that it is impossible for India to become a nation without the abolition of Brahmanism. He described the ideal formula of Brahmins as 'Sarve Bhavantu Sukhinah Sarve Santu Niramayah, Sarve Bhadrani Pashyantu Ma Kashid Dukh Bhagabhet' as plain rhetoric.

VERMAJI, A GREAT CHAMPION OF EQUALITY AND SOCIAL JUSTICE

ere, it is very clear that Varmaji was a great supporter and propagator of humanism and social justice. He wanted to remove the fog of mind of the people trapped in Brahmanism. Brahmanism and wanted to enable the people to see a clear path for humanism in all the four spheres of life social, economic, cultural and political. Varmaji was a great social reformer of the modern era and the brave warriors of equality and social justice like Mahatma Jyotiba Phule, E. Like V. Ramasamy Naykar alias Periyar and Babasaheb Dr. Ambedkar, he was completely aggressive on Brahmanism and superstition and raised his voice vigorously n favour of backward communties advocating for equality and social justice. Trully, he was a great champion of equality and social justice.

BOOKS BY RAMSWAROOP VERMA

i. *Manavwadi Prashnotri* (Humanist Question-Answers), Lucknow: Arjak Sangh, 1984.

v. *Kranti Kyon aur Kaise* (Revolution: Why and How?), Lucknow: Arjak Sangh, 1989.

v. *Manusmriti Rashtra ka Kalank* (Manusmriti a National Shame), Lucknow: Arjak Sangh, 1990.

v. *Niradar kaise mite?* (How to Remove Disrespect?) Lucknow: Arjak Sangh, 1993.

v. *Achuton ki Samasya aur Samadhan* (The Question of Untouchables and its Solution) Lucknow: Arjak Sangh, 1984.

REFERENCES

*https://www.google.com/searchq=ram+swaroop+verma+hd+image&rlz=1C1ONGR_enIN98
2IN982&sxsrf=ALiCzsZ1So6hUNFgO_biLyb2xgBXPh3Wyw:1666265116753&source=lnms
&tbm=isch&sa=X&ved=2ahUKEwidx4qj2e76AhV44TgGHZZyBoAQ_AUoAXoECAIQAw&biw=
1920&bih=860&dpr=1

1. Arjak Sangh Siddhanta Vaktavya - Vidhan - Karyakram (Principles, Statute and Programmes of Arjak Sangh), Patna: Arjak Sangh, ninth edition, 2001.
2. "Ramswaroop Verma: A committed Ambedkarite". Forward Press. Archived from the original on 17 March 2021. Retrieved 17 November 2020.
3. Ramendra and Kawaljeet, Rationalism, Humanism and Atheism in Twentieth Century Indian Thought (Patna: Buddhiwadi Foundation, 2015), pp.255-56.
4. "My memories of Ramswaroop Verma". Forward Press. Retrieved 6 December 2020.
5. Badri Narayan (2011). The Making of the Dalit Public in North India: Uttar Pradesh, 1950–Present. Oxford University Press. p. 89. ISBN978-0199088454. Retrieved 17 March 2021
6. Ramendra and Kawaljeet, Rationalism, Humanism and Atheism in Twentieth Century Indian Thought (Patna: Buddhiwadi Foundation, 2015).
7. mediavigil.com

Source: Ramswaroop Verma - Wikipedia
"रामचरतिमानस और राम के बारे में क्या थी महामना रामस्वरूप वर्मा की राय?". Forward Press. Archived from the original on 17 March 2021.

CHAPTER SIXTEEN

B.P. MANDAL

Source*

INTRODUCTION

Being a leader from backward community, B.P. Mandal was a great advocate of equality and social justice. He was an influential and renowned political leader too whom leaders of casteist mindset could not tolerate and even attacked him for becoming the Chief Minister being a Shudra. When B.P. Mandal was the Chief Minister of Bihar, due to an oil leakage in the Barouni refinery the river Ganga had caught fire. In the Bihar legislative assembly then, an oppressor-caste member Vivekanand Jha made a casteist remark, *"**If a Shudra becomes a chief minister, it is bound for the water to catch fire.**"* B.P Mandal had then riposted, *"The fire in Ganga has been caused due to an oil leakage, but the fire in your heart which has been caught due to a son from the Backward community becoming the Chief Minister; can be felt by all."*

Such was the casteist attitude of oppressor castes towards OBCs reaching leadership positions, and hitherto, it prejudicially persists to be so. Amidst circumstances so adverse, B P Mandal as an elected member of the Lok

Sabha and the Vidhan Sabha in multiple terms; as the Health Minister and then the Chief Minister of Bihar; and then as the Chairman of the Backward Classes Commission; took steps that not only harbingered inclusive representation in society; but also induced a contemporary fervor, self-respect, and assertion amongst OBCs. (https://feminisminindia.com/2021/08/25/remembering-b-p-mandal-the-imperative-voice-for-the-cause-of-obcs/)

EARLY LIFE, AND CASTEISM FACED AT SCHOOL

Born on 25th August 1918 in Varanasi, far away from his village Murho in Bihar, Bindeshwari Prasad Mandal had a life inundated with caste-based discrimination and a revolutionary zeal to not only overcome it; but to construct situations for others to resist it too. His father Rasbehari Mandal was a distinguished freedom fighter and was among the founding figures of the Indian National Congress and unfortunately passed away, just the next day after B P Mandal was born.

Born into a Shudra (OBC) family he was brought up by his mother Sitawati Devi and elder brother Kamleshwari Mandal; B P Mandal faced heinous caste-based discrimination during his higher secondary school where Shudra (OBC) students were given meals only after the oppressor caste students had completed eating. And in the classroom, OBC students could sit on the backbenches only after the so-called upper caste kids had occupied the front benches. At times, OBC students were forced to sit on the floor. Such a casteist system inside educational premises had been normalised ever since. However, for B P Mandal; the man replete with righteous self-worth and voice against violence; this was an unacceptable juncture. Owing to exploitatively extracted social privilege, the number of oppressor caste students in the school was much higher as compared to Bahujan students but B.P. Mandal protested against the administration and ultimately, the practice was ceased. It is to be noted here that Mandal and his Bahujan counterparts were facing casteism in school and they were facing casteist remarks during his tenure as Chief Minister while he was studying in school Even then, Mandal had to face casteist discrimination and even when he became the Chief Minister, he had to face casteist remarks. He was the Chief Minister of the state. That is, no economic advancement or leadership position could eradicate the casteism that they faced at every level. This shows the casteist mindset of caste hindus that they prefare caste as the only basis of merit. Other merits are meaninglss for them.

HIS POLITICAL JOUNEY

B.P. Mandal utilised his comprehensive experience, incisive intellect, and anti-dogmatic leadership skills to commence the uprooting of social ignominies of the caste-based system during his college years as well. At the young age of 23, he was chosen as a member of the Bhagalpur district board and then got appointed as an Honorary Magistrate. However, he resigned later when he faced issues while working for the marginalized. He then won a seat in the first Vidhan Sabha of Bihar.

With multiple terms at the Vidhan Sabha and the Lok Sabha, and the founding of his party named Shoshit Dal; B.P. Mandal had multitudinous achievements to his name. Yet, at every step when he was compelled to compromise, he took a staunch stand. He became the seventh chief minister of the State and it was during his tenure that equitable representation for OBCs was introduced in the cabinet. Though, he resigned within 47 days in opposition to the removal of an inquiry commission meant to investigate the charges on senior leaders and ministers; he went on to again win elections in 1968 and 1972. He then resigned again, protesting against corruption, and then won a seat at the Lok Sabha.

FIGHT AGAINST CASTE-ATROCITIES ON OBCs BY THE OPPRESSOR CASTES

Being a backward leader, B.P. Mandal always favoured social justice and fought against discrimination and atrocities against backwards. When Rajput landowners had attacked a Kurmi-caste (OBC) village in the Pama village in Bihar; and the police had committed atrocities against backward class citizens; B P Mandal had then put a plea during a session of the Bihar assembly for immediate government action against the police and compensation for the victims. However, he was agonizingly pressurized to remove his plea. Immediately, he left the treasury bench and joined the opposition bench to fight against this casteist abuse.

EFFORTS FOR UPLIFTMENT OF OBCs AFTER INDEPENDENCE

Before independence, the roots of backward reservation can be traced in the regime of Shahuji Maharaj who made some serious efforts to uplift backward people introducing reservation system in his princely state, Kolhapur. This can be seen in the chapter on Shahuji Chatrapati Maharaj in this book. In this chapter, we will discuss the efforts to remove backwardness of OBCs after independence. In this connection, in January 1953, the J.L. Nehru government had set up the <u>First Backward Class Commission</u> under thechairmanship of social reformer **Kaka Kalelkar.** The commission submitted its report in March 1955, listing 2,399 backward castes or communities, with 837 of them classified as 'most backwards'. However, the report was never implemented. (https://www.drishtiias.com/daily-updates/daily-news-editorials/30-years-of-mandal-commission)

SETTING UP THE MANDAL COMMISSION-ROAD MAP TO SOCIAL JUSTICE

According to Article 15, it is a constitutional obligation for the government to appoint a commission every 10 years to inquire into the conditions of backward classes in India for the purpose of prohibition of discrimination on grounds of religion, caste, sex or place of birth. And to fulfill the responsibility, the Central Government has so far constituted two Backward Classes Commissions. The first Backward Classes Commission was constituted in 1953 under Kaka Kalelkar. The second commission, on the other hand, seemed to be formed on a partisan basis, composed only of members from the backward castes. Four of its five members were from OBCs; The remaining one, Lr. Naik belonged to the Dalit community, and was the only member of the Scheduled Castes in the Commission.1 It is popularly known as the Mandal Commission, as its Chairman, Shri B.P. There were circles.

The Mandal Commission, or the Socially and Educationally Backward Classes Commission (SEBC), was constituted in <u>India</u> in 1979 by the Janata Party government under Prime Minister Morarji Desai with a mandate to "identify the socially or educationally backward classes" of India. Headed by <u>B.P. Mandal</u>, an Indian parliamentarian, it had to consider the question of reservations for people to redress <u>caste</u> discrimination, and used eleven social, economic, and educational indicators to determine backwardness. In 1980, based on its rationale that OBCs ("Other backward classes") identified on the basis of caste, economic and social indicators made up 52% of India's population, the Commission's report recommended that members of Other Backward Classes (OBC) be granted reservations to 27% of jobs under the Central government and public sector undertakings, thus making the total number of reservations for SC, ST and OBC to 49%.[2]

Though the report had been completed in 1983, the V.P. Singh government declared its intent to implement the report in August 1990, leading to widespread student protests.[3] As per the Constitution of India, Article 15 (4)states, " Nothing in this Article or in clause(2) of Article 29 shall prevent the State from making any provision for the advancement of any socially or educationally backward classes of citizens or for Scheduled Castes and Scheduled tribes". Hence Mandal Commission created a report using the data of 1931 census which was last caste wise census and extrapolating same with some sample studies. VP Singh is accused of using the Mandal Report which was ignored by the Janata government who had initiated it to further his political agenda and to appear as a political Messiah for the backward. Earlier to 1990 the so called backwards were wary of being called backward because in the common language it means a person belonging to inferior caste and are uneducated, uncultured. However, when they found economic gains in being classified as backward the entire outlook changed and they started calling it social revolution and affirmative action. All of a sudden almost 75% of Indian population got preferential treatment in educational admissions and Government employment. Earlier 25% population of India which is SC ST was covered and now more than 50 % of so called Other Backward Class came under reservation. It resulted in huge outrage in the balance population especially students who were depending on Government service in future.[4] The youth went for massive protest in large numbers in the nation's campuses, resulting in many self-immolations by students.[5]

MANDAL COMMISSION'S CRITERIA FOR RESERVATION POLICY TO OBCs

The Mandal Commission adopted various methods and techniques to collect the necessary data and evidence. In order to identify who qualified as an "other backward class," the commission adopted eleven criteria which could be grouped under three major headings: social, educational and economic. 11 criteria were developed to identify OBCs.[6]

<u>Social</u>

1. Castes/classes considered as socially backward by others,
2. Castes/classes which mainly depend on manual labour for their livelihood,
3. Castes/classes where at least 25 per cent females and 10 per cent males above the state average get married at an age below the 17 years in rural areas and at least 10 per cent females and 5 per cent males do so in urban areas.
4. Castes/classes where participation of females in work is at least 25 per cent above the state average.[7]

Educational

1. Castes/classes where the number of children in the age group of 5–15 years who never attended school is at least 25 per cent above the state average.
2. Castes/classes when the rate of student drop-out in the age group of 5–15 years is at least 25 per cent above the state average,
3. Castes/classes amongst whom the proportion of matriculates is at least 25 per cent below the state average,[8]

Economic

1. Castes/classes where the average value of family assets is at least 25 per cent below the state average,
2. Castes/classes where the number of families living in kuccha houses is at least 25 per cent above the state average,
3. Castes/classes where the source of drinking water is beyond half a kilometer for more than 50 per cent of the households,
4. Castes/classes where the number of households having taken consumption loans is at least 25 per cent above the state average.[9]

OBSERVATIONS AND FINDINGS

The commission estimated that 52% of the total population of India (excluding SCs and STs), belonging to 3,743 different castes and communities, were 'backward'.[10] The number of backward castes in Central list of OBCs has now increased to 5,013 (without the figures for most of the Union Territories) in 2006 as per National Commission for Backward Classes.[11] The commission used 1931 census data to calculate the number of OBCs. The population of Hindu OBCs was derived by subtracting from the total population of Hindus, the population of SC and ST and that of forward Hindu castes and communities, and it worked out to be 52 per cent.[12] Assuming that roughly the proportion of OBCs amongst non-Hindus was of the same order as amongst the Hindus, the population of non-Hindu OBCs was considered as 52 per cent.[13]

*   Assuming that a child from an advanced class family and that of a backward class family had the same intelligence at the time of their birth, then owing to vast differences in social, cultural and environmental factors, the former will beat the latter by lengths in any competitive field. Even if an advanced class child's intelligence quotient was much lower compared to the child of backward class, chances are that the former will still beat the latter in any competition where selection is made on the basis of 'merit'.
*   In fact, what we call 'merit' in an elitist society is an amalgam of native endowments and environmental privileges. A child from an advanced class family and that of a backward class family are not 'equals' in any fair sense of the term and it will be unfair to judge them by the same yard-stick. The conscience of a civilised society and the dictates of social justice demand that 'merit' and 'equality' are not turned into a fetish and the element of privilege is duly recognised and discounted for when 'unequal' are made to run the same race.[14]

- To place the amalgams of open caste conflicts in proper historical context, the study done by Tata institute of Social Sciences Bombay observes. "The British rulers produced many structural disturbances in the Hindu caste structure, and these were contradictory in nature and impact .... Thus, the various impacts of the British rule on the Hindu caste system, viz., near monopolisation of jobs, education and professions by the literati castes, the Western concepts of equality and justice undermining the Hindu hierarchical dispensation, the phenomenon of Sanskritization, genteel reform movement from above and militant reform movements from below, emergence of the caste associations with a new role set the stage for the caste conflicts in modern India. Two more ingredients which were very weak in the British period, viz., politicisation of the masses and universal adult franchise, became powerful moving forces after the Independence.[15]

The introduction to the Recommendations section in the report presents the following argument:

As the Commission had concluded that 52 per cent of the country's population consisted of OBCs, it initially argued that the percentage of reservations in public services for backward classes should also match that figure. However, as this would have gone against the earlier judgement of the Supreme Court of India which had laid down that reservation of posts must be below 50 per cent, the proposed reservation for OBCs had to be fixed at a figure, which when added to 22.5 per cent for SCs and STs, remains below the cap of 50 per cent. In view of this legal constraint the Commission was obliged to recommend a reservation of 27 per cent only for backward castes.[16] The overlap between caste and economic backwardness became even more tenuous as a result being that it extended to include the OBC.[17]

MANDAL COMMISSION REPORT — THE SYNONYM TO SOCIAL JUSTICE

Chapter IV (Social Backwardness and Caste) of the first part of the Mandal Commission's Report states, *"If religion was ever used as the opium of the masses, it was done in India, where a small priestly class, by a subtle process of conditioning the thinking of the vast majority of the people, hypnotized them for ages into accepting a role of servility with humility. As laborers, cultivators, craftsmen, etc., Shudras were the main producers of social surplus. Their social labor was the life-blood of India's great civilization. Yet socially they were treated as out-castes; they had no right in private property, they carried the main burden of taxes and the heaviest punishments were awarded to them for minor infringements of the social code. As their low-caste status was tied to their birth, they toiled and suffered without any hope."*

And the Mandal Commission, headed by B.P. Mandal, became the ground to change this devastating status quo. Today, the name 'Mandal' has acquired symbolic prominence as the poecilonym of social justice and self-representation for OBCs.[18]

IMPLEMENTATION OF RECOMMENDATIONS OF MANDAL COMMISSION

Prior to the establishment of the Mandal Commission in India, the state of India faced caste discrimination in terms of social, economic, and political context. Living standards, scheduled castes, scheduled tribes, and OBC households were viewed to be significantly lower than in the mainstream population, comprising Hindu forward castes and other religious groups.[19] In December 1980, the Mandal Commission submitted its Report which described the criteria it used to indicate backwardness, and stated its recommendations in light of its observations and findings. By then, the Janata government had fallen. The following Congress governments under Indira Gandhi and Rajiv Gandhi were not willing to act on the Report due to its politically contentious nature. After being neglected for 10 years, the Report was accepted by the National Front government led by V.P. Singh. On 7 August 1990, the National Front government declared that it would provide 27 per cent reservations to "socially and educationally backward classes" for jobs in central services and public undertaking. Having released the Government Order on 13 August, V.P. Singh announced its legal implementation in his Independence Day speech two days later.[20]

That same year in September, a case was brought before the Supreme Court of India which challenged the constitutional validity of the Government Order for the implementation of the Mandal Report recommendations. Indira Sawhney, the petitioner in this case, made three principal arguments against the Order:[21]

- The extension of reservation violated the Constitutional guarantee of equality of

  opportunity.

- Caste was not a reliable indicator of backwardness.
- The efficiency of public institutions was at risk.

The five-judge Bench of the Supreme Court issued a stay on the operation of the Government Order of 13 August till the final disposal of the case. On 16 November 1992, the Supreme Court, in its verdict, upheld the government order, being of the opinion that caste was an acceptable indicator of backwardness.[22] Thus, the recommendation of reservations for OBCs in central government services was finally implemented in 1992.[23]

However, as reported by the Times of India on 26 December 2015, only 12 per cent of the employees under central government ministries and statutory bodies are members of the Other Backward Classes. The data shows that out of 79,483 posts, employees from the OBCs occupied only 9,040 of them.[24]

SUPREME COURT'S MANDATE IN INDIRA SAWHNEY CASE (1992)

Indira Sawhney challenges the Mandal Commission and Government decision to implement it in the Supreme Court in front of a nine Judge bench. After hearing both sides the bench passed the Act with a provision that maximum reservation can be 50% of the educational seats or job vacancies and creamy layer of income will be applicable. Presently the creamy layer limit is Family income of INR Eight lakhs (Eight hundred thousand rupees) per year. It was implemented in 1992.[25] Even before the Mandal Commission some Indian states already had high reservations for economically poor people like Maharashtra.

PROTEST AND VOILENCE AGAINST RESEVATION TO OBCs

People having casteist and feudal mindset put hurdles in the path of implementation of the Mandal Commission Report since 1980 it was submitted to the government. They averted it for ten years from being implemented it. A decade after the commission gave its report, V.P. Singh, the Prime Minister at the time, tried to implement its recommendations in 1989.[26] The criticism was sharp and colleges across the country held massive protests against it. On 19 September 1990, Rajiv Goswami, a student of Deshbandhu College, Delhi, committed self-immolation in protest of the government's actions. His act made him the face of the Anti-Mandal agitation then. This further sparked a series of self-immolations by other upper-caste college students like him, whose own hopes of getting a government job were now at threat, and led to a formidable student movement against job reservations for Backward Castes in India.[27] Altogether, nearly 200 students committed self-immolations; of these, 62 students succumbed to their burns.[28] The first student protester who died due to self-immolation was Surinder Singh Chauhan on 24 September 1990.[29] Across northern India, normal business was suspended. Shops were kept closed, and schools and colleges were shut down by student agitators. They attacked government buildings, organised rallies and demonstrations and clashed with the police. Incidents of police firing was reported in six states during agitation, claiming more than 50 lives.[30]

HUGE AGITATION AGAINST OBC RESERVATION IN NORTH INDIA

However, according to Ramchandra Guha, the agitation did not gain as much traction in southern India as it did in the North due to certain reasons. Firstly, people in the South were more agreeable to the implementation of the Mandal report recommendations as affirmative action programmes had long been in existence there. Furthermore, while in the South the upper castes constituted less than 10 per cent of the population, the figure in the North was in excess of 20 per cent. Lastly, as the region had a thriving industrial sector, the educated youth in the South were not as dependent on government employment as those in the North.[31] Another remarkable reason behind severe agitation against reservation to OBCs was the existence of potential caste consideration in north Indian than south. In north, there was strong agitation mainly in Haryana.

In brief, B.P. Mandal was a great promoter of equality and social justice. He was an influential and renowned political leader but leaders of casteist mindset could not tolerate him and even attacked him for becoming the Chief Minister being a *Shudra*, a person from OBC community. When during B.P. Mandal's Chief Ministership, the river

Ganga had caught fire due to an oil leakage in the Barouni refinery. Following this incidence, then, an oppressor-caste member Vivekanand Jha made a casteist remark in the Bihar legislative assembly. Such was the casteist attitude of oppressor castes towards OBCs reaching leadership positions. Amidst circumstances so adverse B. P. Mandal as the Chairman of the Backward Classes Commission took steps that not only harbingered inclusive representation in society; but also induced a contemporary fervor, self-respect, and assertion amongst OBCs. This contribution of B.P. Mandal makes him stand in the line of warriors of social justice.

<u>REFERENCES</u>

*https://www.google.com/search=BP+MANDAL&rlz=1C1ONGR_enIN982IN982&sxsrf=ALiCzsY VCD4hlj2YvZNd2KLajUuCiyRudg:1665885018204&source=lnms&tbm=isch&sa=X&ved=2ahUKE wjep_yl0eP6AhWP8DgGHTz6Ao0Q_AUoAXoECAEQAw&biw=1920&bih=860&dpr=1#imgrc=iaW MdOViMCTRlM

1. Maheshwari, Shriram (1991). The Mandal Commission and Mandalisation: A Critique. Concept Publishingk Company. pp. 18–26. <u>ISBN9788170223382</u>.

2. Gehlot, N. S. (1998). Current Trends in Indian Politics. Deep & Deep Publications. pp. 264–265. <u>ISBN9788171007981</u>.

3. "Sunday Story: Mandal Commission report, 25 years later". The Indian Express. Retrieved 18 January 2019.

4. Mandal commission - original reports (parts 1 and 2) - report of the backward classes commission. New Delhi: National Commission for Backward Classes, Government of India. 1 November 1980. Retrieved 26 March 2019.

5. "Mandal commission, 25 years later". The Indian Express. Retrieved 26 March 2019.

6. "Redesigning reservations: Why removing caste-based quotas is not the answer".

7. "Mandal Commission" (PDF). simplydecoded.com.

8. Agrawal, S. P.; Aggarwal, J. C. (1991). Educational and Social Uplift of Backward Classes: At what Cost and How? : Mandal Commission and After. Concept Publishing Company. pp. 59–60. <u>ISBN9788170223399</u>.

9. Agrawal, S. P.; Aggarwal, J. C. (1991). Educational and Social Uplift of Backward Classes: At what Cost and How? : Mandal Commission and After. Concept Publishing Company. pp. 59–60. <u>ISBN9788170223399</u>.

10. Bhattacharya, Amit. "Who are the OBCs?". Archived from the original on 27 June 2006. Retrieved 19 April 2006. Times of India, 8 April 2006.

11. "The Muslim OBCs And Affirmative Action-SACHAR COMMITTEE REPORT".

12. Ramaiah, A (6 June 1992). "Identifying Other Backward Classes" (PDF). Economic and Political Weekly: 1203–1207. Archived from the original (PDF) on 30 December 2005. Retrieved 27 May 2006.

13. "Mandal commission report - salient features and summary" (PDF). simplydecoded.com. Retrieved 7 February 2018.

14. Mandal Commission report, Vol I, pp 23

15. Mandal Commission report, Vol I, pp 31

16. Mandal Commission Report, Vol. 1, Recommendations. pp. 57–60.

17. Borooah, Vani Kant, author. (18 June 2019). Disparity and discrimination in labour market outcomes in India: a quantitative analysis of inequalities. <u>ISBN</u> 978-3-030-16263-4. <u>OCLC1108737729</u>. {{<u>cite book</u>}}: |last= has generic name (<u>help</u>)

18.<u>https://feminisminindia.com/2021/08/25/remembering-b-p-mandal-the-imperative-voice-for-the-cause-of-obcs/</u>)

20. Parchure, Rajas (1 December 2011). "Foreword". Artha Vijnana: Journal of the Gokhale Institute of Politics and Economics. 53 (4). doi:10.21648/arthavij/2011/v53/i4/117540. <u>ISSN0971-586X</u>.

21. "How VP Singh Stirred a Hornet's Nest With the Mandal Commission". The Quint. Retrieved 4 November 2017.

22. Guha, Ramchandra (2017). India After Gandhi: 10th Anniversary Edition. New Delhi: Picador India. pp. 602–604. <u>ISBN9789382616979</u>.

23."Case analysis of Indira Sawhney v. UOI". Legal Bites - Law And Beyond. 15 September 2016.

24. "20 years after Mandal, less than 12% OBCs in central govt jobs - Times of India". The Times of India.

25. Mandal Commission - Wikipedia

19. "Sunday Story: Mandal Commission report, 25 years later". The India Express. 1 September 2015.

26. "Mandal vs Mandir".

27. "The Telegraph - Calcutta : Frontpage". www.telegraphindia.com. Retrieved 30 October 2017.

28. Guha, Ramchandra (2017). India After Gandhi: 10th Anniversary Edition. New Delhi: Picador India. pp. 602–604. ISBN9789382616979

29. Kumar, Anu (29 September 2012). "Mandal memories". The Hindu. ISSN0971-751X.

30. Guha, Ramchandra (2017). India After Gandhi: 10th Anniversary Edition. New Delhi: Picador India. pp. 602–604. ISBN9789382616979.

31. Guha, Ramchandra (2017). India After Gandhi: 10th Anniversary Edition. New Delhi: Picador India. pp. 602–604. ISBN9789382616979

LALAI SINGH YADAV

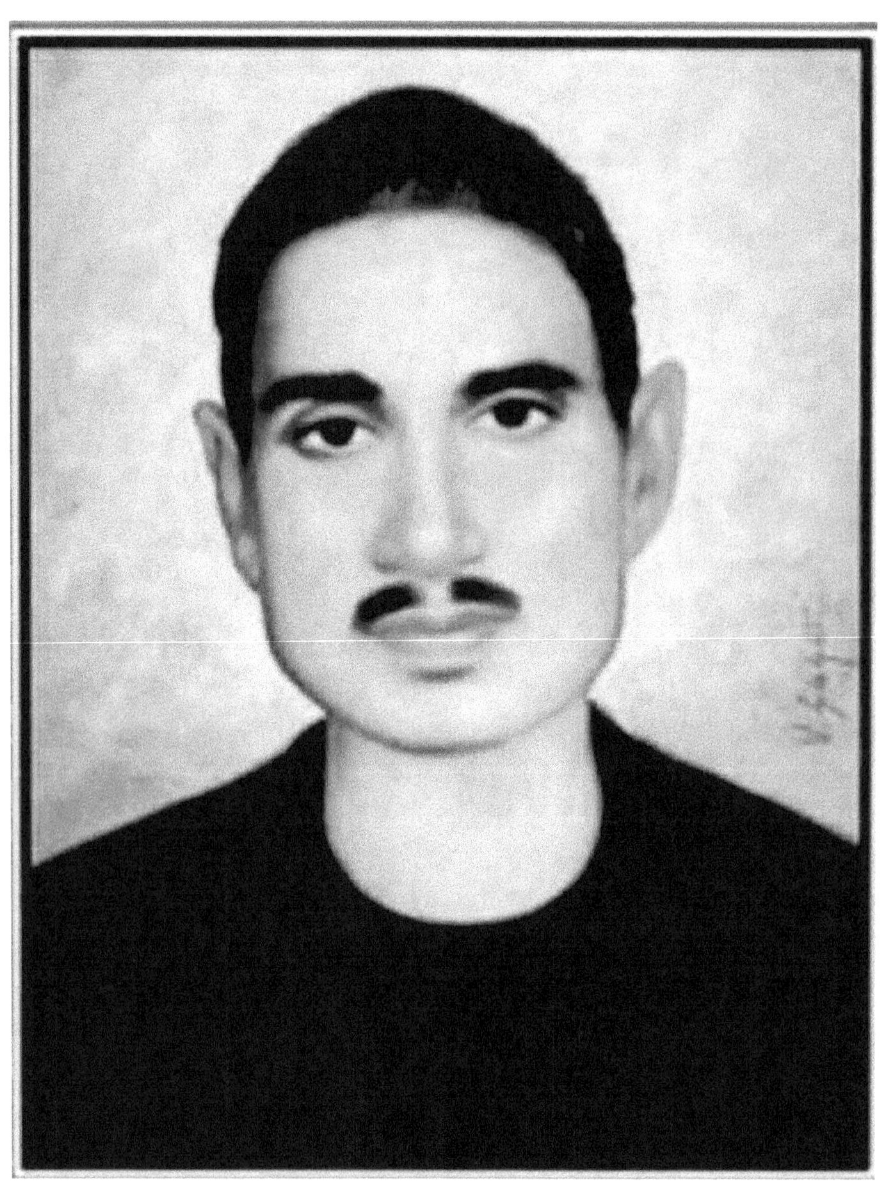

Source*

LIFE AND EDUCATION

Lalai Singh Yadav one of the revolutionary against caste inequality and a champion of social justice was born on 1 September, 1921 at Kathara, Kanpur Dehat district, Uttar Pradesh, later he had been called Periyar of North India who later became a social justice activist and play writer. He wrote plays like *Shambhuk Vadh*. He translated Periyar E. V. Ramasamy's *The Key To Understanding True Ramayan* from Tamil to Hindi as *Sachi Ramayan Ki Chabi*.[1] In 1962, he wrote a book entitled *Baman Vadi Rajya Mein Shoshito Par Rajnaitik Dakaiti*.[2] He fought a free speech case against the UP Government on his book ban.[3] He died on 7 February 1993. Apart from translating True Ramayana, he wrote 5 plays as well, including one on Aṅgulimāla, Shambuka, and Ekalavya.[4] Chaudhary Lalai Singh Yadav (01 September 1911 – 7 February 1993) was a social activist who fought for social justice and wrote many books for his goal of social justice, which were highly controversial.

Lalai was born on September 1, 1911 in a simple farming family in Kathara village of Kanpur Dehat district of Uttar Pradesh. Father Ch. Gujju Singh Yadav was a hardworking Arya Samaji. His mother Mrs. Mooladevi, popular leader of that area, Ch. Sadho Singh Yadav resident of Gr. Makar was a Sadhvi daughter of Dadur Railway Station Rura, District Kanpur. His uncle Ch. Narayan Singh Yadav was a religious and social worker farmer. Despite being religious in the past, this family was not one to run after superstitious stereotypes.

Lalai Singh passed middle class in 1928 by taking Urdu along with Hindi. He was a forest guard from 1929 to 1931. In 1931, he was married to Mrs. Dulari Devi, daughter Ch. Sardar Singh Yadav Mr. Jaraila is near railway station with Rura district Kanpur. In 1933, the Armed Police Company was recruited to the post of constable in District Morena (MP). Saved time from job and got various educations.

LALAI SINGH YADAV'S REVOLT AS A SOLDIER AND HIS REVOLUTIONARY THOUGHTS

Lalai Singh was a soldier and he had concern for other soldiers too. He wanted unexploitive and better conditions for them. In 1946 AD, the Non-Gazetted Employees Police and Army Association was established in Gwalior and elected its president. He wrote the book "Sipahi Ki Tabahi" in Hindi on the 'Soldier of the War' method, which led the employees on the path of revolution. Like the Azad Hind Fauj, he organized a public and government employee for the independence of Gwalior state and organized a strike in the police and army and he insisted upon the need of Roti, Kapra aur Makan (bread, clothing and house). He emphasised upon the hyppocratic life of the casteist people. He awaired the soldiers about the realities of life and gave messages to become strong not only physically but also mentally through the following lines that

BALIDAAN NA SINH KA HOTE SUNA,

BAKARE BALI BEDEE PAR LAE GAE.

(The sacrifice was not heard of the lion; the goats were brought to the sacrification.)

Through these lines, he wanted to give a message that the innocent and vulnerable people are always suppressed and tortured. The powerful and mighty ones do not face difficulty and sufferings.

VISHADHAAREE KO DOODH PILAAYA GAYA,

KENCHUE KATIYA MEIN PHANSAE GAE.

(The venomous was fed milk, earthworms were trapped in the shed.)

NA KAATE TEDHE PAADAP GAE,

SEEDHON PAR AARE CHALAE GAE.

(Crooked plants were not cut; saws were driven on straight lines.)

BALAVAAN KA BAAL NA BAANKA BHAYA

BALAHEEN SADA TADAPAE GAE.

(The hair of the strong should not be banked, but the weak were always tormented.)

Here, he wanted to teach the people from poor and backward families that people belonging to poor and weaker sections always face humiliation and subjugation. The powerful one is not hurted anyway. In this way, he awaked his fellows about suppression and prepared them to fight against exploitation, slavery and subjugation.

LIVED A LIFE OF A PRISONER

On 29.03.47 AD, in connection with the freedom struggle of Gwalior States, under Section 131 of the Indian Penal Code (Military Rebellion), he became a prisoner along with his companions. On 06.11.1947 A.D. Special Criminal

Sessions Judge Gwalior gave the maximum punishment of 5 years' rigorous imprisonment and fine of five rupees for being the President High Commander Gwalior National Army. On 12.01.1948 AD along with civil companions were freed from bondage.

ASSUAULT ON OPPRESSION OF BACKWARDS AND EMPHASISED ON UNITY OF SHUDRAS (BACKWARDS)

Lalai Singh was strongly opposed to the exploitation and oppression of the weaker and backward castes by the upper castes. He had a deep love for studies, so he was engaged in self-study. One after the other he also read Shruti, Smriti, Purana and various Ramayanas. He was stunned by the gross superstition, betrayal and hypocrisy prevalent in the Hindu scriptures. He became distressed from place to place by the conspiracy of Brahmin pride and the mental slavery of the exploited backward oppressed society. In such a situation, he also made up his mind to leave this religion. Now he had come to the conclusion that the two classes of Shudras were created by the contractors of the society with a well thought out trick and conspiracy. One untouchable-Shudra, the other untouchable-Shudra, but a Shudra is a Shudra, whether he is an untouchable or an untouchable. Lalai Singh believed that no matter how rich or educated you are, you are a Shudra in the eyes of Manuvadis. And you cannot get the respect and glory that a Brahmin or a Kshatriya gets. He strongly opposed this discriminatory system. By writing many books, he made a scathing attack on superstition, hypocrisy, exploitation, discrimination and injustice.

VARNA SYSTEM AND HINDU RELIGIOUS BOOKS CAUSE THE ORIGIN OF INEQUALITY

Known as the Periyar of North India Lalai Singh Yadav held Varna system and Hindu religious texts responsible for origin of discrimination and inequality. He was of the opinion that the origin of social inequality is nourished by the Varna system, the caste system, the Shruti, the Smriti and the Puranas. The destruction of social inequality is not contained in social reform but in isolation from this system. By now it had become clear to them that the most powerful medium of dissemination of ideas is short literature. He took this work in his own hands. In 1925, his mother, wife in 1939, daughter Shakuntala (11 years) in 1946 and father Shri Char Mahabhutas died in 1953. He was the only son of his father. He could do second marry after the death of his wife. But being a revolutionary ideology, he did not marry again and said that the next marriage would be a hindrance in the freedom struggle. Whole life he remained a committed revolutionary and critic of discrimination, inequality and injustice. He always echoed his voice for equality and social justice.

WON A LEGAL FIGHT AGAINST BAN ON HIS BOOK *SACHCHI RAMAYAN*

He also got special attention towards the publication of literature. The great revolutionary of South India, Periyar E.V. Ramasami Naicker had several tours in North India at that time. He came in contact with them. When Periyar came in contact with Ramasami Naicker, he showed a special interest in "Ramayana: A True Reading" (in English) written by him. Along with this, there was also a special discussion on the promotion of this book, bringing it to the whole of India, especially in North India. Periyar Ramasami Naicker gave permission for publication of this book in Hindi in North India to Lalai Singh on 01-07-1968.

The publication of this book *Sachchi Ramayana* in Hindi on 01-07-1969 created a panic in the entire North East and West India. Only a year had passed since the publication of the book that the U.P. The order of seizure of the book by the government on 08-12-69 was circulated that this book has been written with the intention of deliberately hurting the religious sentiments of some civilian community of India and insulting their religion and religious beliefs. Against the above order, the publisher Lalai Singh submitted the Criminal Miscellaneous Application in the High Court of Judicature Allahabad on 28-02-70. A special full bench of honorable three judges was formed to hear this case. Free Advocate Shri Banwari Lal Yadav on behalf of the Appellant (Lalai Singh) and Government Advocate on behalf of the Government and his colleague Shri P.C. The arguments of Chaturvedi Advocate and Shri Asif Ansari Advocate were heard for three consecutive days on 26, 27 and 28 October 1970. On 19-01-71, Hon'ble Justice Shri A. Of. Kirti, Justice K. N. Srivastava and Justice Hari Swarup gave the majority decision that -

1. Government of U.P. The order for the seizure of the book 'Sachchi Ramayana' was canceled

2. The confiscated books 'Sachchi Ramayana' should be returned to Appellant Lalai Singh.

3. Government of U.P. on behalf of the appellant Lalai Singh should be given an expenditure of three hundred rupees.

The episode of 'Sachchi Ramayana' published by Lalai Singh Yadav was still going on that Uttar Pradesh. By a special order dated 10 March 1970 by the government, a book titled 'Religion for Honor' in which Dr. Ambedkar had some speeches and a book titled 'Jati Bhed Ka Uchheed' was confiscated by the government of Chaudhary Charan Singh on 12 September 1970. For this also Lalai Singh advocated the case with the help of Mr. Banwari Lal Yadav Advocate. With the victory of the trial, on 14 May 1971, Uttar Pradesh. The confiscation proceedings of these books of the government were canceled and only then the above books could be made accessible to the public. Similarly, in 1973, a case was filed against the book 'Aryo Ka Naitik Pol Prakash' written by Lalai Singh. This trial continued for the rest of his life.[5]

LALAI SINGH YADAV'S CONTRIBUTION DURING FREEDOM MOVEMENT

When Indians formed Gadar Party in America under the leadership of Lala Hardayal, a book called *Soldier of the War* was written to exhort the jawans of Indian army to join the freedom movement. Along the same lines, in 1946, Lalai Singh wrote a book titled *Sipahi Ki Tabahi*. It was not printed but was typed out and distributed among the constables. As soon as the inspector general came to know of it, he ordered its seizure. *Sipahi Ki Tabahi* was written in a conversational style. Had it been published today, it would have been on a par with books like *Kisan Ka Koda* and *Achchooton Ki Kaifiyat* written by Mahatma Phule. Jagannath Aditya has quoted some portions of *Sipahi Ki Tabahi* in which the constable and his wife talk about the miseries of their domestic life. It ends thus: "The fact is that the paradise and hell are imaginations of the priests, pundits and maulvis. But if you want to see a real hell, just visit the home of a constable. The reason this hell exists is the Scindia government's mismanagement. This hell has to be ended; it has to be reversed under any circumstances. All your demands will be accepted when the people will rule over the people." A year later, Lalai Singh led a strike of the Gwalior police and army. He was arrested on 29 March 1947 and was sentenced after trial to five years' rigorous imprisonment. He had to spent nine months in jail. Following Independence and the merger of the Gwalior state with the Indian union, he was released on 12 January 1948.

AS AN EFFECTIVE WRITER AGAINST SOCIAL INJUSTICE

After retirement from government service in 1950, he shifted base to his ancestral village Jhinjhak and stayed there till his death. He started working for societal change and used literature as his tool. He founded a publication named Ashok Pustakalaya and established a printing press called Sasta Press. He was a great playwright, as is evident from his play *Sipahi Ki Tabahi*. He began his writing career with a play. He wrote five plays: *Angulimal Natak, Shambuk Vadh, Sant Maya Balidan, Eklavya* and *Nag Yagya Natak*.

Swami Achhootanand had written *Sant Maya Balidan* in 1926 but had become unavailable. By writing the play, Lalai Singh fulfilled an important need. He also wrote three books in prose: *Shoshiton Par Dharmik Dakaiti, Shoshiton Par Rajnitik Dakaiti* and *Samajik Vishamta Kaise Samampta Ho*. His was a literature parallel to the traditional Hindi literature. The literature of an ideological revolution changed the views of Dalit classes on Hindu heroes and Hindu culture. It was a new discourse that was until then missing from Hindi literature. Lalai Singh's writings created a rebel consciousness among the Bahujans against Brahmanism and sowed the seeds of Shraman culture and ideology in their hearts and minds.[6]

INFLUENCE OF PERIYAR E.V. RAMASAMY ON LALAI SINGH YADAV

In 1967, E.V. Ramasami Naicker came to Lucknow to attend a convention on minorities. At the ti7e, he was the revolutionary leader of the Bahujans of the entire country. Lalai Singh was very impressed with him. He met him and sought his permission to translate his book *The Ramayana: A True Reading* into Hindi. But Chandrika Prasad "Jigyasu" had already got the permission from him to translate this and three other books. So, Periyar advised him to wait for some time. Jigyasu had already had Periyar's three books, *A Pen Portrait* (a brief autobiographical account), *Philosophy* and *Social Reform and Revolution* (written by A.M. Dharmalingam in English) translated by Dayaram Jain and published in a single volume titled *Periyar E.V. Ramasami Naicker* in 1970 under the *Bahujan Kalyan Mala* series. But he could not get *The Ramayana: A True Reading* translated. On 1 July 1968, Periyar wrote a letter to Lalai Singh permitting him to have the book translated and published. He wrote, "The person who was given the permission earlier could not get it published, hence the permission is given to you."

Lalai Singh had the book translated into Hindi and published under the title *Sachchi Ramayan* in 1968. The book kicked up such a row that soon the flag-bearers of Hinduism took to the streets to oppose it. The then Uttar Pradesh Government came under pressure and on 8 December 1969 banned the book and ordered seizure of its copies claiming that the book had hurt religious sentiments. The matter went before the high court, where Advocate Banwari Lal Yadav forcefully argued in favour of *Sachchi Ramayan*. On 19 January 1971, Justice A. Kirti quashed the government's ban order, directed it to return all the seized copies and pay the appellant (Lalai Singh) Rs 300.

LALAI SINGH YADAV – PERIYAR OF NORTH INDIA

Due ot his staunch critic of Brahmanical Hindu religion and strong opposition of social injustice, Lalai Singh was regarded as Periyar of North India. Getting influenced of Peryar and his Book, *The Ramayana: A True Reading*, Lalai Singh had translated the book into Hindi and published under the title *Sachchi Ramayan* in 1968. However, in his original book, E.V. Ramasamy had not given references to prove his contentions. To make up for that deficiency, Lalai Singh wrote a book *Sachchi Ramayan Ki Chabi*, in which he mentioned the references and evidence necessary to understand *Sachchi Ramayan*. Writing about how Lalai Singh became Periyar Lalai Singh, Jagannath Aditya says that Lalai Singh was invited to speak at a condolence meeting on 24 December 1973 after the death of Periyar. Aditya does not mention the venue of the meeting. The south Indian audience at the meeting was so impressed by Lalai Singh's speech that they declared him the next Periyar in the meeting itself. Subsequently, he became famous as the Periyar of the Hindi belt.[7]

ADOPTION OF BUDDHISM AND FREEDOM FROM CASTE

Lalai Yadav was very happy with Babasaheb Dr. Ambedkar's announcement of adopting Buddhism on October 14, 1956. He was inclined towards Buddhism and wanted to embrace Buddhism. He wanted to go to the Buddhist initiation ceremony organized by Dr. Ambedkar but could not go to the initiation ground on 14 October due to asphyxia and vomiting of blood.

But on July 21, 1967, he went to Kushinagar and took initiation in Buddhism at the hands of Mahasthavir Om Chandramani. After receiving initiation Lalai Singh Yadav made a public declaration that 'From today I am a human being, a humanist, from today I am only Lalai. Now I am completely free from caste values and beliefs like Kunwar, Chaudhary, Singh, Yadav, Ahir etc. Now I will not use any caste or feudal terminology with my name'. [8]

To sum up, Lalai Singh Yadav also known as Periyar of North India was a true champion of social justice. He began his journey of social justice as a soldier. Being a soldier, he awakened his fellow soldiers against discrimination and injustice. Writing plays like *Sipahi Ki Tabahi, Shamba Vadh,* Aṅgulimāla and *Ekalavya,* he attacked on discrimination and injustice being done to downtrodden and backwards from ancient period. He translated Periyar E. V. Ramasamy's *The Key To Understanding True Ramayan* from Tamil to Hindi as *Sachi Ramayan Ki Chabi* for which he fought a free speech case against the UP Government on his book ban. In 1962, he wrote a book entitled *Baman Vadi Rajya Mein Shoshito Par Rajnaitik Dakaiti*. He attacked superstition, inequality, discrimination and social injustice without any fear. His famous lines given below expose the discriminatory social, economic and political order about which he continued to awaken the poor, downtrodden and backwards:

Vishadhaaree Ko Doodh Pilaaya Gaya,

Kenchue Katiya Mein Phansae Gae.

Na Kaate Tedhe Paadap Gae,

Seedhon Par Aare Chalae Gae.

Balavaan Ka Baal Na Baanka Bhaya, Balaheen Sada Tadapae Gae.

REFERENCES

*https://www.google.com/searchq=LALAI+SINGH&rlz=1C1ONGR_enIN982IN982&sxsrf=ALi CzsaYzmU6nRbo0nyMfQFYUKNVJQkpw:1665885433171&source=lnms&tbm=isch&sa=X&ved= 2ahUKEwib7-vr0uP6AhU79DgGHU6wBIwQ_AUoAnoECAIQBA&biw=1920&bih=860&dpr=1#imgrc =nyn-SNinsBUI0M

1."Lalai Singh Yadav: Fiery hero of rebel consciousness". Forward Press. 24 September 2016. Retrieved 20 May 2018.

2. Yadav, Lalai Singh (1962). Baman Vadi Rajya Mein Shoshito Par Rajnaitik Dakaiti. Ashok Pustakalaya

Jhinjhak.

3. Bhatia, Gautam (14 January 2016). Offend, Shock, or Disturb: Free Speech under the Indian Constitution. Oxford University Press. ISBN9780199089529.

4. परेयिार ललई सहि यादव को याद करते हुए http://velivada.com/2017/09/01/remembering-lalai-periyarsingh-yadav/

5. (https://hi.wikipedia.org/wiki/%E0%A4%B2%E0%A4%B2%E0%A4%88_%E0%A4%B8%E0%A4%BF%E0%A4%82%E0%A4%B9_%E0%A4%AF%E0%A4%BE%E0%A4%A6%E0%A4%B5)

6. Lalai Singh Yadav: Fiery hero of rebel consciousness | Forward Press

7. Lalai Singh Yadav: Fiery hero of rebel consciousness | Forward Press

8. https://velivada.com/2017/09/01/remembering-lalai-periyar-singh-yadav/

CHAPTER EIGHTEEN

V.P. SINGH

Source*

INTRODUCTION-EDUCATION AND POLITICAL CAREER

Vishwanath Pratap Singh, also known as V. P. Singh, was a prominent politician, successful administrator and good artist (painter). He became a serious contributor to the cause of social justice by taking many bold decisions. He without thinking about reaction of casteist people strengthened the cause of social justice enacting SC/ST (Prevention of Atrocities) Act in 1989 and implementing Mandal Commission Report in 1990. Singh's contribution shows that it is not necessary to be a downtrodden or backward to work for social justice. Person from Savarnas too can contribute. There have been many people belonging to unreserved categories who not only echoed voices for justice but also supported the ideology of social justice and Mr. Singh was one of them. Singh was born on 25 June 1931,[1] the third child of the Hindu Rajput Zamindar family[2] of Daiya, which is located on the banks of the Belan River in the Allahabad district. He was adopted by Raja Bahadur Ram Gopal Singh of Manda and became the heir-apparent. The Last Raj Bahadur of Manda, Ram Gopal Singh, adopted Vishwanath Pratap Singh, who became the 7th Prime Minister of India. He obtained his education from Colonel Brown Cambridge School, Dehradun and got his Bachelor of Arts and Law degree from Allahabad University. He was the elected the vice president of Allahabad University Students Union and later received a Bachelor of Science in Physics from Fergusson College in the Pune University.[3]

He travelled a long and successful political journey becoming MLA, MP, MINISTER and finally Prime Minister. He had been the 7th Prime Minister of India from 1989 to 1990 and the 41st Raja Bahadur of Manda. He is India's only prime minister to have been a former ruler. In 1969, he joined the Indian National Congress party and was elected as a member of the Uttar Pradesh Legislative Assembly. In 1971, he became a Member of Parliament in the Lok Sabha. He served as the Minister of Commerce from 1976 to 1977. In 1980, he became the Chief Minister of Uttar Pradesh and his government exrcuted the encounter of the gang of Phoolan Devi who had turned into a dacait after her brutal rape by the upper caste people. Phoolan Devi avenged her rape and atrocities committed with her by killing some of the Rajput community people.

In 1988, he formed the Janata Dal party by merging various factions of the Janata Party. In the 1989 elections, the National Front, with the support of the BJP, formed the government and Singh became the 7th Prime Minister of India. As far as social justice is concerned, he took some concrete steps in this regard. After 1996, Singh retired from political posts, but continued to remain a public figure and political critic. He was diagnosed with bone marrow cancer in 1998, and ceased public appearances until the cancer went into remission in 2003. Singh died after a very long struggle with multiple myeloma and kidney failure at Apollo Hospital in Delhi on 27 November 2008, aged 77.[4] He was cremated with full state honour at Allahabad on the banks of the River Ganges on 29 November 2008, his son Ajeya Singh lighting the funeral pyre.[5]

AS A LEADER OF JANATA DAL

V.P. Singh was known as the leader of Janata Dal but also he was a voice for social justice. Together with associates Arun Nehru and Arif Mohammad Khan, Singh floated an opposition party named Jan Morcha.[6] He was re-elected to Lok Sabha in a tightly contested by-election from Allahabad, defeating Sunil Shastri.[7] On 11 October 1988, the birthday of the original Janata coalition's leader Jayaprakash Narayan, Singh founded the Janata Dal by the merger of Jan Morcha, Janata Party, Lok Dal and Congress (S), in order to bring together all the centrist parties opposed to the Rajiv Gandhi government, and Singh was elected the President of the Janata Dal. An opposition coalition of the Janata Dal with regional parties including the Dravida Munnetra Kazhagam, Telugu Desam Party, and Asom Gana Parishad, came into being, called the National Front, with V. P. Singh as convener, NT Rama Rao as president, and P Upendra as a General Secretary.[8] The National Front fought 1989 General Elections after coming to an electoral understanding with Bharatiya Janata Party and the Left parties (the two main oppositions) that served to unify the anti-Congress vote. The National Front, with its allies, earned a simple majority in the Lok Sabha and decided to form a government. V.P. Singh was sworn in as India's Prime Minister on 2 December 1989.

ENACTMENT OF *SCHEDULED CASTE AND SCHEDULED TRIBE (PREVENTION OF ATROCITIES) ACT, 1989* – AN ATTACK ON CASTE DISCRIMINATION

V.P. Singh is also known for Sixty-second Amendment, through which the Parliament under his government enacted the Scheduled Caste and Scheduled Tribe (Prevention of Atrocities) Act (popularly known as SC/ST Act) in 1989. that was an immense legal step towards stoping the torture of SCs and STs. Undoubtedly, it was a great step of his government to secure the life and honour of the SC and ST communities. In the year 1989, VP Singh government implemented the SC-ST (Prevention of Atrocities) Act of 1989 to prevent the atrocities against the members of Scheduled Castes and Scheduled Tribes.[9] It was enacted when the provisions of the existing laws (such as the Protection of Civil Rights Act 1955 and Indian Penal Code) were found to be inadequate to check these crimes (defined as 'atrocities' in the Act).[10] Recognising the continuing gross indignities and offenses against Scheduled Castes and Tribes, the Parliament passed the 'Scheduled Castes and Schedule Tribes (Prevention of Atrocities) Act 1989.[11] The objectives of the Act clearly emphasised the intention of the government to deliver justice to these communities through proactive efforts to enable them to live in society with dignity and self-esteem and without fear or violence or suppression from the dominant castes. The practice of untouchability, in its overt and covert form was made a cognizable and non-compoundable offence, and strict punishment is provided for any such offence. The act was finally passed somehow with controversies.[12]

IMPLIMENTATION OF MANDAL COMMISSION REPORT-A HISTORICAL STEP TOWARDS SOCIAL JUSTICE

V.P. Singh government decided to implement the long awaited Mandal Commission report in 1990 and its implementation opened the path for the advancement and empowerment to the other backward castes (OBCs). However, the decision to implement the recommendations of the Mandal Commission was the result of political pressure mounted by Kanshi Ram and his party the BSP. Yet, it was a historical and daring step taken by V.P. Singh as the report was waiting for ten years. Singh himself wished to move forward nationally on social justice-related issues, which would, in addition, consolidated the caste coalition that supported the Janata Dal in northern India, and accordingly decided to implement the recommendations of the Mandal Commission which suggested that a fixed quota of all jobs in the public sector be reserved for members of the historically disadvantaged called Other Backward Classes.[13]The casteist forces and people having Manuist mindset could no digest this decision and it led to widespread protests among the upper caste youth in urban areas in northern India. However, OBC reservation was accepted for OBCs excluding creamy layer OBCs. OBC reservation (less creamy layer) was upheld by the Supreme Court in 2008.[14]

CASTIEST MINDSET VIOLENTLY PROTESTED OBC RESERVATION

People having casteist and feudal mindset put hurdles in the path of implementation of the Mandal Commission Report since 1980 it was submitted to the government. They averted it for ten years from being implemented it. A decade after the commission gave its report, when V.P. Singh tried to implement its recommendations in 1989, the casteist people protested with tooth and nail. The criticism was sharp and colleges across the country held massive protests against it. On 19 September 1990, Rajiv Goswami, a student of Deshbandhu College, Delhi, committed self-immolation in protest of the government's actions. His act made him the face of the Anti-Mandal agitation then. This further sparked a series of self-immolations by other upper-caste college students like him, whose own hopes of getting a government job were now at threat, and led to a formidable student movement against job reservations for Backward Castes in India. Altogether, nearly 200 students committed self-immolations; of these, 62 students succumbed to their burns. The first student protester who died due to self-immolation on 24 September 1990 was Surinder Singh Chauhan.[15]

RAM TEMPLE ISSUE AND SACRIFICATION OF HIS GOVERNMENT FOR SOCIAL JUSTICE AND SECULARISM

Implementation of Mandal Commission Report Ram brought a disaster to V.P. Singh government. His alliance partner, the Bharatiya Janata Party was moving its own agenda forward, which caught speed after V.P. Singh decided to implement the Mandal Commission Report. In particular, the Ram Janmabhoomi agitation, which served as a rallying cry for several Hindu organisations, took on a new life. The party president, L.K. Advani, toured the northern states on a bus converted Rath – with the intention of drumming up support.[16]V.P. Singh decided to attend the call of social justice and secularism rather than saving his government. He strongly opposed the agenda of BJP. Following his opposition to the Ram Rath Yatra, the BJP withdrew its support from the V.P. Singh led National Front government. VP Singh faced the vote of no confidence in the Lok Sabha saying that he occupied the high moral ground, as he stood for secularism, had saved the Babri Masjid at the cost of power and had upheld the fundamental principles which were challenged during the crises. "What kind of India do you want?" he asked of his opponents in Parliament, before losing the vote 142–346.[17] Singh resigned on 7 November 1990.His prime ministerial tenure could last for 343 days only. However, he lost power but he upheld the social justice and secular values of the constitution. Indeed, he sacrificed his government for the cause of social justice and secularism.

BHARAT RATNA AWARD TO BABASAHEB DR. AMNEDKAR

Another significant contribution of V.P. Singh and his government was confirmation of Bharat Ratna Award (the highest civilian award of India) to Babasaheb Dr. B.R. Ambedkar, the main architect of the Indian Constitution and the greatest champion of social justice. Getting influenced of Manyawar Kanshi Ram and BSP's demand of Bharat

Ratna Award to Babasaheb, V.P. Singh government awarded Bharat Ratna Award to Dr. Ambedkar posthumously on March 31, 1990. Really, it was a great step by V.P. Singh towards the cause of social justice as Congress party had not done it and Congress had completely ignored the contribution of Babasaheb and could not award Bharat Ratna to him during its governments. However, it had conferred Bharat Ratna to Jawahar Lal Nehru and Indira Gandhi even during their prime minister-ships. A portrait measuring 7'.3" by 4'.3" was also unveiled by Mr. V. P. Singh, Prime Minister of India on 12.04.1990 in the Central Hall, Parliament House. In this way, V.P. Singh ended the injustice to the greatest champion of social justice, as far as Bharat Ratna Award was concerned. No doubt to say that statues and portraits of Babasaheb Dr. Ambedkar are of vital significance as these works a source of inspiration and motivation to the people to fight against discrimination and echo voices for social justice.[18]

SUPPORT TO DR. K.R NARAYANAN FOR THE POST OF THE VICE PRESIDENT

His another remarkable and worthy task for social justice was his support to Dr. K.R Narayanan for the post of the Vice President of India. In 1992, Singh was the first to propose the name of the future President K.R. Narayanan as a (eventually successful) candidate for Vice President.[19] in other words, V.P. Singh played a significant role for the election of Dr. Narayanan as a first Dalit Vice President of the country. Later on, due to the mounting political pressure of BSP and increasing political consciousness among Dalits, Dr. Narayanan was elected as the President of India that was a historical event in India after independence.[20]

VOICE FOR SOCIAL JUSTICE AFTER PRIMINISTERSHIP

After assassination of Rajiv Gandhi (May 1991), V.P. Singh could not remain active in politics and he later retired from active politics. He spent the next few years touring the country speaking about matters related to issues of social justice and his artistic pursuits, chiefly painting.[21]

In brief, V.P. Singh emerged a serious warrior against discrimination and social injustice. Though, he belonged to a Rajput family but he demonstrated his caliber and dedication to ensure social justice during his short regime. Being Prime Minister, he took many historical steps such as awarding Bharat Ratna to Babasaheb Dr. Ambedkar, enactment of SC/ST Act and implementation of Mandal Commission Report. All three were the major decisions as far as the social justice was concerned. Not only Congress governments from Nehru to Indira Gandhi but also Morarji Desai led Janata Party government and Charan Singh government too have thoroughly neglected Babasaheb while awarding Bharat Ratna Awards. This was a cruel discrimination towards Dr. Ambedkar. V.P. Singh government ended this discrimination and injustice in 1990. By adopting and enacting SC/ST Act, V.P. Singh government provided a grave relief to the SC and ST communities. This act proved a major tool to curb the atrocities being occurred on these people. However, this act did not end all atrocities but it slowed down the brutality and cruelties with the SC/ST communities. This is the significance of this act. Another major and most bold step was the implementation of Mandal Commission Report, which was lieing in the dustbin since 1980. This report proved blessing to OBCs when V.P. Singh government implemented it in 1990 as it opened the door of progress for them.

However, the pressure of giving Bharat Ratna award to Dr. Ambedkar and imperilment the said report was mounted by Manyawar Kanshi Ram and his party BSP since its formation in 1984. But no doubt to say that V.P. Singh and his government took bold decision in favour of social justice and his contribution is enough to call him a supporter of social justice.

REFERENCES

*https://www.google.com/search?q=VP+SINGH&rlz=1C1ONGR_enIN982IN982&sxsrf=ALi Czsap2eJ-oyTbxR0fI7V4ZlLzTUhPQ:1665885646471&source=lnms&tbm=isch&sa=X&ved=2ah UKEwjC0MbR0-P6AhXT3TgGHbErC4IQ_AUoAXoECAEQAw&biw=1920&bih=860&dpr=1#i mgrc=rNdEttRjwyf-JM

1. "List of all Prime Ministers of India (1947-2021)". www.jagranjosh.com. 1 September 2021.

2. Pandya, Haresh (30 November 2008). "V. P. Singh, a Leader of India Who Defended Poor, Dies at 77". The New York Times. ISSN0362-4331.

3. "Remembering VP Singh on his 86th birthday: A grandson reminds us why India needs its political Siddharth". Firstpost. 27 June 2017.

4. V. P. Singh, Bardhan held on U. P. border

(http://www.thehindu.com/2006/08/18/stories/2006081807171200.htm)

5. V. P. Singh, Raj Babbar spring a surprise at Dadri
(http://www.thehindu.com/2006/08/19/stories/2006081913030500.htm)

6. Turmoil and a Scandal Take a Toll on Gandhi. The New York Times. (24 August 1987). Retrieved 14 September 2011.

7. BRASS, PAUL R. (2014). An Indian Political Life: Charan Singh and Congress Politics, 1967 To 1987. Sage Publications India Pvt Limited-Eng. ISBN978-93-5328-895-2.

8. Is the Raja Ready for War, or Losing His Steam?. New York Times. (8 October 1987). Retrieved 14 September 2011.

9. "Exodus of Kashmiri Pandits: What happened on January 19, 26 years ago?". India Today. 19 January 2016.

10. Colonel Tej K Tikoo (2012). Kashmir: Its Aboriginies and Their Exodus. Lancer Publishers. p. 414. ISBN9781935501589.

11. Mustafa 1995, p. unknown

12. "Supreme Court: SC/ST Amendment Act Constitutionally Valid, No Preliminary Enquiry for FIR". The Wire. Archived from the original on 3 August 2020. Retrieved 23 December 2020.

13. "Supreme Court: SC/ST Amendment Act Constitutionally Valid, No Preliminary Enquiry for FIR". The Wire. Archived from the original on 3 August 2020. Retrieved 23 December 2020.

14. Gehlot, N. S. (1998). Current Trends in Indian Politics. Deep & Deep Publications. pp. 264–265. ISBN9788171007981.

15. Kumar, Anu (29 September 2012). "Mandal memories". The Hindu. ISSN0971-751X.

17. India's Prime Minister Loses His Parliamentary Majority in Temple Dispute. New York Times. (24 October 1990). Retrieved 14 September 2011.

18. http://164.100.47.194/loksabha/writereaddata/our%20parliament/List%20of%20Statues%20and%20Portraits.htm

19. For India, Will It Be Change, Secularism or a Right Wing?. New York Times. (24 April 1991). Retrieved 14 September 2011.

20. https://en.wikipedia.org/wiki/Vishwanath_Pratap_Singh

21. Matthews, Roderick (7 August 2020). "Chandra Shekhar had 'solved' Ayodhya issue. But 'petty' Rajiv Gandhi brought his govt down". ThePrint. Retrieved 29 October 2020.

CHAPTER NINETEEN

INDIAN CONSTITUTION:

A DOCUMENT OF SOCIAL JUSTICE

Source-https://www.indialegallive.com/towards-isocracy-the-indian-constitution-as-a-site-of-complex-equality/

INDIAN CONSTITUTION AND SOCIAL JUSTICE

The Constitution of India that was drafted by a Drafting committee headed by Dr. B.R. Ambedkar is the largest constitution of the world. It was a result of a very deliberative and long exercise of 2 years, 11 months and 18 days. The Constituent Assembly under the presidentship of Dr. Rajender Prasad adopted, enacted and gave it to the nation on 26 November, 1949. Its few provisions were implemented from the same day but the whole constitution came into application on 26 January, 1950. Dr. Ambedkar mainly played most significant and vital role in writing the Constitution of India that is why he is regarded as the chief Architect and father of the Indian Constitution.

Being the main architect of the Constitution of India, Dr. B.R. Ambedkar tried his best to institutionalize and practice social justice through the Constitution of India too. For ensuring social justice, he architected constitutional and legal order that safeguards the socially and educationally backwards along with the forward sections of the society. The Constitution of India classifies Dalits as Scheduled Castes (SCs) and Adivasis as Scheduled Tribes (STs).

Dalits are the people who tend to have engaged themselves in occupations such as cultivate the land, mend the shoes, wash the clothes, clean the toilets, scavenge the dead animals or unknown human bodies and do all types of menial works, but share the stigmas of untouchability and are frequently denied the any accessibility to eat, smoke and even seat with the members of upper castes. They are often forced to use separate wells and tube wells from those maintained for others. Several Articles in the Indian Constitution are framed to remove this discrimination.

The Constitution of India through its various articles provide equal status to not only Dalits but also to other segments of society including women. The Constitution of India makes concrete provisions to abolish untouchability and discrimination against them, provisions of fundamental rights to all, equal protection of laws, voting rights and reservation in education, jobs, promotion and political fields to them. Besides these several programs in the form of grants, scholarships, loans, stipend etc. are being provided to Dalit's by the States. It also brings a renaissance in the concept of social justice when it weaves a trinity of it in the preamble, the fundamental rights, and the directive principles of state policies and this trinity is the "the core of the commitments to the social justice". This is the conscience of the Constitution. In this chapter, key parts, articles and provisions have been discussed which are supposed to be components of social justice.

PREAMBLE OF THE INDIAN CONSTITUTION-FOUNDATION OF EQUALITY & SOCIAL, ECONOMIC AND POLITICAL JUSTICE

The preamble of the Indian Constitution is the mirror of Constitutional values an dprincipals such as social justice. It provides social, economic and political justice to the citizen of India, which is a sovereign, socialist, secular, democratic, republic. Each word of the preamble is of great significance and some of them have been written in golden letters in our Constitution. No doubt to say that the preamble of Indian Constitution reflects the basic values and principles required for social justice and to establish an egalitarian and inclusive social, economic and political culture in a country full of diversities. We can read the preamble of the Constitution of India as under-

"**WE, THE PEOPLE OF INDIA,** having solemnly resolved to constitute India into a **SOVEREIGN** *SOCIALIST SECULAR* **DEMOCRATIC REPUBLIC** and to secure to all its citizens:

JUSTICE, social, economic and political;

LIBERTY of thought, expression, belief, faith and worship;

EQUALITY of status and of opportunity; and to promote among them all

FRATERNITY assuring the dignity of the individual and the unity and *integrity* of the Nation;

IN OUR CONSTITUENT ASSEMBLY this twenty-sixth day of November, 1949, do HEREBY ADOPT, ENACT AND GIVE TO OURSELVES THIS CONSTITUTION".[1]

HISTORICAL SIGNIFICANCE OF THE PREAMBLE

The preamble is based on the Objectives Resolution, which was drafted and moved in the Constituent Assembly by Jawaharlal Nehru on 13 December 1946 and adopted by Constituent Assembly on 22 January 1947.[2] Dr. B. R. Ambedkar said about the preamble:

It was, indeed, a way of life, which recognizes liberty, equality, and fraternity as the principles of life and which cannot be divorced from each other: Liberty cannot be divorced from equality; equality cannot be divorced from liberty. Nor can liberty and equality be divorced from fraternity. Without equality, liberty would produce the supremacy of the few over the many. Equality without liberty would kill individual initiative. Without fraternity, liberty and equality could not become a natural course of things.[3]

The Supreme Court of India originally stated in the Berubari case presidential reference that the preamble is not an integral part of the Indian constitution, and therefore it is not enforceable in a court of law. However, the same court, in the 1973 *Kesavananda* case, over-ruled earlier decisions and recognized that the preamble may be used to interpret ambiguous areas of the constitution where differing interpretations present themselves. In the 1995 case of Union Government Vs LIC of India, the Supreme Court once again held that the Preamble is an integral part of the Constitution.

AMENDMENT IN THE PREAMBLE

As originally enacted the preamble described the state as a "sovereign democratic republic", to which the terms "Secular" and "Socialist" were later passed by a Captive Parliament during The Emergency in the 42nd Amendment.[4]

The preamble was amended only once on 18 December 1976, with most of the opposition being jailed during the Emergency in India, the Indira Gandhi government pushed through several changes in the Forty-second Amendment of the constitution. Through this amendment, the words "socialist" and "secular" were added between the words "Sovereign" and "democratic" and the words "unity of the Nation" were changed to "unity and integrity of the Nation".[5] The ammendment procedure of the Indian constitution is provided under Article 368.

INTERPRETATION OF THE BASIC VALUES AND PRINCIPLES OF THE CONSTITUION OF INDIA

Indian Constitution is a detailed document which contains 395 (now 448) Articles, 8 (now 12) Schedules and 22 (now 25) parts including the Preamble. There are many features of this constitution but its basic values and principles have been outlined in the Preamble which are as under.

1. *Sovereignty*

Indian constitution through its Preamble declares India a sovereign state. Sovereign means the independent authority of a State. It means, that it has the power to legislate on any subject; and that it is not subject to the control of any other State/external power.

According to the preamble, the constitution of India has been pursuance of the solemn resolution of the people of India to constitute India into a 'Sovereign Democratic Republic', and to secure well-defined objects set forth in the preamble. Sovereignty denotes supreme and ultimate power to take decisions regarding internal and external affairs of the country. It may be real or normal, legal or political, individual or pluralistic. In monarchies, sovereignty was vested in the person of monarchs. But in republican form of governments, which mostly prevail in the contemporary world, sovereignty is shifted to the elected representatives of the people. According to D.D Basu, the word 'sovereign' is taken from article 5 of the constitution of Ireland. 'Sovereign or supreme power is that which is absolute and uncontrolled within its own sphere'. In the words of Cooley, "A state is sovereign when there resides within itself supreme and absolute power, acknowledging no superior".

Sovereignty, in short, means the independent authority of a state. It has two aspects- external and internal. External sovereignty or sovereignty in international law means the independence of a state of the will of other states, in her conduct with other states in the committee of nations. Sovereign in its relation between states and among states signifies independence. The external sovereignty of India means that it can acquire foreign territory and also cede any part of the Indian territory, subject to limitations (if any) imposed by the constitution.

On the other hand, internal sovereignty refers to the relationship between the states and the individuals within its territory. Internal sovereignty relates to internal and domestic affairs, and is divided into four organs, namely, the executive, the legislature, the judiciary and the administrative. Though India became a sovereign country on 26 January 1950, having equal status with the other members of the international community, she decided to remain in the Commonwealth of Nations. Pandit Nehru declared that India will continue – "her full membership of the Commonwealth games of Nations and her acceptance of the King as the symbol of the free association of the independent nations and as such the Head of the Commonwealth". Her membership of the Commonwealth of Nations and that of the United Nations Organization do not affect her sovereignty to any extent. It is merely voluntary association of India and it is open to India to cut off this association at her will, and that it has no constitutional significance.

2. *Socialism*

However, the term, socialist was added to the preamble of the constitution by the 42nd Amendment in 1976 by Indira Gandhi led Congress government, the Constitution had socialist content in the form of certain Directive Principles of State Policy provided in the fourth part of the constitution. The term socialist used here refers to democratic socialism, i.e. achievement of socialist goals through democratic, evolutionary and non-violent means. Essentially, it means that (since wealth is generated socially) wealth should be shared equally by society through distributive justice, not concentrated in the hands of few, and that the government should regulate the ownership of land and industry to reduce socio-economic inequalities.

3. Secularism

Secularism is another substantial principle of the constitution which is vested under Right to Equality, Right to Liberty and Right to Freedom of Religion in the third part of the constitution. By the 42nd Amendment in 1976, the term "Secular" was also incorporated in the Preamble. Secular means that the relationship between the government and religious groups are determined according to constitution and law. It separates the power of the state and religion. There is no difference of religion *i.e.* Hinduism, Buddhism, Jainism, Sikhism, Christianity and Islam are equally respected here. There is no state religion too. State is not permitted to discriminate on the basis of religion. All the citizens of India are allowed to profess, practice and propagate. Explaining the meaning of secularism as adopted by India, Alexander Owics has written, "Secularism is a part of the basic structure of the Indian Constitution and it means equal freedom and respect for all religions." The Right of Freedom Of Reliogion has benn provided to all Indian citizens as a Fundamental Right under Articles 25 to 28.

4. Democratic System of Government/Democracy

The framers of the constitution decided to adopt a democratic form of government. Democracy is the system of governance where people rule directly or indirectly. In the words of former President of U.SA. Abraham Lincoln, Democracy is the government of the people, for the people, by the people. Thus India is a democracy where the people of India elect their governments by a system of universal adult franchise, popularly known as "one person one vote and one value". Every citizen of India having18 years of age or older and not otherwise debarred by law is entitled to vote. The word *democratic* refers not only to political democracy but also to social and economic democracy.

5. Republic State

Republic State is the state where the head of state is elected by people directly or indirectly for a fixed tenure. The head of state is not a hereditary monarch. The head of the state uses executive power on the behalf of the people of the state. The constitution of India constitute India into a republic state and its head of the state is the president who is indirectly elected and has a fixed term of office. There's an absence of a privileged class and all public offices are open to every citizen without discrimination. Anyone whom the people of the country will prefer can become the president of India following the constitutional procedure.

6. Justice

Justice stands for rule of law, absence of arbitrariness and a system of equal rights, freedom and opportunities for all in a society.

India seeks social, economic and political justice to ensure equality to its citizens.

(i) Social Justice:

Social Justice means the absence of socially privileged classes in the society and no discrimination against any citizen on grounds of caste, creed, color, religion, gender or place of birth. India stands for eliminating all forms of exploitation from the society.

(ii) Economic Justice:

Economic Justice means no discrimination between man and woman on the basis of income, wealth and economic status. It stands for equitable distribution of wealth, economic equalities, the end of monopolistic control over means of production and distribution, decentralisation of economic resources, and the securing of adequate opportunities to all for earning their living.

(iii) Political Justice:

Political justice means equal, free and fair opportunities to the people for participation in the political process. It stands for the grant of equal political rights to all the people without discrimination. The Constitution of India provides for a liberal democracy in which all the people have the right and freedom to participate. (https://en.wikipedia.org/wiki/Preamble_to_the_Constitution_of_India)

7. Liberty

Liberty is also an important value of our constitution and without which an individual cannot develop his /her personality. The idea of Liberty refers to the freedom on the activities of Indian nationals. This establishes that there are no unreasonable restrictions on Indian citizens in term of what they think, their manner of expressions and the way they wish to follow up their thoughts in action. However, liberty does not mean freedom to do anything, and it must be exercised within the constitutional limits.

8. Equality

The term 'equality' means the absence of special privileges to any section of society, and the provision of adequate opportunity of all the individuals without any discrimination. Indian Constitution makes provision under Article 14 for 'equality before law and equal protection by law' that means law is supposed to treat all Indians equally without consideration of discrimination on the basis of caste, creed, religion, sex and place of birth. Discrimination has been prohibited under Article 15. There is provision of equal opportunity to all under Article 16. Another important provision is of 'abolition of untouchability' under Article 17. In this way, Indian Constitution has endorsed the value of equality by legally terminating the practice of upper and lower caste consideration.

9. Fraternity

Our constitution believes in fraternity without which we cannot imagine of unity and integrity of the nation. Fraternity refers to a feeling of brotherhood and sisterhood and a sense of belonging with the country among its people of different castes and religions. The Preamble declares that fraternity has to assure two things—the dignity of the individual and the unity and integrity of the nation. The word 'integrity' has been added to the Preamble by the 42nd Constitutional Amendment (1976).

10. Dignity of Individual

The Preamble reflects the basic intention and goals of the Constitution of India out of which assuring the dignity of individual is one. The constitution of India assures to create an atmosphere in which all individuals will live a life of respect and dignity without any fear and insecurity. Indeed, it is the most valuable principle of our constitution as it secures dignity of all which was absent in the pre-independence India.

11. Unity and Integrity of the Nation

Our constitution adopts a vision of national unity and integrity. As our constitution assures the dignity of the individual that is the foundation of the fraternity and which in turn ensures the unity and integrity of the country. The dream of the constitution makers was fraternity and unity and integrity of the nation and to achieve this goal they made necessary provisions in the constitution to ensure the dignity of the individual, in absence of which we cannot fulfil the sought goal.

To sum up, it can be said that the basic values and principles are reflected in our constitution's preamble which is the mirror of our constitution really. In true sense, the Preamble of our constitution works as the foundation of the equality and social, economic and political justice.

FUNDAMENTAL RIGHTS: PROTECTION SHIELD OF SOCIAL JUSTICE

Part III of the Constitution (Art 12 to 35)

Part III of the Constitution deals with fundamental rights that is the worthiest part dealing with social justice. Indian Constitution makes provisions of six fundamental rights for all the citizens without any discrimination of caste, race, religion, gender and place of birth. These are as under:

1. Right to Equality (Art. 14 to 18)
2. Right to Freedom (Art. 19 to 22)
3. Right against Exploitation (Art. 23 to 24)
4. Right to Freedom of Religion (Art. 25 to 28)
5. Cultural and Educational Rights (Art. 29 to 30)

6. Right to Constitutional Remedies (Art. 32)

The fundamental rights mainly Right to Equality (Art 14-18) and Right against Exploitation (Art 23-24) inculcate the sense of reconstruction and foster social revolution by generating equality among all, prohibiting discrimination on the grounds of caste, religion, sex, creed, place of birth, abolishing untouchablity and making its practice punishable by law, banning trafficking in human beings and forced labour. Moreover, the Indian Constitution under Art 15 (4) and 16 (4) has empowered the states to make special provisions for the advancement of any socially, educationally backward classes and also for the Scheduled Caste and Scheduled Tribes. Fundamental rights also secure the minority rights and provides them full space to develop themselves. Right to Constitutional Remedies under Article 32 provides protection shield to not only other fundamental rights but also to the social justice. That's why this has been regarded as the heart and soul of the Constitution. In brief, by providing fundamental rights to all citizens of the country, the discrimination has been hampered and the equality and justice are promoted. Fundamental rights are necessary for all people to develop their personality and live a life of respect and dignity. No doubt, fundamental rights have brought significant changes to the life of ordinary people. These have motivated them to live a life of dignity.

DIRECTIVE PRINCIPLES: A DETAILED PLAN OF SOCIAL AND ECONOMIC JUSTICE

Part IV of the Constitution (Art 36-51)

The important part of the Social justice is the part IV of the Constitution as directive principles of state of policy. Although this part of Constitution is not enforceable by any court but the directive principles of state policy undoubtedly express in categorical terms for equality, economic empowerment and social justice through various provisions as under.

- Article 38 of the Constitution requires the state inter-alias to minimize the inequalities in income and endeavor to culminate inequalities in status, facilities and opportunities, not amongst individual, but also amongst group of people residing in different areas or engaged in different vacations.
- Article 39- The State shall aim for securing right to an adequate means of livelihood for all citizens, both men and women as well as equal pay for equal work for both men and women. The State should work to prevent concentration of wealth and means of production in a few hands, and try to ensure that ownership and control of the material resources is distributed to best serve the common good. Child abuse and exploitation of workers should be prevented. Children should be allowed to develop in a healthy manner and should be protected against exploitation and against moral and material abandonment
- Article 39A- The State shall provide free legal aid to ensure that equal opportunities for securing justice is ensured to all, and is not denied by reason of economic or other disabilities.
- Article 40- The State shall also work for organisation of village panchayats and help enable them to function as units of self-government.
- Article 41-The State shall endeavor to provide the **right to work**, to education and to public assistance in cases of unemployment, old age, sickness and disablement, within the limits of economic capacity.
- Article 42- provide for just and humane conditions of work and maternity relief. The State should also ensure living wage and proper working conditions for workers, with full enjoyment of leisure and social and cultural activities.
- Article 43A-The State shall take steps to promote their participation in management of industrial undertakings.
- Article 44-the State shall endeavor to secure a uniform civil code for all citizens.
- Article 45- the State shall provide early childhood care and education for all children until they complete the age of six years. This directive regarding education of children was updated by the 86th Amendment Act, 2002.[6]
- Article 46- the state should work for the economic and educational upliftment of scheduled castes, scheduled tribes and other weaker sections of the society.
- Article 47-The directive principles commit the State to raise the level of nutrition and the standard of living and to improve public health, particularly by prohibiting intoxicating drinks and drugs injurious to health except for

medicinal purposes.

Through the Directive Principles, the Constitution requires the state to make available to all the citizens adequate means of livelihood, to distribute ownership and control of material resources. The state is also required to provide equal justice through the mechanism of free legal aid in order to ensure that opportunities for securing justice are not denied to any citizen by reason of economic or other disabilities. to provide right to work, to education and public assistance in cases of unemployment, old age, sickness and disablement and other cases of undeserved want, to make provision for securing just and humane conditions of work ensuring a decent standard of life and full enjoyment of leisure and social and cultural opportunities, to secure the participation of works in the management of under taking establishment or other organizations engaged in industry, to secure for all the citizens uniform civil code throughout the country, to provide free and compulsory education for children below the age of 14 years, to promote the educational and economic interests of the Scheduled Castes and Scheduled Tribes and other weaker sections, to raise the level of nutrition and standard of living and to improve the public health.

The contents of Ambedkar's concept of social justice included unity and equality of all human beings, equal worth of men and women, respect for the weak and the lowly, regard for human rights, benevolence, mutual love, sympathy, tolerance and charity towards fellow being. Humane treatment in all cases dignity of all citizens, abolition of Caste distinctions, education and property for all and good will and gentleness, He emphasized more on fraternity and emotional integration. His view on social justice was to remove man-made inequalities of all shades through law, morality and public conscience, he stood for justice for a sustainable society. Ambedkar stood for a social system in which man's status is based on his merit and achievements and where no one is noble or untouchable because of his/her birth. He advocated the policy of preferential treatment for the socially oppressed and economically exploited people of the country. The Constitution of India, which was drafted under his chairmanship, contains a number of provisions that enjoins the state to secure to all its citizens, justice, social, economic and political, along with liberty, equality and fraternity. It also contains a number of provisions that guarantee a preferential treatment to the downtrodden people in various sectors. Article 17 of the Indian Constitution declares untouchability as abolished. Ambedkar, in his speech before the Constituent Assembly for the passage of the Constitution, said 'I have completed my work; I wish there should be a sunrise even tomorrow. The new Bharat has got political freedom, but it is yet to raise the sun of social and economic liberty.[7]

CONSTITUTIONAL PROVISIONS REGARDING RESERVATION

Indian Constitution has validated the idea of social justice by making necessary provisions for affirmative action or reservation in political institutions, education and government services for deprived and depressed people of the country. Reservation has been provided to ensure their political representation and participation in education and government jobs.

- **Article 15(4) and 16(4)** of the Constitution enabled the State and Central Governments to reserve seats in government services for the members of the SC and ST.
- The Constitution was amended by the **Constitution (77th Amendment) Act,** 1995 and a new **clause (4A)** was inserted in **Article 16** to enable the government to provide reservation in promotion.
- Later, **clause (4A)** was modified by the Constitution (85th Amendment) Act, 2001 to provide consequential seniority to SC and ST candidates promoted by giving reservation.
- Constitutional 81st Amendment Act, 2000 inserted **Article 16 (4B)** which enables the state to fill the unfilled vacancies of a year which are reserved for SCs/STs in the succeeding year, thereby **nullifying the ceiling of fifty percent reservation** on total number of vacancies of that year.
- **Part XVI** deals with reservation of SC and ST in Central and State legislatures.
- **Article 330 and 332** provides for specific representation through reservation of seats for SCs and STs in the Parliament and in the State Legislative Assemblies respectively.

- **Article 335** of the constitution says that the claims of STs and STs shall be taken into consideration constitutionally with the maintenance of efficacy of the administration.
- **Article** 340 of the Constitution of India opens the door for empowerment and reservation to other backward castes (OBCs). This article provides **for the appointment of a Commission to investigate the conditions for the improvement of backward classes** within the territory of India and the difficulties under which they labour and to make recommendations as to the steps that should be taken by the Union or any State to remove such difficulties and to improve their condition and as to the grants that should be made for the purpose by the Union or any State and the conditions subject to which such grants should be made, and the order appointing such Commission shall define the procedure to be followed by the Commission. To adhere the Article 340, two backward castes commissions were constituted in 1953 (Kaka Kalelkar Commission) and 1978 (B.P. Mandal Commission) respectively.
- **Article 243D** provides reservation of seats for SCs, STs and women in every Panchayat.
- **Article 233T** provides reservation of seats for SCs, STs and women in every Municipality.

When India got freedom (1947) and its new Constitution was drafted and implemented (1950), three types of reservation was provided for the Depressed Classes to secure their political, educational and economic representation in independent India. Thus, Article 330 of Indian Constitution makes a provision for the reservation in the Lok Sabha, the lower house of Indian Parliament. Article 332 provides reservation to the SCs and STs in the state Legislative Assemblies. Though, political reservation provided under Articles 330 and 332 respectively was temporary and was to be reviewed in 1960 that whether it would need continuance or not. Article 335 gives reservation to the mentioned communities in the government services and posts.

Provisions for promotion of educational and economic interests are made under Directive Principles of the State Policy (Article 46) in *The Constitution of India*. It was done to ensure the representation of the deprived people in the process of development and growth. Here one thing is clear that political reservation had been provided to SCs and STs to ensure their inclusion and representation in the law making bodies - Lok Sabha and State Legislative Assemblies was temporary but reservation in education and appointments was given unconditional and without any time limit. In other words, reservation in education and appointments is to ensure the social, educational and economic empowerment of the SCs and STs and it is permanent.

93ʳᵈ Constitutional Amendment allows the government to make special provisions for "advancement of any socially and educationally backward classes of citizens", including their admission in aided or unaided private educational institutions. Gradually this reservation policy is to be implemented in private institutions and companies as well. This move led to opposition from non-reserved category students, as the proposal reduced seats for the General (non-reserved) category from the existing 77.5% to less than 50.5% (since members of OBCs are also allowed to contest in the General category).

Article 15(4) of our constitution empowers the government to make special provisions for advancement of backward classes. Similarly, Article 16 provides for equality of opportunity in matters of employment or appointment to any post under the State.

"Clause 2 of article 16 lays down that no citizen on grounds of religion, race, caste, sex, descent, place of birth, residence or any of them be discriminated in respect of any employment or office under the State."

However, clause 4 of the Article 16 provides for an exception by conferring a certain kind of power on the government: *"It empowers the state to make special provision for the reservation of appointments of posts in favour of any backward class of citizens which in the opinion of the state are not adequately represented in the services"*. Thus two conditions have to be satisfied: 1. The class of citizens is backward. 2. The said class is not adequately represented.[8]

In brief, the policy of reservation was intended to eradicate the vast inequalities between the privileged and neglected sections of Indian society and ensure socio-economic democracy in absence of which political democracy was meaningless as according to Dr. Ambedkar, the main architect of the Indian constitution. Dr. Ambedkar was of the opinion that the social and economic democracy was necessary to support political democracy. He observed, "Political democracy cannot succeed where there is no social and economic democracy. Social and economic democracy is the tissue and fibre of a political democracy. The tougher the tissue and fibre, the greater the strength of the body politic" (S.N. Busi, 1997)[9].

OBJECTIVES OF RESERVATION

- To correct the **historical injustice** faced by backward castes in the country.
- To provide a **level playing field** for backward section as they cannot compete with those who have had the access of resources and means for centuries.
- To ensure **adequate representation** of backward classes in the services under the State.
- For **advancement** of backward classes.
- To **ensure equality** as basis of meritocracy i.e. all people must be brought to the same level before judging them on the basis of merit.

(source-https://www.drishtiias.com/to-the-points/paper2/reservation-in-india)[10]

IMPACT OF RESERVATION POLICY TOWARDS SOCIAL JUSTICE

Representation of SCs/ STs has increased in all the Groups viz. A, B, C and D during last six decades. At the dawn of independence representation of SCs/STs in services was very little. As per available information, representation of SCs in Groups A, B, C and D as on 1.1.1965 was 1.64%, 2.82%, 8.88% and 17.75% respectively which has increased to 12.5%, 14.9%, 15.7% and 19.6% respectively as on 1.1.2008. Likewise, while representation of STs as on 1.1.1965 in Group A, B, C and D was 0.27%, 0.34%, 1.14% & 3.39% respectively, it has increased to 4.9%, 5.7%, 7.0% and 6.9% respectively as on 1.1.2008. Total representation of SCs and STs as on 1.1.1965 was 13.17% and 2.25% respectively, which has increased to 17.51% and 6.82% respectively on 1.1.2008.

(https://persmin.gov.in/DOPT/Brochure_Reservation_SCSTBackward/Ch-01_2014.pdf)[11]

The credit of increasing representation and participation of SCs and STs ultimately goes to the reservation policy that was included in the constitution because of Dr. B.R. Ambedkar. He wanted equality and social, economic and political justice to the deprived and depressed people, therefore he made concrete provisions in the constitution to ensure their empowerment.

SUPREME COURT AS CUSTODIAN OF THE CONSTITUTION AND JUSTICE

The **Supreme Court of India which has been provided under article 124** is the supreme judicial body of India and the highest court of the Republic of India under the constitution. It is the most senior constitutional court, and has the power of judicial review. The Chief Justice of India is the head and chief judge of the Supreme Court, which consists of a maximum of 34 judges and has extensive powers in the form of original, appellate and advisory jurisdictions.[12]

As the apex constitutional court in India, it takes up appeals primarily against verdicts of the high courts of various states of the Union and other courts and tribunals. It is required to safeguard the fundamental rights of citizens and settles disputes between various government authorities as well as the central government vs state governments or state governments versus another state government in the country. As an advisory court, it hears matters which may specifically be referred to it under the Constitution by the President of India. The law declared by the Supreme Court becomes binding on all courts within India and also by the union and state governments.[13] As per the Article 142 of the Constitution, it is the duty of the President of India to enforce the decrees of the Supreme Court and the court is conferred with the inherent jurisdiction to pass any order deemed necessary in the interest of justice. The Supreme Court has replaced the Judicial Committee of the Privy Council as the highest court of appeal since 28 January 1950.

SUPREME COURT AS A KEY TO RULE OF LAW AND SOCIAL JUSTICE

The basic foundation of the constitution is the dignity and the freedom of its citizens which is of supreme importance and cannot be destroyed by any legislation of the parliament. Whereas the fair trial to examine the validity of the ninety-ninth constitutional amendment dated 31 December 2014, to form National Judicial Appointments Commission for the purpose of appointing the judges of the Supreme Court and high courts, was conducted on utmost priority and the Supreme Court delivered its judgement on 16 October 2015 (within a year) quashing the constitutional amendment as unconstitutional and ultra vires stating the said amendment is interfering with the independence of the judiciary. Under checks and balances as provided in the Constitution, it is the duty of the judiciary/Supreme Court to establish the rule of law at the earliest by rectifying any misuse of the Constitution by Parliament and the executive without colluding with them and to remove perceptions of people that rule of law is side lined and a section of its citizens are subjected to discrimination. Really, having significant provisions for welfare and upliftment of the common people, Indian Constitution is a document of social justice.

RFERENCES

1.Baruah, Aparijita (2006). Preamble of the Constitution of India: An Insight and Comparison with Other Constitutions. New Delhi: Deep & Deep. p. 177. ISBN978-81-7629-996-1. Retrieved 12 November 2016.

2. M Laxmikanth (2013). "4". Indian Polity (4th ed.). McGraw Hill Education. p. 4.5. ISBN978-1-25-906412-8.

3. "Fundamental rights in The Preamble,Free Law Study material,IAS Law Notes,material for Ancient India Law". www.civilserviceindia.com.

4. "The Constitution (Forty-Second Amendment) Act, 1976". Government of India. Retrieved 1 December 2010.

5. "The Constitution (Forty-Second Amendment) Act, 1976". Government of India.

6. "Article 141 of the Constitution of India"

7. (Source-https://www.ijcrt.org/papers/IJCRT2012278.pdf)[7]

8. (https://www.youthkiawaaz.com/2011/02/educational-reservations-india-solutions/)[8]

9. S.N. Busi, 1997: Mahatma Ganghi and Babasaheb Ambedkar: Crusaders Against Caste And Untouchability, Saroj Publications, Andhra Pradesh, p. 199.

10. (SOURCE-https://www.drishtiias.com/to-the-points/Paper2/reservation-in-india)[10]

11. (https://persmin.gov.in/DOPT/Brochure_Reservation_SCSTBackward/Ch-01_2014.pdf)[11]

12. "Rule of law index 2016". Archived from the original on 29 April 2015. .

13. "History of Supreme Court of India" (PDF). Supreme Court of India. Archived from the original (PDF) on 22 December 2014.

CHAPTER TWENTY

CONCLUSION: WHY SOCIAL JUSTICE?

AND HOW TO PROTECT SOCIAL JUSTICE?

This book highlights the life, struggle and contribution of the great champions of equality and social justice who echoed strong voice for social justice. This chapters makes a serious effort to bring the solid and appropriate answer to the question, why social justice and how to protect social justice? In recent years, the term "social justice" has become just as prominent as "human rights." What does social justice mean exactly? In the simpler sense, it is essentially a concept of fairness within a society which advocates for equality and discrimination free social, economic and political environment. It applies to fairness in wealth, opportunities, basic needs, and more.[1]

CASTE AND CASTE SYSTEM: ROOT CAUSE OF DISCRIMINATION AND SCOCIAL INJUSTICE

The roots of the caste system, which has been tarnishing Indian society for centuries, lie in the Chatur-Varna system described in the book 'Manu-Smriti' written by Manu. However, the varna system was based on karma and it categorized and organized human beings on the basis of karma. This system based on division of work was similar to the three-class ideal state of the Greek philosopher Plato. But over a period of time, this varna-system became the basis of the devious and complex caste system that broke the Indian society in to different segments. Human beings got divided into different castes, which had serious consequences in the form of repeated external attacks on India. The varna system and caste system continued to get spiritual and ideological support. For example, Maharishi Tulsidas may be quoted here. Tulsi Das clearly appeared to support caste and caste oppression, he wrote in 'Ramcharitmanas' that,

"Dhol, fool, shudra, animal, woman all deserves chastisement."

This type of thinking played a special role in providing strength and encouragement to caste discrimination, oppression and social injustice.

As far as the efforts to reform of Hinduism and to fight for the abolition of caste and caste based discrimination are concerned, such efforts had already been started from the time of Tathagata Gautam Buddha. Buddha gave the message of social and religious equality, influenced by which millions of Sanatani people became his followers. The shackles of caste were definitely weakened by the efforts of Gautam Buddha, but could not be broken completely. Inspired by the teachings of Tathagata Buddha, Mauryan emperor Ashoka the Great discouraged caste discrimination and high and low tendencies to a great extent by ending slavery and created an atmosphere of social harmony. Emperor Ashoka's Dhamma-policy was also against all kinds of discrimination and based on the welfare of humanity.

But, during the reign of Pushyamitra Sung, caste discrimination and feelings of high and low got encouragement again. Pushyamitra Sunga was a great supporter of Manuvad and Brahmanism. The caste-based discrimination gained a lot of strength even during the later Gupta rule. The condition of the untouchable community during the Gupta period was very painful and pathetic. However, during the Gupta period there was unprecedented progress in various fields, due to which some historians have underlined the Gupta period as the golden age. But the feeling of inequality, social discrimination, casteism and social injustice and the condition of Shudras and Ati Shudras reached a very pathetic condition.

Downward, we are going to discuss the two serious questions 'why social justice' and how to protect social justice? In this chapter, sufficient arguments have been given in favour of social justice and some measures to protect social justice too have been suggested.

A FOUNDATION OF FRATERNITY AND NATIONAL UNITY

It is the social justice which functions as foundation of fraternity and national unity. It strengthens the unity and integrity of the country. Without social justice in a society, we cannot imagine of fraternity and national unity. Unity among the citizens of any country depends on the presence of social justice. It leads people to live a life based on fraternity. Within a social and political system based on social justice, people feel happy. It enhances the social harmony which in turn strengthen national unity. Social justice leads to tolerance and preserves social diversity. Social justice is not against any community and individual. It loves all and believes in power sharing not power snatching. It believes in inclusive development and progress of all. It echoes voice for the upliftment of lagging behind. It is not a voice to pull-down anyone. In short, as a foundation of fraternity and national unity, it preserves the interests of all and create an atmosphere of social harmony.

AN INSTRUMANT OF EQUALITY

In a democratic political system, justice is the foundation which makes the democracy stable as without justice people will be not in a position to escape from discrimination. Social justice stands for social equality which is absence of discrimination on the grounds of caste, creed, sex, religion etc. Itprotects against various forms of discrimination. One of the most significant focuses within social justice is to protect against and reduce discrimination of all types; it's safe to say that discrimination is one of the most common and prevalent forms of social injustice. Race, ethnicity, and gender are only a few examples of discrimination that someone can face. Whether it's within the professional world or the justice system, it happens every day. When social justice becomes something that's regularly practiced within our society, it brings us closer to putting an end to the discrimination that occurs so often.[2]

The political system based on social justice ensures people to be treated with respect and promote social justice within schools, colleges, universities, other educational institutes, hospitals, nursing homes, community centres etc. Social justice as an instrument of equality promotes social development and change. Social justice supports social, economic and political rights to citizens in an equal proportion. It favours for equality of opportunity to all so that each can develop his/her personality.

Social Justice helps promote gender equality

Along with many discrimination, discrimination based on gender is one of the oldest forms of injustice around the world. Women and girls are the most oppressed group in history, and it gets worse for them if they are also members of another oppressed population, like a certain race, caste or religion. Social justice strives to bridge the gap between sexes and empowers women. Social justice is pro gender equality and favours women empowerment. It advocates freedom and rights for women equal to men. Despite constitutional and legal termination of gender discrimination, women are facing injustice in political spectrum and their representation is very low. In our 17th Lok Sabha, only 78 women have got elected which is about 14 percent. Whereas, their population is almost half of the total population. Hence, social justice favours reservation to women in politics so that they could be well represented in the parliament and state legislative assemblies.

It helps promote economic equality

As far as economic status of the people is concerned, there is a huge gap between the rich and the poor. This gap is expanding rather than decreasing. The fact that some people struggle to buy enough food for their children while others get millions of dollars in a severance package. There is complete unequal distribution of economic resources in our country. On one hand, few people who are about 20 percent owns 80 percent resources. On the other hand, 80 percent people depend on 20 percent resources. India is moving rapidly towards a capitalism. Rich are becoming richer and poor are becoming poorer. It is simply not fair and against the principles of equality and social justice. Such a gap creates an imbalanced society which is not healthy for the unity and stability of the nation too. However, Equality doesn't mean that everyone is rich, but it should mean that everyone is able to meet their basic needs and live without being afraid that one setback could put them on the streets. Social justice is about securing everyone's economic stability.

<u>Social Justice promotes equal rights to all segments of the society</u>

Today's civilizations are almost heterogeneous and full of diversities. Almost countries are multicultural. In case of India, people belonging to different castes, cultures and religions live together. It protects people from religion-based discrimination also. A person's religion is a central part of them, and freedom from religious discrimination falls right into the lap of social justice. Many countries have laws that discourage religious freedom, while others fail to enforce protections. Social justice advocates want all religions to be free and safe, including a person's right to *not* follow any religion.[3] To ensure equality and social justice, we have taken concrete steps and constitutional measures and commitment. In this way, Social justice works as a tool or an instrument of equality which proves relevance of social justice.

EQUAL OPPORTUNITIES FOR ALL IN EDUCATION AND GOVERNMENT JOBS

<u>Social justice favours educational opportunities for all.</u>

It favours inclusive education that provides opportunities to all children and teaches them without discrimination of caste, religion, gender etc. A good <u>education is crucial</u> to ending cycles of poverty and giving everyone the opportunity to fulfill their dreams. However, countless people are unable to get an adequate education simply because of where they live or because they're facing other discrimination. Social justice wants everyone to be able to learn in a safe place that's encouraging and that provides equal opportunities. All of society benefits when children get educated.

<u>Social justice recommends equal opportunities to all in government jobs.</u>

Social justice recommends equal opportunities to all in government jobs too so that an inclusive administrative structure can be evolved. In other words, by providing equality in opportunities, social justice can be achieved and maintained. Despite, constitutional provisions for reservation to the backward people, they are lagging behind in all fields. They have almost zero representation in the judiciary. SCs, STs and OBCs have nominal representation on the posts of Professors in universities. Their presence is very on the top posts in bureaucracy. Dominance of few or any particular community can prove dangerous for not only justice but also for social harmony. Therefore, to build an unbiased democracy, we need to design a bureaucratic and judicial system committed to social justice through the mechanism of equality in opportunity. All segments of the society should reflect and be represented in the government services.

SPECIAL PROVISIONS FOR THE ADVANCEMENT OF SOCIALLY AND EDUCATIONALLY BACKWARD CLASSES

Social justice stresses upon making special provisions for the advancement of any socially, and educationally backward classes such as the Scheduled Caste, Scheduled Tribes, Other Backward Castes and women. It is necessary to uplift the lagging behind sections of the society so that they can live life of dignity and respect. The Constitution of India that is based on equality and social, economic and political justice promotes advancement of SCs, STs, other backward castes and women. Social justice promotes betterment and empowerment of the poor and depressed through constitutional and legal measures. Therefore, the Constitution of India which promotes social justice, makes following provisions for the advancement of socially and educationally backward people as under:

- **Article 15(4) and 16(4)** of the Constitution enabled the State and Central Governments to reserve seats in government services for the members of the SC and ST.
- The Constitution was amended by the **Constitution (77ᵗʰ Amendment) Act,** 1995 and a new **clause (4A)** was inserted in **Article 16** to enable the government to provide reservation in promotion.

Article 15(4) of our constitution empowers the government to make special provisions for advancement of backward classes. Similarly, Article 16 provides for equality of opportunity in matters of employment or appointment to any post under the State.

"Clause 2 of article 16 lays down that no citizen on grounds of religion, race, caste, sex, descent, place of birth, residence or any of them be discriminated in respect of any employment or office under the State."

However, clause 4 of the Article 16 provides for an exception by conferring a certain kind of power on the government: *"It empowers the state to make special provision for the reservation of appointments of posts in favour of any backward class of citizens which in the opinion of the state are not adequately represented in the services"*. Thus two conditions have to be satisfied: 1. The class of citizens is backward. 2. The said class is not adequately represented.*(https://www.youthkiawaaz.com/2011/02/educational-reservations-india-solutions/)*[4]

PROTECTION TO PEOPLE WITH DISABILITIES

Social justice protects people with disabilities too. Disability rights have been ignored and neglected for many years, but with social justice on the rise, these people are finally getting a voice. Those with both visible and invisible disabilities (like mental illness) are often discriminated against in their workplace, in health-care, and more. Social justice rejects discrimination and humiliation in all forms. Discrimination is discrimination whether it is against deprived or disables. Hence, social justice believes truly in justice for all and it advocates for rights of disables.

A TOOL OF INCLUSIVE DEMOCRACY

Today, we are living in a multicultural and heterogeneous societies which are full of diversities. People of different religions, cultures, castes and languages live together in a democratic system. But any heterogeneous society and state can survive only when there is unity and mutual fraternity. Unity and fraternity depend on existence of social justice in a heterogeneous society. Almost countries and mainly India have a majority and minorities. Both stratas majority and minority need freedom and rights to develop themselves. Without freedom and rights, no one can not develop himself or herself. Therefore, social justice favors minority rights and their empowerment through administrative policies. It supports political rights to all including minorities. Social justice advocates all social, economic, political and cultural rights to minorities in the degree as the majority group enjoy. The presence of minority rights maintains unity, peace and harmony among citizens in a county. In this way, social justice being fair to all citizens works as a tool of inclusive democracy by giving them representation or adequate share in power and providing necessary opportunities for going ahead in life.

POLITICAL REPRESENTATION TO ALL COMMUNITIES INCLUDING WOMEN

Social justices favours representation to all communities including women not only in education and administration but also in political power too. It believes in power sharing that is participation and involvement of all sections of the society in the governance. Political representation and social justice are complimentary to each other as both promote each other. By securing the interests of all and giving political representation to deprived, backwards, women, minorities and other legging behind people, social justice minimises the chances of civil war and prevent the division of the country. It supports power sharing to all the communities and weaker sections, which makes them supportive to the country. For example, political representation has been given to the SCs and STs in our country through the mechanism of reservation, which has prevented the further division of the country.

Social justice promotes a well-representative and inclusive administrative and political system. It is necessary to crystalize the bonding and belonging-ness of all the citizens to the country and make realise them happy. It inculcates the spirit of nationalism in the citizens as they enjoy all rights and political representation. But ignoring any community in political and administrative representation is a very dangerous thing for the unity and integrity of any nation. We cannot live united for a long time if we ignore any particular group of people in political and administrative representation. It can lead to upheaval and instability that can lead to civil war and finally to division of the land. Srilanka is the example, where civil war was burst when Sinhalese got hegemonic position ignoring Tamils in education, government services and politics. Due to the majoritarian and hegemonic political culture, Srilanka hardly could avert the partition of the country. To secure social justice and end the racial discrimination, Blacks of America steered a long struggle for civil rights under the leadership of Martin Luther King Junior. Finally, their struggle proved fruitful and they got political and civil rights.

PRESENT CONSTITUTION OF INDIA AND RESERVATION SYSTEM – THE PROTECTION SHIELD OF SOCIAL JUSTICE

Indian Constitution makes necessary arrangements for social justice and inclusive and participatory democracy through its various provisions. Provisions of Fundamental Rights, Directive Principles and Reservation are effective tools to protect and promote social justice in the country. Reservation in education and government services for lagging behind sections of the society has been an effective mechanism to ensure an inclusive and participatory educational and administrative system. Political Reservation that is reservation in Lok Sabha and state Legislative Assemblies ensures power sharing for SCs and STs. It makes them feel satisfied and cement their bond with the nation. But what will happen when there will not be this constitution and reservation system. Hence, it is true to say that we cannot imagine of social justice in absence of the present constitution. Social justice will stay as long as the present constitution and reservation stay. Therefore, we need to protect our constitution as well, if we want social justice to survive in India.

Indian Constitution provides 15% and 7.5% reservation to SCs and STs respectively in Lok Sabha and central government jobs. But the census of 1991 shows the population of Dalits belonging to the three religions, Hindu, Buddhism and Sikhism, is 138,223,277 out of a total population of 846,320,688 (*Presidential* order). According to the announcement made by census commissioner on July 11, 2004, the total population of the country was 1,02,87,37,436 and the percentage of SCs and STs was 16.2 and 8.2 respectively[5]. Therefore, to strengthen the social justice, the respective quotas of SC and ST categories must be increased as according to their increased ratios in population of the country. OBC reservation too must be increased as according to their populous number. Now the time has come to increase the quota above its limit of 50 percent. However, this limit has been broken by central government giving 10 percent reservation to economically weaker sections (EWS) among general category. In this way, the present constitution of India and the reservation policy are the protection shield of the social justice.

NEED TO REJECT SUPERSTITION AND THEORIES OF *PUNARJANMA* AND *BHAGYAWAD* – HUGE OBSTACLES TO THE PATH OF SOCIAL JUSTICE

Brahmanical religion that has taken new avatar in form of Hindu religion has great faith in the concepts of *punarjanma* (re-carnation) and *bhagyawad* (destiny). It believes that the people face pleasure and sorrow due to their past birth and fate. The God has written people' destiny at the time of birth and no one is responsible for the sufferings of a man despite their own deeds in the past birth. These ideas have been inculcated in the minds of people by the Brahmins on the basis of religious books. The revolt against exploitation is warned as revolt against the divine order. Hence, parents too start to inculcate these thoughts in the minds of children from childhood. They learn to bear the oppression and exploitation from childhood and hardly protest. They don't demand for rights and justice. In this way, it can be understood that the ideas of punarjanma and bhagyawad work as powerful and effective weapons against the social justice. Babu Jagdev Prasad Kushwaha had hardly hit on the theories of punarjanm aur bhagyavaad. He emphatically used to say that punarjanm aur bhagyavaad, inse janma brahmanvad (Belief in rebirth and Fatalism has given birth to Brahmanism) that put social justice to the deep ditch and the exploitation and discrimination continued. Therefore, if we want social justice, we will have to reject superstition and the theories of punarjanma and bhagyawad, which are huge obstacles to the path of equality and social justice.

CULTURAL HEGEMONY BASED ON CASTE AND RELIGION- A THREAT TO SOCIAL JUSTICE

Antonio Gramsci, an Italian philosopher opines that cultural hegemony promotes the interests of haves or the holders of resources. Cultural hegemony supports the exploiter to continue the exploitation of the not haves. Due to cultural hegemony, the exploited do not revolt against the exploiter. As far as India is concerned, caste is the unique feature of Indian society that differentiate people on the basis of birth. Due to the caste mechanism, some people become upper and superior by default as they are born in particular castes but some are lower or inferior. Caste system divides the whole society broadly into two segments such as the forward and the backwards but again narrowly divides backwards into thousands of communities. According to the Self-Respect Movement and Periyar, the root of all social evils can be found in religion. It believed that without destroying the superstitions based upon religion and tradition, it could not affect any social change. In its opinion, the caste system was closely intervened with the Hindu religion. So, in order to reform the society, it felt that there was a dire need for changing some of the basic practices in the religion.

In the words of Babasaheb Dr. Ambedkar, Caste is not the division of labour but the division of labourers. It is done to make sure the majority of the people who have been stratified among thousands of sections could not unite against the haves. In other words, the caste system is a Brahmanical system which makes a smart and strategic order in favour of the forward people who have been succeeded in maintaining their cultural, social, economic and political hegemony over the rest. The caste system supported by the religion has been favouring the inequality and discrimination for centuries. This cultural hegemony makes the Bahujans who are eighty-five percent in number as according to Manyawar Kanshi Ram, dependent on the mercy of few socially, economically and politically. Cultural hegemony promotes subjection of deprived and backwards, exploitation of poor and suppression of women. In this way, caste and religion based cultural hegemony of the supporters of inequality is a huge threat to the social justice. The supporters of social justice will have to dismantle the cultural hegemony of the forward. Without dismantling it, social justice can not be achieved in its full form.

MAJORITARION AND THEOCRATIC STATE – A THREAT TO SOCIAL JUSTICE

Illustrations of Srilanka and some Islamic countries demonstrate that a majoritarian and theocratic states can not be conducive for social justice. Indeed, these are not only bigger hindrances but also a huge threat to the cause of social justice. Majoritarian and theocratic states which rule as per emotions of larger group of the country and religious texts and traditions respectively. Religion and religious books such as Bible, Qur'an, Manusmriti etc. play primary role in governing the country. Such states are undemocratic and fully biased. They do not take care of minority groups and habitually ignores their interests. Hence, such states are anti social justice. Therefore, we need to make every possible effort to stop our country from becoming either majoritarian or theocratic. It is democracy only that serves interests of all and ensures social justice by providing freedom and rights to the all citizens of the country without giving importance to caste, religion, gender, language etc. In short, we need to strengthen our democracy and by doing so we can protect the social justice in our country.

PSEUDO WELFARISM – A THREAT TO SOCIAL JUSTICE

The dominant forces always try to maintain their hegemony by grabbing political power, as without political power, social and economic hegemonies cannot be retained. Therefore, they take the help of pretend welfarism to attract the people. In the name of welfare of the poor, they make some manipulated policies which proves ineffective to abolish the poverty. Theses welfare schemes are not concrete to pull out them from deprivation, subjugation and marginalization. People get mislead due to these welfare schemes which are illusionary only. Under the influence of pretend welfarism, the poor and backward people vote to even such political parties which are anti-social justice. The ordinary people do not recognize them and push away the social justice. Pretend welfare policies cannot flourish the cause of social justice. Social justice is not only to achieve some facilities such as grain, food items, tabs, laptops, clothes etc but it is proper representation and participation in education, government service, army, judiciary, politics, other employments, business, land and other resources so that the people can live a life of respect, dignity and prosperity. In this way, pretend welfarism is a threat to the cause of social justice as this mislead and throw them away from the idea of social justice. The deprived, backward and poor should identify their true well wishers who can bring them a life full of respect and prosperity and who can provide them free education, free medical treatment, justice, security and representation in all fields.

SOCIAL JUSTICE AND CASTE-BASED CENSUS

Social justice favours caste-based census, which is an opportunity to backwards or lagging behind sections of the society of getting inclusion in mainstream and empowerment. It is necessary to conduct caste based census as it will bring true figure of their numbers in the population of the country. But forward and dominant castes are opposing caste based census. Caste based census is essential to ensure social justice in India as it will give accurate data of lagging behind people. According to Vivek Kumar, Professor at JNU, the people incapable to understand meaning and functioning of caste-based census fear of it. Hence, they are tossing an unexpected and utopian question giving it a political colouring. If anyone presents caste based census linking it with national unity and integration, he is neglecting the socio-political realty of Indian society. No doubt to say that communal tussle is a danger to the unity and integrity of the nation as we have seen in 1947. But yet we are doing census based on religion and languages. He further said that world history has been witness to the fact that most of countries are products of religious and linguistic bases. No nation is thoroughly based on a particular caste or race. No caste can do it as it has no sufficient numbers to demand a separate country. Therefore, it can be said that if any person is linking it with national unity and integration, then he is misleading the country[6]. Hence, it is need of hour that to protect social justice, we must conduct a caste based census so that backward people may be benefited in a proper sense.

SOCIAL JUSTICE AIMS AT POWER SHARING AND POLITICAL REPRESENTATION TO ALL

Social justice aims at political representation to all mainly weaker and lagging behind sections of the society. Political representation is not necessary only to political empowerment of all communities in a country full of diversities but also it is necessary to protect social justice. But social justice is not possible without political will and governmental support. As the voice for social justice is the voice for social change which is difficult to achieve without political power. It the political power, which makes the social justice and social change possible through governmental policies. Our constitution is no doubt a document of social justice and has will and plan to make India a social and economic democracy without which political democracy is meaningless. But this is the responsibility of the people in power to implement or not implement the constitutional will. In his final speech in the Constituent Assembly, dated November 25, 1949, Babasaheb Dr. Ambedkar himself had spoken: "However good a constitution may be, if those who are implementing it are not good, it will prove to be bad. However, bad a constitution may be, if those implementing it are good, it will prove to be good". This clearly shows that the implementation of the constitutional will depends on the will of people in power or the government. Hence, there is need of political unity of all who believes in social justice. All the intellectuals, thinkers, leaders, activists and journalists should work together to bring power to the people who can implement the will of our constitution that is social justice along with economic betterment of the poor, Dalits, tribes, backwards, minorities and women.

PRIVATISATION AND LATERAL ENTRY-A THREAT TO RESRVATION POLICY

No doubt, reservation is the protection shield of social justice in India but since 1991 a new trend has taken place which is based on New Economic Policy. The liberlisation, privatization and globalisation are the backbone of the New Economic Policy. For last few years, privatization is taking place in employment and it is increasing day by day. Increasing privatization in education and employment is a huge threat to not only reservation but also to social justice as the privatization does not support reservation on the one hand and it promotes exploitation of the poor and less educated people on the other hand. There is complete unequal distribution of economic resources in our country. On one hand, few people who are about 20 percent owns 80 percent resources. On the other hand, 80 percent people depend on 20 percent resources. India is moving rapidly towards a capitalism and rich are becoming richer and poor are becoming poorer. In a capitalist society, social justice cannot survive as capitalism is based on private profit not on welfare of poor. As stronger will be the capitalism, the social justice will be the weaker. A new trend of lateral entry too has been developed in the country through which government is giving lateral entry of employees in government jobs. Recently, Government of India has selected some civil servants from the corporate sector surpassing UPSC's examination system. This is straight dent to the reservation policy. Hence, it is easy to understand that privatization of government jobs and lateral entry to government jobs are a threat to the reservation policy and it is real threat to social justice as well. Whereas, reservation is essential to promote and protect social justice. Hence, if governments believe in social justice than these must not adopt privatization and stop lateral entry program in administration.

POLITICAL POWER: MASTER KEY TO SOCIAL JUSTICE

Babasaheb Ambedkar was of the opinion that "Political Power is the Master Key." It means political power holder is always in position to make crucial decision in favour of the citizens of the country. They have authority to solve social, economic and political issues. Hence, no doubt Babasaheb was fully correct when he said that Political Power is the Master Key. Obviously, political power is a master key by which we can open all the doors of progress. It has been proved right that by grabbing political power, BSP had played remarkable role to ensure empowerment of downtrodden, backwards and women, in which it registered amazing success too. By acquiring master key in U.P., BSP started many Universities in Uttar Pradesh In 1994, BSP laid foundation for Sahu Mahraj University in Kanpur. In 1996, it opened Mahatma Phule University and Dr. Ambedkar University. Beside it all, BSP government founded Gautham Buddha University in NOIDA. It created seventeen new districts of which the last one is Buddha Nagar. BSP government built splendid memorials and parks to honour Bahujan warriors of social justice such as Babasaheb Dr. Ambedkar, Mahatma Jyotiba Phule, Shahuji Maharaj, Mata Svitribai Phule, Manyawar Kanshi Ram etc. BSP government launched number of schemes to empower the poor and downtrodden. In brief, it is true to say that political power is the master key. And the poor, downtrodden and backwards should unitedly make serious efforts to acquire the political power, which is really a master key not only to true welfare of downtrodden, backwards and minorities but also to social justice.

SOCIAL AND POLITICAL UNITY OF ALL STAKE HOLDERS OF SOCIAL JUSTICE - A NEED OF HOUR

However, we have adopted social justice as our constitutional obligation but we need to take another better steps to strengthen the social justice. But the social justice can be weakened by the office bearers at any time. The power holders who are against the idea of social justice can either damage it or put it on hold. Therefore, the stake holders of social justice are required to be vigilant and united on the issue of social justice. Togetherness or social and political unity is the only tool which can safeguard the social justice not only in present but also in future. Today, all the supporters of social justice seem fractured due to their political obligations and selfishness. They have their personal aspirations too. Due to selfish attitude, they seem to fight against each other, whereas they need to work f` or the protection of social justice unitedly. If the supporters of social justice will live divided, they possibly face social injustice. In brief, political unity of SCs, STs, Backwards and minorities is the need of hour to save the social justice and establish an egalitarian society and a social and economic democracy as well, as envisioned by Dr. Ambedkar.

EDUCATION, ETERNAL VIGILENCE AND CONSTANT STRUGGLE- KEY TOOLS TO PROTECT SOCIAL JUSTICE

There is no doubt to accept that the education is the most significant asset that can elevate a man to the heights of success. It is also the most effective weapon to fight against injustice. Education pulls people out of ignorance and superstition and trains them to live life logically and scientifically. On the other hand, it is education only which makes people vigilant and prepares them to fight against discrimination, exploitation and injustice. An educated person is more vigilant about their rights and he can raise their voice more vibrantly for social justice as compared to an illiterate person. Therefore, it is the primary need to educate our generations. By educating them, we can protect the social justice and will be in position to uproot inequality and injustice. People will have to be eternal vigilant and conscious to save their rights and freedoms. People will have to respond strongly against injustice. It is the eternal vigilance which can hamper the discrimination. As Laski says, "Eternal vigilance is the real price of liberty", it also can be said that it is the real price of social justice too. They will have echo their voice vibrantly. Beside vigilance, people will continue their struggle and fight against discrimination and injustice through democratic and constitutional means following Dr. Ambedkar and Mahatma Gandhi. Satyagrah and democratic non-violent movements will prove effective weapons to fight against discrimination, deprivation, inequality and social injustice. In short, education, eternal vigilance and constant struggle in a democratic manner are very effective tools to fight for social justice.

NEED OF PROLIFERATION OF THOUGHTS AND PHILOSOPHY OF THE CHAMPIONS OF SOCIAL JUSTICE

No doubt to say that the thoughts and philosophy of social justice is weakening in India for few years and we are much far from the goals set by our great champions of social justice specially Babasaheb Dr. B.R. Ambedkar. He had dreamt of social and economic democracy beside political democracy to be established in our country. But still India has not fulfilled the dream of Babasaheb. Still social inequality and discrimination is existed. Still economic disparity and huge poverty exist. Still the aim of social justice is unfulfilled. Amid increasing threat to social justice, we need to go back to the thought and philosophy of social justice. It is a matter of grave concern that our Youth are not enthusiastic towards the cause of social justice. They seem either unconscious or reluctant towards the social justice. It is why, they do not study the great champions and scholars of social justice. Our younger generations both men and women must read the famous books like *Ghulamgiri, Annihilation of Caste, The Untouchables, Buddha and his Dhamma. Chamcha Yug,* andthe *Constitution of India* that reflect the thoughts and philosophy of social justice. we should study the books authored by the warriors of the equality and social justice. We need to propagate and proliferate the ideology and philosophy of social justice throughout the country with focus on rural India, where social injustice is prevalent. We need to concretize the Bahujan ideology that is based on social justice. By doing so, social justice can be protected and a strong voice can be echoed for social justice that is very important to keep the country united and integrated. We must not only pay great respect and grateful-ness to the great champions of social justice who echoed their vibrant voices for the cause of equality and social justice. In short, by following the thoughts and philosophy of the great warriors of social justice, we can not only strengthen social harmony but also consolidate the unity and integrity of the country.

<u>**EFERENCES**</u>

1. https://www.humanrightscareers.com/issues/10-reasons-why-social-justice-is-important/

2. https://thriveglobal.com/stories/the-importance-of-social-justice/

3. https://www.humanrightscareers.com/issues/10-reasons-why-social-justice-is-important/

4. https://www.youthkiawaaz.com/2011/02/educational-reservations-india-solutions/

5. Mukul, Akshya (2006). "Striking AIIMS docs live in a glass house", Times of India, New Delhi, 23 May.

6. Kumar, Vivek (2010). "Jati Ka Buniyadi Sawal", June 2, Dainik Jagran

www.ingramcontent.com/pod-product-compliance
Lightning Source LLC
Chambersburg PA
CBHW060601120726
48002CB00010B/2775